£1

THE RUCK

A Selection of Rugby Writing

OUT OF THE RUCK

A SELECTION OF RUGBY WRITING

EDITED BY
DAVID PARRY-JONES

PELHAM BOOKS

First published in Great Britain by
Pelham Books Ltd
27 Wrights Lane
Kensington
London W8 5TZ

British Library Cataloguing in Publication Data

Out of the ruck: a selection of rugby writing.
1. Rugby football
I. Parry-Jones, David
796.33′3′0922 GV945

ISBN 0 7207 1698 5

Printed and bound in Great Britain by
Butler & Tanner Ltd, Frome and London

Contents

CONTENTS

Foreword

Some folk might point to video-tape recordings as the sporting anthologies of our time. Certainly the sales of compilations like *The Crowning Years*, a review of Welsh rugby triumphs of the 'seventies, and *Scotland's 1984 Grand Slam* have been phenomenal. The colour, the spectacle, and the second (and third) scrutiny afforded by action replay have permitted fans to gorge themselves on quick-moving, high quality entertainment. Decisive editing has eliminated from such tapes not only stoppages for injury but also the hiatuses in which twenty-nine players stand idle while one kicks at goal.

Yes, video-tape is the fast food of spectator sport. But however often the exchanges between two teams are viewed, there endure the complementary desires to share experiences and compare notes. The first of these is what motivates observers and critics to set down an account of events as witnessed by them; the second prompts the purchase by readers of a favourite newspaper or a volume of essays. As a general rule 'sound' opinions will find favour with consumers – that is, they are seeking confirmation of their own judgements; but there is also a role for provocative and controversial writing.

The validity of such speculation is surely borne out by the undiminished space which the Press devotes the morning after to big rugby, despite what may have appeared on TV in *Grandstand*, and by the proliferation of memoirs published by star players. It would appear, therefore, that just as televising the Brontës and Dickens and Galsworthy tempts viewers to acquaint themselves with the original texts, so *Rugby Special* and related programmes, far from satisfying inquisitiveness about the Irvines and the Davieses and the Mouries, actually stimulate it.

Such considerations emboldened my approach to Pelham Books with a suggestion that a modern anthology of rugby writing might not be untimely. It is some years, as far as I can tell, since a comparable volume appeared, and in that time Rugby Football's media standing has changed radically. The game has administered many shots in the arm to itself, providing more meat into which critic and reader can bite. There has been growth in the sheer number of writers, for newspapers which used to employ a single correspondent now find space for two or three.

I have to thank Dick Douglas-Boyd, himself a rugby enthusiast, for taking the idea on board. The volume we have put together perhaps falls into the 'miscellany' rather than the 'anthology' category, since the single highly arbitrary criterion for the inclusion of material is that it has for one reason or another appealed to the Editor. Thus the writing is not necessarily ornate; nor the event described earth-shattering; nor the players portrayed world-beaters; nor the humour side-splitting – though there are examples of all these things. No, the contents are simply a wide-ranging pot-pourri of pieces, well crafted by men with a confident grasp of their subject.

The writers included, a goodly proportion still active by the way, are a fairly representative group. They are mainly from the Home Countries, though some examples are by overseas correspondents. Everyone approached was generous with permission to reproduce material he had written; and copyright holders too placed no obstacle in my path. Besides acknowledging excerpts in context, I extend warm thanks here to those who gave clearance.

As for the reader, I hope this will strike you as the kind of volume which can be read anywhere – but, best of all, can be kept at your bedside to dip into, before dropping contentedly off to sleep with a mind full of pleasant thoughts and colourful images.

DAVID PARRY-JONES
Llandaff, Cardiff, 1986.

Every effort has been made to trace the copyright owners of the material used in this book. The Editor and Publisher apologise for any omissions, and will be pleased to hear from those whom they were unable to trace.

THE GAME

The Spirit of Rugby

Just as it is proper to begin this Anthology with a section on the Game, so it is hard to think of anyone better qualified to lead a team of authors out onto the field than William Wavell Wakefield. He won thirty-one caps for England – a phenomenal number in days before regular tours – and is thought of as the architect of organised forward play.

And his summation of Rugby Football's appeal and the spirit of the Game can scarcely be improved upon. Published in 1927, it reads as though it had been written yesterday.

Without doubt it is a hard game, and that is one of its chief virtues. A man who plays it must be ready to give and take hard knocks, but he will take and give them with a grin. He will need courage and determination and a sense of humour, and he must learn the meaning of unselfishness. It may be that Rugger has an element of danger about it, and people often ask whether it is worth risking serious injury in what, after all, is only a game. It would, I think, be a poor sort of game that had no sort of risk to be faced, and it is one of the glories of Rugger that you can put your shoulder into a man with all your strength and bring him down with a crash, knowing that if you stave in a rib or two of his he will bear no grudge against you, while if he knocks your teeth out in handing you off it is merely your own fault for tackling him too high. Such accidents are relatively rare, but when they do happen they are just the fortune of war.

There really is the crux of the matter, for Rugger is war, though it is friendly and controlled war, if such a conception be possible. We all have our primitive instincts, and one of the strongest is the love of a good fight, which no amount of civilisation has been able to eradicate. I see no reason, as a matter of fact, why it should be eradicated, for it is merely the natural desire of a healthy man to pit his strength against another's, and for this desire we have in Rugger the best possible outlet. Of all games it is the least hampered by restrictions, and though a player may not be a Hercules, he may

England forwards enjoy a half-time breather during the 1923 Twickenham encounter with Wales in which the visitors were beaten 7–3. Wavell Wakefield, then at Cambridge, is third from right. (*BBC Hulton Picture Library*.)

have speed or subtlety to put to the test, and in modern conditions every quality and every physique has its chance. It is because of the freedom of Rugger and its consequent risks that it breeds hardiness, which in these days of cocktails and lounge-lizards is a quality to be encouraged.

But I do not want to give the impression that Rugger is no more than brute force directed by courage rather than intelligence. If it were only that it would not be so increasingly popular, nor would it be so widely played in the schools. It is above all the game for the tactician and for the man who is mentally alert, for so quickly does it move and so unexpected are its phases, that only a keenly intelligent player can seize openings which come and are gone in a flash, or can check his opponents when prompt decision and action are essential.

There is, moreover, a deep theory underlying every move and counter-move on the field, and to learn and apply this theory successfully a man must have all his wits about him. But that is not all, for just as in a game you try your strength against an opponent, so also you must pit your mentality against his, altering the play of your team to strike at the weak links in your opponents' armour. Plainly there is more in Rugger than mere strength, and I would go so far as to say that it calls for quicker and deeper thought than any other game. But though I have tried to show how it breeds courage and hardiness, unselfishness, self-control and strength of character and mind, I have said nothing of the spirit underlying it all.

The spirit of any game is an elusive quantity, for we play without analysing our motives. There is, however, something in the spirit of Rugger which is worth defining, difficult though it is to express. Mrs Battle demanded for her whist 'a clean hearth and the rigour of the game', and somehow that expresses my feelings about Rugger. A clean hearth – well, that is plain enough; our game is to be played swept clean of all those mean and petty infringements of the rules which could so easily creep in; infringements and obstructions which no man who understands the spirit of Rugger could ever practise. And the rigour of the game, that we must have, a wholehearted joy in the hardness of it, a desire to do our best, to play fair and ask no favour. And, above all, there is no fear of defeat, but simply an effort to win because that is the object of the game. If defeat comes our way, it is a lesson rather than a loss, while if we win we are satisfied that our best should have proved good enough.

Rugger. W.W. Wakefield and H.P. Marshall. Longman, Green and Co.

The clubs, in whom the Game is enshrined, recognise such ideals and struggle towards them – some more energetically than others. Few have taken the trouble to think through their approach and attitude to the staging of fixtures, and the obligations owed to players and spectators; and to find a credo spelled out in a match programme is rare indeed. But then the club which plays at Stradey Park has much about it that is unique ...

As in the past, the philosophy of the Llanelli Rugby Football Club will continue to be to try to provide entertainment and excitement for its supporters by playing adventurous and effective winning Rugby in a style which will be enjoyable for both player and spectator alike. Hopefully, it will be Rugby Football of quality, which incorporates the belief that such an approach involves the taking of risks, especially in running the ball from our own line and behind.

Obviously Rugby played with such style requires players of calibre, and therefore the degree of entertainment provided will depend on the level of skill and the confidence of the players involved. This will necessitate shifts of emphasis in the pattern of play and the coaching thereof; and the club will continue to do its utmost to see that the Rugby provided at Stradey Park will be consistently among the best in the country, providing both excellent value for money and pleasure for our many supporters who always expect something special from the Scarlets.

Llanelli RFC Match Programme.

Rugby is often called a 'players' Game'. But what does that mean? Surely it cannot signify that they owe nothing to anyone or anything else – to team-mates, spectators or to the imponderable 'spirit' of rugby.

One of the great mid-century players was Bleddyn Williams, a man who enjoyed every honour the Game could offer him and gave it a great deal both as a player and later as a broadcaster and writer. His retirement in 1956 prompted these reflections on the blend of opportunities and obligations with which playing rugby had presented him.

It is a hard thing to make a complete break with something that has been a vital ingredient in one's everyday way of life. It is like giving up smoking or turning teetotal. It is a heart-warming sight to see the sea of faces around one from the middle of Twickenham, Murrayfield and other famous grounds. That pulse-quickening roar from thousands of throats as the ball curves into the air from the kick-off. The impact of the crash-tackle, or the wildly ecstatic feeling as a swift burst or side-step sweeps one through an off-balance defence. Anxiety. Dogged desperation. A player is conscious of all these emotions; and they are all part of the game, accepted as such and never feared, but taken for granted. They are part of a rugby player's life – my life. Such experiences can never be replaced; and they can never be taken away. Those memories will always remain.

Rugby watchers often say: 'I could hardly bear the strain. Tension was too taut.' How do the players themselves engaged in the tussle feel about it? People never think about their feelings! Yes, our players

Bleddyn Williams: 'Rugby should be enjoyed by each individual ... I give priority to an ardent desire to gain maximum enjoyment out of the game.' (*Western Mail & Echo Ltd.*)

felt just as frustrated as the thousands of Welshmen who saw Cardiff almost conquer the famous Springboks in October 1951. We felt the oppressive intensity of defence stretched to its limit when the All Blacks scrummaged ominously beneath the Cardiff posts in another match of splendour and thrills. It is like the thrill of the chase; only, often, we were the hunted.

This is an aspect of the game that very few people consider. Too often players are criticised for attempting something the crowd feels too risky to be tried. If he fails, that player is condemned. Should he succeed he is a one-match genius. I feel consideration should always be shown and allowances made for the nature of the game and conditions existing on the field. I have known players hurried into further errors after an initial mistake had brought groans from the crowd. Players try too hard and too anxiously to regain favour through an act that will invoke cheers. This is not good for the game or the players themselves. Rugby should be enjoyed by each individual, a personal satisfaction being derived from the knowledge that one is fitting into a team and contributing a full share with due allowance for error.

I considered it a duty to supply my wing with an acceptable pass. But there has yet to be the player who never passed an uncatchable ball. We all make mistakes. Perhaps it was because I took a personal pride in passing accurately that when I missed my target the Arms Park resounded with groans! I never let it upset my methods. An imperturbable outlook is an incalculably valuable possession in big-match rugby. But other qualities are also necessary to become a world-famous player. Some of them are almost indefinable; but I give priority to an ardent desire to gain maximum enjoyment out of the game.

I enjoyed football. Success is a stimulant, and I well remember my determination to regain a place in the national side after Wales had won the Triple Crown without me in 1950 for the first time for thirty-nine years. The spotlight of publicity has a fierce glare, and often it can scorch a player's mental approach. Press criticisms never worried me. The fact that Wales had won the Triple Crown without Bleddyn Williams set me a target. The 'Old Man' might have put on weight, lost a little of the 'dazzling' form the Press spoke about, but he was not feeling any older, I can say. And I was back in the Welsh Triple Crown winning side of 1952 with three other Cardiff backs in Rex Willis, Cliff Morgan and Alun Thomas.

It revitalised me. All players suffer an off-form period of some kind or another, often at the peak of their career. This has been noticeable with many leading post-War players. Cliff Morgan, for example, had many unhappy experiences during 1954–55. But that is where the enthusiasm I rate so highly as an essential attribute for the game comes in. Form can be recaptured as long as players do not brood on their misfortunes – or listen to the Press, who say they are 'finished'. It was not until 1953, after playing seventeen games for Wales, that I was honoured with the captaincy. And in that (for me) memorable match at Murrayfield I scored two tries. I had 'come back'.

I shall continue to enjoy rugby football. It is far too fine a game to lose sight of for even a winter. Enthusiasm as a player will now be turned to enthusiasm as a watcher. And I look forward to many happy years of excitement and contentment, watching the game through the eyes of one who has known the quick surge of pounding action on the field. I wonder if I will watch the game with the same wise solemnity as the owl that once frowned down on us from the lofty top of a goal-post at Stradey Park? I fancied him as just another of my critics!

Rugger My Life. Bleddyn Williams. Stanley Paul.

Men like Wavell Wakefield and Bleddyn Williams were 'into' Rugby from their short-pants days. To others it is a matter of regret that they were not introduced to the game at an earlier point in their life; and the admission comes with particular conviction from one distinguished in other sports – in this case C.B. Fry, who played soccer and cricket for England, held the world long-jump record for a spell, but could get no further than the Barbarians at Rugby! Hence the wistful note in the Preface he wrote for a book by his friend E.H.D. Sewell.

Once on a day, pre-Hitler, my Editor, having regarded me for years as an amateur in everything but Cricket, suddenly found out that I had played Rugger for Oxford University, the Barbarians and Blackheath. So he said would I do Blackheath *v* Cardiff at the Rectory Field next Saturday. So I said, certainly.

So my pre-Hitler motor-driver Jimmy Brooks (now mending and wiring Spitfires and last heard of over the air in 'Lunchtime War Workers', introduced as 'Public Enemy Number 1', he being an accomplished revue artist in the style of Max Miller) – Jimmy, I say,

[15]

drove me to Blackheath. He also 'phoned my copy to the *Evening Standard* and drove me home.

We left the field in reverent silence. But after half a mile he said: 'Excuse me, Sir . . .'

'Well, Mr Brooks?' said I.

'Well, Sir,' said he, 'now I call it a man's game, this Rugby Football.'

Now Jimmy Brooks had spent 1914–15 in the Flanders trenches, had seen life in the Halls and, with me, any number of Soccer Cup-ties and League matches.

So I cross-examined him, as one whose opinion counted.

It transpired that (a) this Rugby is pretty well a free fight and tough at that; (b) further, that the scragging was pretty well all-in wrestling; (c) further, did I see the Cardiff chap make a swallow dive at full speed and fling the Blackheath chap, also going full speed, at least ten yards head over heels? And (d) that in this game a man could run full bat without having to palter. And (e) all this, all this, Sir, with no-one losing his temper so as you'd notice it.

Now if I, Charles Fry, who spent most of my Football years playing Soccer for the Corinthians and for Southampton in League matches and Cup-ties, say that I liked Rugger better than Soccer and found it a finer game, all I do is to give a personal opinion, liable to paradox.

But Jimmy Brooks is, I assure you, a good cross-section of observant quick-witted democratic experience. That is why I give the story.

For myself I would say that, being a wing three quarter who could take a pass and leg it pretty well in even time for the 100 yards, naturally I liked Rugger. The game is so full of plot interest and drama.

True, I never compassed the swallow dive at the ankles of a full-speed opponent: I never got lower than the thighs. But as I began at the neck when I first played for Wadham I don't call that so bad.

The chief interest of this is that I was at a Soccer school and even played for England at Soccer, so I must be rated a not altogether despicable convert.

And I do wish to this day that my Public School had played Rugger instead of Soccer.

Preface by Captain C.B. Fry, RNR,
from *Rugger – The Man's Game*. E.H.D. Sewell.
Hollis and Carter. Reprinted by permission of Bodley Head.

Some people assume that rugby players' attitude to Association Football is frigid and unappreciative. Wrong: certainly in Wales the 'other' code is viewed with great enthusiasm, and stars like Gareth Edwards and Phil Bennett are not strangers to the VIP lounges at Ninian Park or the Vetch Field for midweek games. The same lively curiosity extends to almost any other sport that can be named – with one exception. It is enjoined that Rugby League, the professional version of the handling game, be shunned. The merest contact with it can deprive a man of his amateur status and the right to any participation whatsoever in Union affairs – theoretically this would apply to a householder who simply answered the door to a League scout.

There are historic reasons for this attitude, which is strait-laced in southern England and borders on the hysterical in Wales (the further north you go, until you reach Scotland, the more tolerant it becomes). Some time before the end of this century a mellowing is likely to take place among the amateurs, partly forced on them by changing circumstances and attitudes. For the time being, however, it is rare to come across candid admissions like those committed to paper, no doubt with a twinkle in his eye, by Watcyn Thomas a year or two before his death. A great captain of Wales, he played for most of the thirties in the North with amateur Waterloo, while training with professionals!

Unbeknown to the Welsh Rugby Union I trained on the St Helens Recs ground, mixing freely with the players. Three great forwards of theirs were Smith, Fildes and Mulvanney, called the Three Musketeers, and the terror of the opposition. Mulvanney was a great character and as strong as any man I've known – woe betide a policeman who intruded into the dressing room for he would be hoisted onto a big hook behind the door and left there to dangle helplessly. On his retirement Mulvanney became landlord of a local public house, and if you were pestered by a scrounger he had a novel way of getting rid of him: he would tinkle a bicycle bell in his private apartments and say you were required on the phone whereupon, having answered it, you made your escape.

Welshmen were prominent players in the town rugby league. One of them was almost bald, no chicken by any means. He had bluffed the club into signing him on by producing the birth-certificate of a much younger friend of his, of the same name, who lived in the same valley. Some Welsh players have had secret trials with Rugby League clubs unbeknown to the Welsh Rugby Union. One of them, who was not a success, claimed £20 in expenses and when his claim was queried and examined it included train fare and taxi to the ground;

[17]

when the club secretary expostulated that a bus would have taken him to the ground the secret triallist exclaimed, 'If you had the rheumatics like me, you would have taken a taxi too!'

While in St Helens I saw many a League game, mainly in midweek and on some Saturdays when I was unfit to play Rugby Union with Waterloo RFC. Rugby League was not a game to which I could take a liking, for it had too much of a sameness and predictability, with none of the fluidity of Rugby Union. I speak of those days when I was resident in St Helens. The Rugby League have tried to introduce more variety into the game but basically it is still the same. Then, after each tackle, a player was allowed to get up, tap the ball along the ground with his foot if only an inch or two in a forward direction, and re-start the game; his colleagues meanwhile being lined up in support behind him and his opponents lying well up in defence. So the game was renewed from scratch (as it is now) and there was no variety stemming from line out and quick heeling from loose mauls, when opponents can be overlapped. Scrums were a farce, with the three front row forwards standing almost upright when the ball was thrown in, with the middle man (hooker or 'striker' as they called it) ending up prostrate on the ground. Possession was essential, for successful results counted for bonus money, and I must admit that the resultant deft handling of the ball by backs and forwards combined was the acme of rhythm. Knocks-on meant loss of possession and this skill is something which Rugby Union forwards should cultivate.

Some South Wales rugby players still 'go north', but in lesser numbers, since unemployment is not so rife as in the bad old days and Rugby Union playing is a strand in the pattern of life in South Wales; going Rugby League would mean giving up much that you love. Regrettably there is still an undefinable hiatus between ex-Rugby League players who return home and the natives; but this state of affairs is changing and I've even seen current and ex-League players in Union clubhouses in the Midlands.

Rugby-Playing Man. Watcyn Thomas. Pelham Books.

Back in pursuit of the Game, and an elusive, evasive definition to fit it. R.C. Robertson-Glasgow, as witty and elegant an essayist as ever graced the columns of the Observer *and other organs, put in a series of light-hearted tactical probes – before confessing himself defeated.*

[18]

'Like the game?' asked my old friend G., as we strolled from the ground, then, with unreported skill, swerved past a motor-bus, gave the dummy to a boy riding a bicycle with his hands in his pockets, side-stepped just for practice, and grounded ourselves for a try on the far pavement. 'Like the game?' 'Yes,' said I, 'Both of them'; then, as we settled ourselves and notions in the train: 'but, as to the game inside the ground, which *was* the game?'

I meant it, too; though it sounds like the start of some one-sided bout between a professor of philosophy and a pupil whose companions are safe in the pictures. I have felt, and chewed, this same helpless question at many spectacles – at cricket, the circus, boxing, and in the public gallery of the House of Commons; but never more than at Rugby football. How much and how little we see. And which is the Game?

There is the scrum half. A link which, when missing (no offence, sir), divides the team, like earth-worms by the careless spade, into two still animate but bewildered segments. The scrum half is a game in himself; a round game, of earth and mirth, of trounce and bounce, of trick and come again. The forwards, once down in the tight, never see the scrum half unless they are contortionists; but they hear the little ... er ... man; 'coming in right, coming in left'; then it doesn't come at all. Scrum halves; coxswains; short-legged sergeant-majors in the Brigade of Guards: all are little men who order big men about with impunity.

But where, still, is the game? The three-quarters, of course. The day is fine; they have more than half the fun, you say, and nearly all the publicity. The day is wet; the touch-judge loses mileage against the wind; and the three quarters watch that lurching morass of malediction so felicitously called the scrum, watch the fly-half, famed for his manual dexterity, dropping the one pass which, in half a freezing hour, survives the so-called liaison of foot and hand. And, as they watch, their thoughts wander, like those of head clerks who with disciplined patience wait for the senior partner to fill in his pools, and they miss the tackle that costs the match.

Maybe you'll find the game at full back. Sometimes you could watch only him and have superabundant worth of money and delight; Dan Drysdale, Vivian Jenkins, H.G. Owen Smith; or whatever hero the fancy picks and the memory catches.

Dodging, swaying, weaving game. Will you run it to earth among the critics, or the Selectors? Ah; that, as the innkeeper remarked of his York ham, is a secret between me and me. But the groundsman; he will know where and what it is. I asked once. For years he had been employed, as they say, by a famous Rugby club. 'The game?' he answered; 'Why, yes; didn't you never see Meredith play at outside right for Wales?'

Rain Stopped Play. R.C. Robertson-Glasgow. Dennis Dobson.

Quite early in Rugby's history it is clear that women enjoyed attending matches and cheering on their menfolk from vantage points in the grandstands. As is still the case, some were evidently noisier and less inhibited than others. Certainly those at Rodney Parade on 23 December 1905, when the All Blacks beat Newport 6–3, caught the fancy of the Daily Mail *correspondent; and his colour piece in turn found favour with an editor out in New Zealand, who promptly reproduced it.*

The game at Newport (says a writer in the *Daily Mail*) produced a remarkable effect on the hundreds of ladies who watched its varying fortunes from the stands. The average woman in Newport, judging from the expert feminine criticisms punctuating Saturday's play, apparently knows nearly as much of the science of Rugby as any man; and their patronage of the game, it is said, has not a little to do with the Newport club's brilliant career. They enter heart and soul into every contest, urging on their players with impassioned cries of approval and encouragement, visiting their failures and shortcomings with mournful wails of disappointment that very often drown their brothers' and fathers' gusts of despair.

There is scarcely a trick of the game with which the Newport girl is not familiar. Her long drawn 'Oho' of regret or quick triumphant 'Aha' afford a sure index of the progress of the game. She is not a bit like the Blackheath or Richmond girl, who goes to a football match more because it is 'the thing' socially than for any real pleasure she derives from watching the struggle. The Newport girl, on the other hand, enters into the spirit of the contest with all the ardour and abandon of her brother. And not only the Newport girl, but the Newport matron too, and in not a few cases even the Newport grandmother.

On Saturday the most vehement cries of denunciation and encouragement on the principal stand came from several smartly-attired elderly ladies, who unquestionably possessed footballing sons, if not footballing grandsons. Some of them leaped to their feet during exciting periods with wild cries of fear and hope and no-one around them seemed to think that the exhibition was at all unfeminine or out of place. 'Merely a matter of temperament, my boy – don't be afraid,' said a cold-blooded Saxon reassuringly to a startled 'All Black' whose first introduction this was to the feminine possibilities of the game.

But, if it may be urged against the participation of the fair sex in so vigorous and manly, not to say rough, a game as football that it tends to blunt the delicate edge of their refinement and familiarises with the coarser side of the human animal, still their presence may have the effect in the long run of bringing a softening influence into the play. They possess a wondrous sympathy for any player – especially if he belongs to their own side – who receives a bad bump or bites the dust of a vigorous tackle, and their pained murmurs of gentle consolance are calculated to act as a magic salve to the wounded victim of a ruthless 'knock-out'.

'Poor Willie!' cooed one fair maiden as a mud-begrimed Usksider crawled from beneath a mountain of flesh heaped around one tremendous bully. 'What a shame to treat our boys like that.' 'Willie', however, seemed to be quite enjoying himself.

From the *Daily Mail*, December 1905, via *The Press* (Christchurch, New Zealand).

The early years of the century confirmed Rugby as a spectator sport; but the new fans, women included, who flocked through the turnstiles did not necessarily preserve the stiff upper lip of earlier generations as they furthered their appreci-ation of the Game and familiarity with its players. Seasoned critics felt the need to deliver small, stern lectures directing what should be 'done' and 'not done' on the sidelines. E.H.D. Sewell's homily was penned in 1922.

A little prophecy really does nobody any harm and it is such a joy to all who, having become wise after the event, thereupon proceed to rend the poor prophet! He, for his part, enjoys that joke as much as most people. What would our games be but for their prognosticators and trixies? For, to be sure, one has to include the ladies nowadays in these matters, as is evident from a glance at any assembly on the occasion of an International match. If they do not here, as elsewhere, outnumber the male sex, it is surely near the mark to say that thirty per cent of an average International company at

Twickenham is made up of the fair sex. I cannot, in truth, admit that as yet they know much about the game, judging mainly from the acts they applaud and their subsequent conversation; but much the same thing may be said of many of their cavaliers since, to go to Rugby matches having become the vogue, one consequence thereof is the presence of large numbers of men who have never played a game of Rugby. Inasmuch as some of those who do play seldom read or know the rules, it is only logical to assume that most of the newcomers are even more handicapped.

This presence of a section of the public which is 'foreign' to our game was vividly illustrated at Twickenham at half time during the Irish match last February. Hundreds of the ring-seat spectators rushed across the ground in order, presumably, to have a nearer view of the players during their less mobile moments. In other words, to put into practice a form of idolatry which is excessively disagreeable to every Rugby Union player and which, that apart, is a practice that has other objections. To crowd round the players at half time in an International match is one of those things which simply is 'not done'. There are several things in decent society that are 'not done' and for the not doing of which it would not always be an easy matter to provide an adequate reason. But, in Rugby Foot-ball, there are several adequate reasons why this particular thing should not be done and why the Union, which issues the ring-seat tickets, should print thereon some words to the effect that the buyer does not buy with the price of his seat the right to walk on the football pitch at any time before, during or after the match. There was a time when the public understood the limits surrounding the places where it is 'not wanted', but the war has changed all that, and with this absurd spirit of communism and 'what's yourn's mine' everywhere rampant, the uninitiated portion of the public obeys no such unwritten laws of decent usage and civilised gentlefolk. It just trespasses whether wanted or not. One reason why the public is *de trop* in the vicinity of the players at half time is that this period of rest is often, almost invariably, used by the teams as one for holding an informal council of war. In this council a member or members of the selection committee concerned often play a part and such necess-ary adjuncts to an International match cannot be carried out – indeed they have been prevented – when the public has come nosing in, gaping at the players at short range, sometimes offering extremely stupid advice, and at others giving way to the insensate autograph mania. Another reason why the half-time interval is no place for the public is that since time immemorial those minutes have been considered sacred to the somewhat astringent but therefore very refreshing lemon. This morsel of fruit may be a small matter to the comfortable spectator, who has perhaps a Thermos flask of tea handy, but I can assure non-players that the absence of just that small amount of liquid refreshment makes a very great difference to the physical comfort, and subsequent effort, of the players. A very necessary reform of the future is, as I have indicated, some such warning notice printed on the ring-seat tickets. The best-behaved crowd in the whole gamut of games is the Rugby Union crowd which assembles at Twickenham; Inverleith; Richmond; Queen's Club; the Officers' Ground, Portsmouth; and at both universities. A very small hint from an official quarter is needed, and would be obeyed. Those who disregarded such a printed notice would find public opinion very strongly against them.

Reform, too, is needed in another direction. This is, that in all International matches players should be numbered. There was a time when I was in agreement with the large number of people who are very much opposed to this practice, but the official arrangements for the game must progress with the game. Men come from far and wide and pay a lot of money to see eighty minutes' football. Under the existing system many go away quite legitimately dissatisfied in that they were unable to know who it was brought off that fine tackle in the first ten minutes; who was that chap who saved an almost certain try by going down to the Scots pack in full cry; who kicked that penalty goal from long range with a side-wind handicap; yes, and who was it that played foul football that time when he tripped an opponent with a trip so deliberate as to make it astonishing how it escaped the referee? In numbering the players the governors of Rugby have one of the most powerful, though silent, forces in their hands towards *preventing* foul or unfair play that there is. A man with a 5 on his back, the figure being about fifteen inches in size, thinks twice, for instance, before he tackles an opponent who has passed the ball or puts the ball unfairly into the scrum. One or two rather ugly incidents might not have taken place this last season had this deterrent been at hand.

Rugby Football Up To Date. E.H.D. Sewell. Reprinted by permission of Hodder & Stoughton Ltd.

Richard Burton: 'Never mind the bloody ball – where's the bloody actor?' (*Gianni Bozzacchi/Rex Features Ltd.*)

Richard Burton's stature as a considerable stage and screen personage is acknowledged. His other accomplishments often come as a revelation to those who knew only Burton the actor; for example, when he found time to pick up a pen or sit at a typewriter he could produce colourful, readable prose. The year 1964 saw the publication by Heinemann of his brief A Christmas Story, *and in 1971, for the celebration of the Rugby Football Union's Centenary, he contributed the essay which follows (and which is reproduced by permission of the RFU) to the publication* Touchdown. *It indicates a certain sensitivity to the heartbeat of rugby football.*

And it is proof of another accomplishment – the ability which Burton once possessed to give a good account of himself between the touchlines as well as before the footlights.

It's difficult for me to know where to start with rugby. I come from a fanatically rugby-conscious Welsh miner's family, know so much about it, have read so much about it, have heard with delight so many massive lies and stupendous exaggerations about it and have contributed my own share, and five of my six brothers played it, and I mean I even knew a Welsh woman from Taibach who before a home match at Aberavon would drop goals from around forty yards

[24]

with either foot to entertain the crowd, and her name, I remember, was Annie Mort and she wore sturdy shoes, the kind one reads about in books as 'sensible' though the recipient of a kick from one of Annie's shoes would have been not so much sensible as insensible, and I even knew a chap called Five-Cush Cannon who won the sixth replay of a cup final (the previous five encounters having ended with the scores 0–0, 0–0, 0–0, 0–0, 0–0 including extra time) by throwing the ball over the bar from a scrum ten yards out in a deep fog and claiming a dropped goal. And getting it. What's more I knew people like a one-armed inside half – he'd lost an arm in the First World War – who played with murderous brilliance for Cwmavon for years when I was a boy. He was particularly adept, this one, at stopping a forward bursting through from the line out with a shattering iron-hard thrust from his stump as he pulled him on to it with the other. He also used the mis-placed sympathy of innocent visiting players who didn't go at him with the same delivery as they would against a two-armed man as a ploy to lure them on to concussion and other organic damage. They learned quickly, or were told after the match when they had recovered sufficiently from Jimmy's ministrations to be able to understand the spoken word, that going easy on Jimmy One-Arm was first cousin to stepping into a grave and waiting for the shovels to start. A great many people who played unwarily against Jimmy died unexpectedly in their early forties. They were lowered solemnly into the grave with all match honours to the slow version of 'Sospan Fach'. They say that the conductor at these sad affairs was noticeably .one-armed but that could be exaggeration again.

As I said, it's difficult for me to know where to start so I'll begin with the end. The last shall be first, as it is said, so I'll tell you about the last match I ever played in.

I had played the game representatively since the age of ten until those who employed me in my profession, which is that of actor, insisted that I was a bad insurance risk against certain dread teams in dead-end valleys who would have little respect, no respect or outright disrespect for what I was pleased to call my face. What if I were unfortunate enough to be on the deck in the middle of a loose maul ... they murmured in dollar accents? Since my face was already internationally known and since I was paid, perhaps overpaid, vast sums of money for its ravaged presentation they, the money men, expressed a desire to keep it that way. Apart from wanting to preserve

[25]

my natural beauty, it would affect continuity, they said, if my nose was straight on Friday in the medium shot and was bent towards my left ear on Monday for the close-up. Millions of panting fans from Tokyo to Tonmawr would be puzzled, they said. So to this day there is a clause in my contracts that forbids me from flying my own plane, ski-ing and playing the game of rugby football, the inference being that it would be all right to wrestle with a Bengal tiger five thousand miles away, but not play against, shall we say, Pontypool at home. I decided that they had some valid arguments after my last game.

It was played against a village whose name is known only to its inhabitants and crippled masochists drooling quietly in kitchen corners, a mining village with all the natural beauty of the valleys of the moon, and just as welcoming, with a team composed almost entirely of colliers. I hadn't played for four or five years but was fairly fit, I thought, and the opposition was bottom of the third class and fairly beatable. Except, of course, on their home ground. I should have thought of that. I should have called to mind that this was the sort of team where, towards the end of the match, you kept your bus ticking over near the touchline in case you won and had to run for your life.

I wasn't particularly nervous before the match until, though I was disguised with a skull-cap and everyone had been sworn to secrecy, I heard a voice from the other team asking, '*Le ma'r blydi* film star '*ma?*' (where's the bloody film star here?) as we were running on to the field. My cover, as they say in spy stories, was already blown and trouble was to be my shadow (there was none from the sun since there was no sun – it was said in fact that the sun hadn't shone there since 1929) and the end of my career the shadow of my shadow for the next 80 minutes or so. It was a mistaken game for me to play. I survived it with nothing broken except my spirit, the attitude of the opposition being unquestionably summed up in simple words like, 'Never mind the bloody ball, where's the bloody actor?' Words easily understood by all.

Among other things I was playing Hamlet at that time at the Old Vic, but for the next few performances after that match I was compelled to play him as if he were Richard the Third. The punishment I took had been innocently compounded by a paragraph in a book of reminiscence by Bleddyn Williams with whom I had played on and off (mostly off) in the RAF. On page thirty-seven of this volume Mr Williams is kind enough to suggest that I had distinct possibilities as a player were it not for the lure of tinsel and paint and money and fame and so on. Incidentally, one of the curious phenomena of my library is that when you take out Bleddyn's autobiography from the shelves it automatically opens at the very page mentioned above. Friends have often remarked on this and wondered afresh at the wizardry of the Welsh. It is in fact the only notice I have ever kept.

Anyway, this little snippet from the great Bleddyn's book was widely publicised and some years later by the time I played that last game had entered into the uncertain realms of folk-legend and was deeply embedded in the subconscious of the sub-Welshmen I submitted myself to that cruel afternoon. They weren't playing with chips on their shoulders, they were simply sceptical about page thirty-seven.

I didn't realise that I was there to prove anything until too late. And I couldn't. And didn't. I mean prove anything. And I'm still a bit testy about it. Though I was working like a dog at the Vic playing Hamlet, Coriolanus, Caliban, the Bastard in King John, and Toby Belch, it wasn't the right kind of training for these great knotted gnarled things from the burning bowels of the earth. In my teens I had lived precariously on the lip of first class rugby by virtue of knowing every trick in the canon, evil and otherwise, by being a bad loser, but chiefly, and perhaps *only*, because I was very nippy off the mark. I was 5 ft 10½in in height in bare feet and weighed soaking wet no more than 12½ stone, and since I played in the pack, usually at open side wing forward, and since I played against genuinely big men it therefore followed that I had to be galvanically quick to move from inertia. When faced with bigger and faster forwards I was doomed. R.T. Evans of Newport, Wales and the Universe for instance – a racy 14½ stone and 6 ft 1½ in in height – was a nightmare to play against and shaming to play with, both of which agonies I suffered a lot, mostly, thank God, the latter lesser cauchemar. Genuine class, of course, doesn't need size, though sometimes I forgot this. Once I played rather condescendingly against a Cambridge college and noted that my opposite number seemed to be shorter than I was and in rugby togs looked like a schoolboy compared with Ike Owen, Bob Evans or W.I.D. Elliot. However, this blond stripling gave me a terrible time. He was faster and harder and wordlessly ruthless, and it was no consolation to find out his name afterwards because it meant nothing at the time. He has forgotten me but I haven't forgotten him. This anonymity was called Steele-Bodger and a more onomatopoeic name for its owner would be hard to find. He was, I promise you, steel and he did, I give you my word, bodger. Say his name through clenched teeth and you'll see what I mean. I am very glad to say that I have never seen him since except from the safety of the stands.

In this match, this last match played against troglodytes, burned to the bone by the fury of their work, bow-legged and embittered because they weren't playing for or hadn't played for and would never play for Cardiff or Swansea or Neath or Aberavon, men who smiled seldom and when they did it was like scalpels, trained to the last ounce by slashing and hacking away neurotically at the frightened coal-face for $7\frac{1}{2}$ hours a day, stalactitic, tree-rooted, carved out of granite by a rough and ready sledge hammer and clinker; against these hard volumes, of which I was the soft-cover paper-back edition, I discovered some truths very soon. I discovered just after the first scrum, for instance, that it was time I ran for the bus and not for their outside half. He had red hair, a blue-white face and no chin. Standing up straight his hands were loosely on a level with his calves and when the ball and I arrived exultantly together at his stock-still body, a perfect set-up you would say, and when I realised that I was supine and he was lazily kicking the ball into touch I realised that I had forgotten that trying to intimidate a feller like that was like trying to cow a mandrill, and that he had all the graceful willowy-give and sapling-bend of stressed concrete.

That was only the outside half.

From then on I was elbowed, gouged, dug, planted, raked, hoed, kicked a great deal, sandwiched and once humiliatingly taken from behind with nobody in front of me when I had nothing to do but run 15 yards to score. Once, coming down from going up for a ball in a line-out, the other wing forward – a veteran of at least 50 with grey hair – chose to go up as I was coming down, if you'll forgive this tautological syntax. Then I was down and he was up and to insult the injury he generously helped me up from being down and pushed me in a shambling run towards my own try-line with a blood-curdling endearment in the Welsh tongue, since during all these preceding ups and downs his unthinkable team had scored and my presence was necessary behind the posts as they were about to attempt the conversion.

[28]

I knew almost at once and appallingly that the speed, such as it had been, had ended and only the memory lingered on, and that tackling Olivia de Havilland and Lana Turner and Claire Bloom was not quite the same thing as tackling those Wills and Dais, those Twms and Dicks.

The thing to do I told myself with desperate cunning was to keep alive and the way to do that was to keep out of the way. This is generally possible to do when you know you're outclassed without everybody knowing, but in this case it wasn't possible to do because everybody was very knowing indeed. Sometimes in a lament for my lost youth (I was about 28) I roughed it up as well as I could but it is discouraging to put the violent elbow into the tempting rib when you prescience tells you that what is about to be broken is not the titillating rib but your pusillanimous pathetic elbow. After being gardened, mown and rolled a little more I gave that up and asked the captain of our team if he didn't think it would be a better idea to hide me deeper in the pack. I had often, I reminded him, played right prop, my neck was strong and my right arm held its own with most. He gave me a long look, a trifle pitying perhaps, but orders were given and in I went to the maelstrom and now the real suffering began. Their prop with whom I was to share cheek and jowl for the next eternity didn't believe in razor blades since he grew them on his chin and shaved me thoroughly for the rest of the game, taking most of my skin in the process, delicacy not being his strong point. He used his prodigious left arm to paralyse mine and pull my head within an inch or two of the turf, then rolled my head around his, first taking my ear between his fore-finger and thumb, humming 'Rock of Ages' under his breath. By the end of the game my face was as red as the setting sun and the same shape. Sometimes, to vary the thing a bit, he rolled his head on what little neck he had, under and around again my helpless head. I stuck it out because there was nothing else to do, which is why on Monday night in the Waterloo Road I played the Dane looking like a Swede with my head per-manently on one side and my right arm in an imaginary sling, intermittently crooked and cramped with severe shakes and invol-untary shivers as of one with palsy. I suppose to the connoisseurs of Hamlets it was a departure from your traditional Prince but it wasn't strictly what the actor playing the part had in mind. A melancholy Dane he was, though. Melancholy he most certainly was.

I tried once to get myself removed to the wing but by this time our captain had become as, shall we say, 'dedicated' (he may read this) as the other team and actually wanted to win. He seemed not to hear me and the wing in this type of game, I knew, never got the ball and was, apart from throwing in from touch, a happy spectator and I wanted to be a happy spectator. I shuffled after the pack.

I joined in the communal bath afterwards in a large steamy hut next to the changing rooms feeling very hard-done-by and hurt though I didn't register the full extent of the agonies that were to crib, cabin and confine me for the next few days. I drank more than my share of beer in the home team's pub, joined in the singing and found that the enemies were curiously shy and withdrawn until the beer had hit the proper spot. Nobody mentioned my performance on the field. There was only one moment of wild expectation on my part when a particularly grim, sullen and taciturn member of the other side said suddenly with what passed shockingly for a smile splitting the slag heap of his face like an earth tremor,

'Come outside with us, will 'ew?' There was another beauty with him.

'Where to?' I asked.

'Never 'ew mind,' he said, 'you'll be awright. Jest come with us.'

'OK.'

We went out into the cruel February night and made our way to the outside Gents – black-painted concrete with one black pipe for flushing, wet to the open sky. We stood side by side in silence. They began to void. So did I. There had been beer enough for all. I waited for a possible compliment on my game that afternoon – I had after all done one or two good things if only by accident. I waited. But there was nothing but the sound of wind and water. I waited and silently followed them back into the bar. Finally I said, 'What did you want to tell me?'

'Nothing,' the talkative one said.

'Well what did you ask me out there for, then?'

'Well', the orator said. 'Well, us two is brothers and we wanted to tell our mam that we'd 'ad a. . .'

He hesitated; after all I spoke posh except when I spoke Welsh which oddly enough the other team didn't speak to me though I spoke it to them. 'Well, we jest wanted to tell our mam that we had passed water with Richard Burton,' he said with triumphant care.

'Oh 'ell,' I said.

I went back to London next day in a Mark VIII Jaguar driving

very fast, folding up and tucking away into the back drawer of my
subconscious all my wounds, staunched blood, bandaged pride,
feeling older than I've ever felt since. The packing wasn't very well
done as from time to time all the parcels of all the games I'd ever
played wrapped up loosely in that last one will undo themselves,
spill out of the drawer into my dreams and wake me shaking to the
reassuring reaching-out for the slim cool comfort of a cigarette in the
dead vast and doomed middle; and with a puff and a sigh mitty
myself into Van Wyk, Don White and Alan Macarley and, winning
several matches by myself by 65 points to nil, re-pack the bags.

'I was playing Hamlet at that time at the Old Vic but for the next few performances
I was compelled to play him as if he were Richard III'. Richard Burton.
From *Touchdown*, published by the RFU.

The Scots tell a story about Colin Meads at Murrayfield in 1967 – a
happy one, to balance the sad sending-off that took place.

Marking the big All Black at the line-outs was a new cap called
Erle Mitchell. Soon after the kick-off there was a lull while an injured
man received attention. Meads took the chance to explain to Mitchell
in lurid detail what damage he would be doing to him as the game
went on, with a warning that it would be better for the young Scot if
he neither resisted nor hit back. This harangue lasted until the referee
re-started the play.

Afterwards the Scottish XV, beaten but not disgraced, heard a
first-hand account from Mitchell of the Meads speech. The room went
very quiet. Then a team-mate asked, 'What did you say to him in
reply, Erle?'

Said the youngster, 'I told him to bugger off. But, hoots, I didna
say it too loud!'

PLAYERS

Men of Gift and Genius

Though Rugby Football is a great democracy, some participants are more equal than others by virtue of their special gifts or the affection in which they are held, or just occasionally through the mark they have left on the game. This section on the players begins with such a man.

It is clear from works like Tom Brown's Schooldays *that until the 1870s Rugby was essentially a huge, protracted maul from which the ball emerged but rarely – 'in they go, straight to the heart of the scrummage, bent on driving that ball out on the opposite side. My sons, my sons! you are too hot; you have gone past the ball, and must struggle now right through the scrummage and get round and back to your own side, before you can be of any further use.'*

Probably because smaller, slighter boys shunned such physical confrontations, backs gradually evolved into a separate, specialist unit; and soon tacticians came on the scene to organise and streamline their activities. Such a man was F.E. – Frank – Hancock, one of ten brothers from Wiveliscombe in Somerset, who came to Cardiff to work in the family brewery, joined the local club and scored two tries on his debut in February 1884. After that he could not be left out of the team for the next game though the man for whom he had deputised was now fit; so Cardiff fielded four three quarters against Gloucester instead of the customary three. By accident Hancock had revolutionised the game.

However, there was nothing accidental about his skill as a player nor about the way he subsequently skippered his team, as the archives of the club confirm.

He was elected captain of the Club by the unanimous vote of the members, and it is not too much to say that never before was a similar appointment received with so large amount of favour by the outside public. It was admitted and felt by all that the right man had been put in the right place, and a prosperous season for the Club was predicted. How far these expectations have been fulfilled, the achievements of the 'Welsh Invincibles', as the Club has lately been termed, best show. That a great deal of their success is due to Mr Hancock there can be little or no doubt. A brilliant and unselfish player himself, he has striven to impart some of his own good qualities to those who follow him, and he has not striven in vain. Under his captaincy the team play as they never played before, and have made for themselves a reputation second to none in the football world. As all our readers know Mr Hancock's place on the field is at three quarter, and few men are more thoroughly fitted for this important post. He is somewhat deficient in pace, perhaps, but more than makes amends for this by his dodging powers. Every Cardiff spectator is familiar with 'Hancock's "corkscrew" runs'. But what has contributed most of all to his popularity – apart from a frank, genial disposition and utterly unaffected manner – is the thorough unselfishness of his play. If he possesses one fault it is that he is too unselfish. He tackles cleanly and well, and as a rule the man who can manage to hand him off deserves to get away. In other respects he is a model captain, always ready to detect where the enemy's weakness lies, and to take steps accordingly. He also keeps a sharp look-out on his own men, and any shirking or bad play elicits prompt condemnation. He is not much addicted to praising, and for this reason the 'well played so-and-so' with which he occasionally greets some unusually smart piece of play is all the more highly esteemed by the individual to whom the remark is addressed. Of Mr Hancock's performances outside his own club this season it will only be necessary to say that he captained the Welsh team against Scotland, and the South Wales fifteen in their matches with Blackheath and Oxford University. It may be added that three of his brothers play at present for Wiveliscombe, one of these being P. Froude Hancock, who although only about eighteen years of age has this year played for Blackheath on several occasions, for England against Scotland and Wales, and in other first class matches.

Cardiff RFC: History and Statistics. C.S. Arthur. 1906.

Rugby Football's popularity saw it transplanted swiftly around the English-speaking world, and in 1875 – shortly after the Rugby Union was founded in London – Army officers stationed in Cape Town introduced the game to those parts. By the turn of the century the South Africans were capable of winning Tests, and early in the twentieth century their first tour of Britain took place. They won twenty-five games out of twenty-eight; and as is so often the case owed much to the skills and inspiring example of one player in particular.

[33]

To Paul Roos belongs the unique distinction of having led the first South African rugby team on a tour overseas and it was he who told reporters that his players should be called 'De Springbokken', a happy choice, soon to be shortened to 'Springbokke' or 'Springboks'. Paul Roos, therefore, was the spiritual father of all those who were to represent South Africa on the rugby field for the next 70 years, as he will be of all those who will earn that honour for all time to come. Destiny could not have given us a more solid foundation on which to build a tradition.

He was a forward, big and strong enough for his era, but rather small and light by today's standards. He had superb qualities of leadership, however, and his impeccable character and innate charm earned him the respect and affection of his players as well as his opponents.

To the end of his days he maintained that a man's motto should be 'Let the stumbling blocks be your stepping stones', and in his own life he added to that utter devotion to duty and principles.

As a teacher he was a strict disciplinarian who never spared the rod, but those who knew him remember him for his fierce interest in the welfare, material and spiritual, present and future, of each and every one of his pupils. It is a fact that once, on hearing that one of his former pupils preferred the bright lights to his studies at Stellenbosch, he marched into Wilgenhof hostel with his cane and gave the erring student four of the best.

He was appallingly absent-minded, invariably late for everything and to have been a passenger in a car driven by him was, according to one who did have the doubtful pleasure, tantamount to a peep into the Valley of Death! It was said that he held all records for speeding between Stellenbosch and surrounding towns. He never hesitated to lend his car to a student, but always with this advice: 'Now look, my boy, you have just as much a right to be on the road as any other driver, but just be careful of trains!'

He was constitutionally unable to arrive for any appointment on time and this used to drive his team-mates to distraction. People and their problems mattered far more to him than did clocks or watches. Once, when he was captain of Stellenbosch, his team had already gathered at the station for the trip to Cape Town where they were to play Newlands and still there was no sign of Polla, as he was usually called. Finally it was time for the train to depart, but fortunately the station master was a keen rugby fan and he gave instructions to the

Captain of the First Springboks of 1906, Paul Roos sits with the ball in the middle of the second row. His team won twenty-six of their twenty-nine games, losing only to Scotland and Cardiff. (*S & G Press Agency Ltd.*)

machinist to wait. Another fifteen minutes ticked by with everybody growing more frantic with every passing second. Just when it looked as if even the co-operative station master had run out of patience, Roos came cycling up at a furious pace. Hurling his bike against the waiting-room wall, he rushed into the compartment to join his team, sagged back into the seat and panted, 'Wow! Just made it in time, eh!'

As a back-bencher in Parliament he was a most impressive sight; big and powerful in his conservative suit with a stiff and formal wing collar, his hair thick and grey and his drooping soup-strainer moustache a bristling symbol of his individuality. At first the other Members delighted in teasing the old Springbok and headmaster, but he had too much natural dignity and commonsense to rise to the obvious bait and soon he was listened to in silence.

It is rather indicative of the man's character that his last speech in Parliament dealt with helping the underprivileged. Political correspondents who knew him well wrote at the time that the speech was not delivered in his usual flamboyant style, that the big dark eyes so startling under the bushy eyebrows were, as usual, in eloquent support of his words but that his emphasising gesticulations were conspicuously missing. Only a few hours after completing his appeal for better housing for the poor Paul Roos was dead.

Springbok Saga. Chris Greyvenstein. Nelson and Toyota, South Africa.

[35]

Although stop-watch specialists say authoritatively that players' possession of the ball in an average game amounts to no more than seconds, certain men do appear to the retrospective eye to have dominated the exchanges through handling skills, or feats of strength, or bravery, or capacity to side-step or outstrip the opposition or jump higher than the rest. Such participants excite admiration in all onlookers and hero-worship in the young and impressionable. A.A. Thomson wrote that the England players in the first International match he saw, at Twickenham in 1912, seemed to be 'built in heroic mould'. He was evidently spellbound by the backs, and by one man in particular.

The English three quarter line of 1912 must live perennially in the memories of those who saw it; apart from the swift and determined Chapman, the line might be described as the creation of the strategist and team-builder Adrian Stoop, who was himself playing that day at stand off half, with J.A. Pym, of Blackheath, as his partner. J.G.G. Birkett was a three quarter with the build of a forward, a human fore-runner of the Conqueror tank; to any full back faced with the agonising problem of tackling him, he must have seemed a moving mountain.

The other wing was Henry Brougham, a dashing and dangerous fellow anywhere near the line. The left-centre, the fourth of that line, was Ronald William Poulton, who was without exception the most beautiful player I ever saw. It is difficult for a lad not to have an idol, and Poulton was mine. Rugby footballers, like cricketers and indeed like most other groups of men, can fall into two broad categories. They may be puritans or cavaliers, artisans or artists, honest toilers or dazzling charmers. Both kinds are of undoubted value and the game, and the world, would be the poorer without either. But one kind is far more numerous than the other. There are many artisans (bless them all) but few artists; there are many honest toilers, but very few enchanters. And, alas, enchanters grow fewer every day.

Ronald Poulton was a cavalier, a supreme artist, a dazzler of dazzlers. There have been few like him, none quite like him. I do not know which other footballers are regarded as having consistently dazzled spectators and opponents (and, it must be confessed, occasionally friends); Obolensky, perhaps, with his never-to-be-forgotten try against New Zealand in 1936, by a breath-taking diagonal run ending on the 'wrong' side of the field; Catcheside, who leaped to fame over the French full back's head; Ian Smith, whose speed on the wing anticipated the guided missile by half a century, and R.A. (Dickie) Lloyd who was capable of dropping a goal with virtually the second kick of a match. These were a shining company. All of them were individualists and artists with resplendent skills all their own. But none of them was like Poulton.

Cricketers are easier to assess. Everyone has an idea of what is mean by the brilliance of 'Ranji', K.L. Hutchings or Frank Woolley; the Denis Compton who flashed through the season of 1947 had it too. If Poulton reminded me of any cricketer, it was of Victor Trumper. There was in the art of both these men a swiftness, a panache, a chivalry, a sheer enchantment that caught the breath. It used to be said that the secret of Trumper's glory was his unshakeable belief that no bowler could really bowl. When you saw Poulton flying through a defensive gap that had not been there a split second before, you instantly had the feeling that the opposition did not really exist. He went through a ruck of players as the prince in some fairy tale might pass by a touch of his magic sword through a castle wall. He would move with his rhythmic stride towards a waiting full back and, hey presto, Poulton was over the line and the unhappy back was clutching the air. The swerve was so accurate and yet so slight that you had the optical illusion of seeing him go, not past the full back but right through him. Spectators who stood behind the goal line and watched him approach had a slightly different illusion; they declared that it was the defenders trying to tackle him who appeared to swerve. Poulton, as they saw him, seemed to run dead straight. Like Trumper, he had some of the swift, shining quality of a rapier. And, also like Trumper, he was a man, masculine but full of charm, whose character and personality stood right out from those of his fellows.

Rugger My Pleasure. A.A. Thomson. Museum Press. 1955.

Some players provoke excellent writing about them; but sometimes, tragically, assessment turns into obituary through circumstances.

C.M. Pritchard (Newport); fourteen caps; forward; 1904–1910. Before dawn broke on August 13, 1916, a 33-year-old captain in the 12th Battalion, South Wales Borderers, was brought into No.1. Casualty Clearing Station in France badly wounded. He had been carried back after taking part in a raid on the German trenches, which had achieved its objective of taking prisoners. He had been at the Western Front for just over two months. His last reported words were as follows: 'Have they got the Hun?' Reply: 'Yes, he's all right.' 'Well, I have done my bit.' He died without leaving the Station the following day.

It sounds like a film script, but it is not. It is the official record of the death of 'Charlie' Pritchard. For his part in the action he was mentioned in dispatches. His death was seen to epitomise the glorious sacrifice of the 'best sort' of young British manhood in the Great War.

The descriptions of him in life bear out the manner of his dying. He was like a lion on the field; off it he was extremely gentle, tender and lovable. In his play he was an untiring worker with almost inexhaustible energy. Although not a specialist, he more often than not played in the back row. He played with great fire and exuberance and was a very difficult player to stop. He had an excellent swerve in open play and always seemed to sustain a resolute forward momentum in the mauls and tight play. His passing was excellent while he could scrummage and dribble as well as any player. But his most important asset was his deadly tackling. George Travers said of his performance against the 1905 All Blacks, 'He sent 'em down like ninepins.'

He stood an inch or so under six feet and was about 13 st 10 lb.

A Century Of Welsh Rugby Players. Wayne Thomas. Ansells Ltd.

Arguments about the relative strengths of teams from different eras and the players included in them have been – and surely always will be – a strong undercurrent in rugby conversation. How would the 1950–51 Springboks have fared against the 1967 All Blacks? Could the Welsh sides of the middle and late seventies have defeated those of the early fifties? Was the British Isles team of 1974 a better one than that of 1971? The beauty of such questions is that since they do not possess answers anyone can pronounce with authority upon them.

Certainly supporters argued fiercely in 1924 when Cliff Porter's New Zealand side remained unbeaten throughout a long tour of Britain and France. Its predecessors of 1905 had a blot on their copybook, the defeat by Wales (the outbreak of war meant that there was no All Black tour in the century's second decade).

Writers and critics strove to be balanced as they weighed up the merits of two great tour sides. Here is the careful assessment of a Westcountryman who won a lot of caps in the thirties.

Pride of place must go to the rock-like George Nepia, the full back, who played in all the 28 games, kicked and tackled with tremendous skill and zest and never let the side down. A great full back, this, who will be remembered for many years to come for his outstanding displays throughout the tour. I frequently hear comparisons made between Nepia and R.W.H. Scott, the All Blacks' full back of the 1953–4 tour, and fine player though Nepia undoubtedly was, I consider Scott an even better full back. Whilst Nepia was the better tackler, Scott's amazing accuracy, positional sense and versatility earns him a place among the really great players of our time.

As a scoring machine the All Blacks' back division, once they had settled down, were a thoroughly efficient combination. Short, quick passing in close formation and straight running were the successful formula. Individually they were no faster or more resourceful than many of our half backs and three quarters with whom they were matched, but the additional thrust and determination, allied to the complete understanding which they quickly developed and maintained, made them a formidable striking force which, given a fair share of the ball, could be relied upon to score tries. Their defence was sound, and if a gap was found by an opposing player, the reliable Nepia was always there as the last line of defence.

I have often heard the relative merits of this 1924 All Black side and their predecessors of 1905 debated, sometimes with heat, and

A blazer once owned by George Nepia found its way to Penarth RFC's Trophy Room. When the 'rock-like' All Black full-back of 1924 returned to Wales to support the 1982 Maoris, he tried it on at the invitation of club officials Kevin Bush (left) and Cyril Lewis. It still fitted him! (*Western Mail & Echo Ltd.*)

for the very good reason that I was not old enough to see the 1905 team I am not qualified to enter into this controversy. It seems to me, however, that in attempting to draw such a comparison due allowance should be made for the fact that the 1924 side visited these islands at a time which was something of a vintage period for English rugby football; such players as H.J. Kittermaster, H.M. Locke, R. Hamilton-Wickes and A.T. Young were then in their prime behind the scrum, and in one of the strongest packs ever fielded by England the names of W.W. Wakefield, G.S. Conway, R. Edwards, A.T. Voyce, J.S. Tucker and R. Cove-Smith will bring back vivid memories to rugby followers of my generation.

Yet the 1924 All Blacks had little difficulty in defeating all the English county club sides, most of them by a comfortable margin, and finished gloriously with a 17–11 victory over England at Twickenham early in January. But then, I suppose, the 1905 protagonists will counter the point I have made by reminding me of the strength of Wales at that time, and will argue from this that the standard of opposition which the 1905 All Blacks came up against was at least as high as in the later tour.

Let us, then, leave it to the septuagenarians to carry on the argument; for my part I am content to accept the outstandingly successful results of the games played by both the 1905 and 1924–5 All Blacks as evidence of their great strength and all-round ability.

'Part II: The 1924–5 Tour', by L.J. Corbett from *Fifty Years Of The All Blacks*, compiled by Wilfred Wooller and David Owen. J.M. Dent and Sons Ltd.

Whereas a fair number of cricketers have found it possible to defy the march of time and re-appear in a new era – the names of Washbrook, Graveney and Bradman himself spring to mind– the trick is harder to bring off in rugby since careers are relatively shorter. Where it is possible, however, there is a distinct spin-off for spectators, who feel as if a little of their own youth has been restored. Certainly that would have been the case after World War II: when pre-War Internationals won post-War caps they must indeed have confirmed the view that, after the six-year Hitler hiatus, life was back to normal.

Jack Heaton was one such player, first chosen by England in 1935 and captain of his country as late as 1947. What follows, however, is an all-too-familiar tale of a player whose gifts and genius were either misunderstood, or imperfectly understood, or simply not considered a good risk by national selectors. All countries have known their Jack Heatons.

Jack Heaton had the misfortune to be an attacking general in an age when the England selectors were more interested in stolid, safe defence. The choice he posed the selectors in the nineteen-thirties was simple: either build a back division around him and attack; or make the pivotal player Moseley's Peter Cranmer, who had a basically defensive approach, and be certain of safety.

Most of the time England adopted the latter course. When Heaton did play for his country it was in an atmosphere alien to his genius for inspiring combination in the backs. In 1939, for example, it was his accuracy as a place kicker that England put to greater use than anything else. When his talents were belatedly rewarded with the England captaincy after the War it was too late. Heaton was by then in his mid-thirties, past his prime and on the brink of retirement.

[41]

It was a tragedy for rugby. While Wales were exploiting the comparable qualities of Wilfred Wooller, England were squandering the talents of a man who was considered the greatest attacking centre his nation had produced for years. The result was that despite twelve war-interrupted years of being in and out of the national side Heaton ended up with only eight International caps, excluding the 1946 Victory Internationals. The measure of his greatness, then, can only be really taken from his play with Lancashire and Waterloo.

Heaton was a great leader on the field. He was used to captaincy from an early age, leading Cowley School and then Liverpool University. He encouraged and inspired others to follow his approach to the game, which revolved around the simply obvious fact that if you fail to attack your opponents' line you will not score tries. He was strong on ensuring that the man with the ball was always supported, and believed that the one sure way to win was attack, attack and attack again, probing for weakness that could be exploited. He was a master of counter-attack and also believed that one of the best ways to demoralise the opposition was to attack from your own line, gaining surprise, when safety first was uppermost in most players' minds. Inevitably this approach had its risks and England selectors before the War were not prepared to take them.

It was Heaton's performances for Lancashire that first brought him national fame. Lancashire reached three county finals and two semi-finals in six seasons from 1929, then won the title in 1934–5. Heaton was the star of the final and, with Graham Meikle on one wing and Roy Leyland in the centre, was alongside Waterloo players with whom he had great rapport. Inevitably he and Leyland were picked for England, though hardly in a manner which enabled them to be truly effective. This was because the selectors dithered appallingly. Cranmer was the other centre in contention and the resultant shuffles saw both him and Leyland capped on the wing in different games. This completely wasted Heaton's genius, which Leyland's understanding of his play (as well as his own considerable talents) accentuated. In combination, the pair played well beyond the sum of their individual abilities. The result of such selectorial incompetence in the 1935 Internationals was, in effect, to isolate Heaton on the field. His style required backs to combine in support of each other in running play and he never got the chance to show this off. The isolation left him unsupported and ripe to be marked out of the game – which he then was, relentlessly.

When out of the England side during the period 1936–8 Heaton continued to give everyone lessons in attacking rugby. One of the best ploys he developed was to shout 'Run left!' at his stand-off, who then did exactly that, drawing the wing forwards while the ball was passed by the scrum half to Heaton breaking right, usually with his cousin Richie – Dicky Guest– in support. Waterloo were chalking up impressive victories and so were Lancashire, who won the county title again in 1937, beating Surrey 24–12 in a final where Heaton and Leyland attacked time after time. That year the Barbarians recognised his worth by picking him for a side that included two other world-class attackers, Cliff Jones of Wales and Louis Babrow of South Africa. How the Baa-Baas' style and approach must have suited Heaton's own.

Probably, it was such company that Heaton needed completely to fulfil his enormous potential. At club and county level, which were almost identical given Waterloo's contribution to Lancashire, he could be devastating. If he could have played alongside similarly great attackers of the period at the next level of the game, who knows what the world would have seen? Alas – he had just started work as an architect in 1938 and had to decline the invitation to tour South Africa with the Lions. War prevented the opportunity ever arising again.

Heaton and George Key kept rugby alive at Blundellsands during the War and, although ageing as a player, Heaton carried on after-wards, leading Lancashire to the county final yet again in 1946–7. On the way the county scored 171 points in eight games, and then beat Gloucestershire in a replayed final after the first match had been drawn. Appointed England captain in all four matches, he missed one through injury. England won three and shared the title with Wales. It was the end of Heaton's International career, though two years later he was to turn down a request to train up for International rugby again. He told the selectors that the game at that level was too hard for a man of thirty-six.

His county days were not yet over, however. He led Lancashire to the championship in 1947–8 and 1948–9 to complete a post-war hat-trick. He even captained a combined Lancashire-Cheshire XV to victory over the Australian tourists. When he retired from serious representative rugby in 1949 a giant passed out of the game. The tragedy was that he might have been even greater.

Waterloo Centenary Brochure. 1982. Ian Hamilton Fazey.

Clubs and countries always look on families of rugby players as something
special, and there is charisma in the achievements of the Browns and Bruce-
Lockharts, the Ellas and the Clarkes.

Surely the most notable, though, have been the Williamses of Taffs Well,
a riverside village in Glamorgan. For fifty years the brothers have graced the
ranks of Cardiff RFC (and Wales), first as players and latterly perpetuating
the link as committee-men.

Their names and achievements were summarised by Cardiff's great archivist,
Danny Davies.

I arrive in this alphabetical chapter at the names of probably the
greatest family group of rugby players, the Williams brothers, whose
remarkable achievements for their club and country have spread
across the world of rugby football. Eight brothers in all – and in
addition the son of one of them, named Bleddyn Ashley – have
played for Cardiff with great distinction. I give their Christian names
in order of the seasons in which they first played for the club:

GWYN, a forward, 1934–5 to 1938–9. A most robust back row
man who really did put half backs on the deck. Gained his senior
cap in 1935–6. A police officer, he turned professional for Wigan and
during the last War was severely wounded in action.

BRINLEY, a centre, 1938–9, 1946–7 and 1949–50. Played for both
Cardiff's senior teams in over twenty matches while also assisting his
local village club, Taffs Well.

BLEDDYN made his debut in 1938–9 against Ebbw Vale (Brinley
also played) and continued until season 1954–5, playing 283 first-
team games. Captain of his club 1953–4, when he led it to victory
over the touring All Blacks. A Barbarian, captain of Wales with
twenty-one caps and a member of the British Lions team to New
Zealand and Australia in 1950. Holder of his club's highest scoring
record of forty-one tries in the season of 1947–8. One of the greatest
centre three quarters of all time.

LLOYD, scrum half, 1952–3 to 1963–4, a well-built and outstanding player who followed after Rex Willis. Twice captained the
club, 1960–1 and 1961–2, and Wales also on three occasions, with
thirteen International caps to his credit. He had two Welsh Youth
International caps before making his senior club debut. He made

310 first team appearances before his retirement. Lloyd has served on the rugby club committee since season 1965–6.

VAUGHAN, centre three quarter, was not as successful as his brothers and played only three matches in all for the club in 1969–70, remaining faithful to his village club Taffs Well.

CENYDD. This brother, who gave excellent service in the period 1956–7 to 1961–2, was equally at home at centre or outside half. A neat, almost classical player, he graduated via Cardiff Juniors and gained First XV and Athletic caps. Like Bleddyn, Lloyd and Tony, he was a Barbarian and made 115 1st XV appearances before turning professional with the St Helens club.

ELWYN. This excellent back row forward has served the club since 1958–9 after playing for Cardiff Juniors whom he captained in 1957–8. He gained a Welsh Youth International cap, Athletic and 1st XV caps, and one for Wales Under-23 against Canada in 1962; and has been a Welsh senior International triallist. A modest and likeable player, probably one of the most versatile of any forwards, able to play in almost any position in the backs as well. Up to September 1972 he made 338 1st XV appearances, plus those in Sevens.

TONY. The youngest, but not the least remarkable of the family, at home at stand off half or centre, Tony graduated to the seniors via Christ College, Brecon, and Cardiff Juniors, then to the Athletic XV in 1959–60. He won his Athletic cap in 1960–1 and his 1st XV cap in the following season. A sterling player of cleverness and tactical ability and a great tackler, he has been worthy of International honours. Captain of the Athletic XV for 1972–3 and 1973–4, he also played no fewer than 328 1st XV games for the club. Made a great name for himself in Sevens and, like Elwyn, is seemingly evergreen. Tony – Anthony D. – was elected to the rugby committee for 1975–6.

ASHLEY, the son of Bleddyn, no doubt to his dad's regret, did not mature like some of his uncles, but he did assist the club in Junior matches between 1964–5 and 1968–9 and played 28 matches for Cardiff Extras including an odd game with Cardiff Athletic.

Such then, is the brief story of this remarkable family of rugby players who, from their humble schooling in Taffs Well have made this unique contribution to Cardiff and Wales and probably one without parallel in the world of rugby football. At least one of the brothers played for Cardiff in every season since Gwyn's debut in 1934–5 until 1972–3 (and as many as four appeared in the same team for Cardiff 1st XV in 1959–60). Excluding the War years, 1940–4, these brothers have covered a span of thirty-four consecutive seasons with the Cardiff club.

Cardiff Rugby Club: History and Statistics. D.E. Davies.

Because of their exploits in open play backs tend to catch the eye and hence the major part of appreciative and even adulatory writing tends to be about them, whereas forwards mainly generate esteem and affection for their semi-clandestine work in areas nick-named the 'power-house' or the 'engine room'. So far, this section reflects that preponderance, and it is time to redress the balance. How better than with this genial essay by Bill McLaren on a fellow Border Scot, Hugh McLeod.

He was, in every sense, a combative forward and, though not primarily disruptive, he none-the-less would 'sort out' anyone causing his hooker discomfort. With a determined glint in his eye he would ask his middle-man: 'Will I fork them for you, son?'

Originally a tight-head prop (as successor in his club fifteen to a former cap, Stewart Coltman), McLeod was forced on the 1955 Lions tour to switch to the loose head because three of the four props – himself, T. Elliot (Gala and Scotland) and C.C. Meredith (Neath and Wales) were regular tight-heads. He was even versatile enough to deputise on that tour as a hooker. Though he had no preference he played most of the remainder of his career as a loose head and it is a testimony to his remarkable strength and sound technique that on only one occasion do I recall seeing him genuinely troubled by an opposing prop – in the 1961 South of Scotland v South Africa match at the hands of that incredibly strong Boland farmer Piet du Toit. Not surprisingly, McLeod has rated du Toit top of his list of opponents along with the Irish trio, B.G.M. Wood, A.R. Dawson and S. Millar, whom he regarded as the hardest trio to scrummage against, and he has paid tribute too to the guidance he received on the 1955 tour from W.O. Williams (Swansea).

Acutely conscious of his line-out obligation to his specialist jumpers, McLeod was rock-solid in his 'blocking', preferring the

Hugh McLeod (left) with Robin Roe (centre) and Tom Elliott before the 1955 British Lions' departure for South Africa. On tour McLeod demonstrated versatility by switching to loose-head prop from his normal tight-head side – and even stood in as an emergency hooker. (*S & G Press Agency Ltd.*)

wedge onto his lock with forward drive rather than the turned-back technique favoured by some of his contemporaries. He would deal ruthlessly with any opponent attempting illegally to drive through and though he never regarded himself as an auxiliary jumper, one was not alone in believing that he carried immense additional value as a surprise line-out catcher, for his power in the upward spring was astonishing as he frequently displayed in sevens. Latterly he utilised his keen sense of judgement and timing in providing peel linkage round the line-out tail and one of the most breathtaking sights in the game was that of McLeod, head lowered, thundering into a ruck and the shudder that inevitably ran through the edifice as he struck!

Despite lack of early tuition, he proved outstandingly skilled at a time when forwards were having to reach out for a higher standard of basic technique. His receipt and delivery of passes were copybook. One recalls in particular his perfectly-timed delivery after appearing out of some private trap door to give Arthur Smith a scoring overlap against Ireland in the 1961 Dublin match. This was typical of him and it is hardly surprising that he had no peer in seven-a-sides where his skill in linkage and his sense of positioning came to the fore as well as commendable basic speed which frequently belied his broad contours and heavy bow legs. I remember gasping in surprise when McLeod chopped down an admittedly overworked John Ranson (Rosslyn Park) from behind with a scalding burst at the Twickenham sevens in 1963 and one has heard the famous Herbert Waddell describe in ecstatic terms how McLeod succeeded so often in arriving second or third man to the breakdown following a set scrummage. It was typical of McLeod's thoroughness, too, that he taught himself to punt most acceptably with either foot and there was a time when he was principal goalkicker for his club seven.

Like all successful front row men, he could be totally uncompromising – and brutally frank into the bargain.

The story is told of one club game in which a brash youngster went into his first scrummage against McLeod with the sarcastic comment to his colleagues: 'I wonder what lesson we'll have from the famous McLeod today.' Unfortunately for him the youngster had a habit of placing his outside hand on the pitch for balance and McLeod – said hand having been firmly stamped into the ground – politely remarked: 'And there endeth your first lesson, sonny boy.' He stood on no ceremony! On one famous occasion he upbraided a Union official before the whole Scottish fifteen for having sent him a letter beginning 'Dear McLeod.' He had another joust with authority before the Scottish tour of South Africa in 1960 when he wanted to play for his club seven a week before tour departure and they wouldn't let him in case of injury. He told the massive lock Frans ten Bos (London Scottish) on the eve of a French International in Paris: 'If I was half your size I'd pick up the first two Frenchmen who looked at me tomorrow and I'd throw both of them right over the bloody stand.' It was at the practice session prior to Wales v Scotland at Cardiff in 1962 that McLeod showed the bluntness of speech that could inspire his colleagues. He had been pressed, reluctantly, into leading the Scottish pack but the practice was not getting off the ground because too many of his colleagues were voicing differing opinions. So he called them together with a 'Come here my wee disciples' and told them in the most forthright terms that he did not want to lead the pack but had been forced to do so; that if any one of them fancied himself as a boss man he need only

[48]

inform McLeod who would sponsor him for the pack leadership among the hierarchy; but, failing that, any one thereafter who opened his bl——y mouth would feel McLeod's boot at his backside! All this was spoken, vehemently, in a strong Border dialect and it is said that one of the Anglo-Scots turned to a friend and whispered: 'Well, I didn't understand a word but it all sounded damned impressive.' In any event McLeod regained absolute control and, on the morrow, the pack went like bombs in Scotland's first win at Cardiff for 35 years, a famous occasion in which *McLeod surpassed J.M. Bannerman's long-standing Scottish record of 37 caps.

'Hugh Ferns McLeod' by Bill McLaren, from *Rugby: The Great Ones*, edited by Cliff Morgan. Pelham Books.

For more than a decade in the late fifties and sixties New Zealand packs were the world's best and although other nations enviously recognised the great contribution of men like Gray, Lochore, Tremain and Nathan, the granite-hard, unflinching quality of All Black forward play was best epitomised by the lock forward Colin Meads.

The skill was there certainly – the comprehension of a big forward's role at ruck and maul; but more, there was a capacity for covering ground doggedly like an infantryman under fire – a shock-absorbing shake of the head, followed by the remorseless advance which guaranteed the half back good ball. Meads also possessed the mean streak required for a lock to be a world-beater.

His already high reputation in Britain was further boosted in 1971 when, as his country's beaten Test skipper, he showed that he could take defeat gracefully. Such qualities prompted John Hopkins to seek him out during the next Lions' tour.

When I met Colin Meads I was struck by his sheer physical size, the size of his hands and the brusqueness of his welcome. Yet I sensed that the brusqueness was not a lack of warmth but an inability to make himself at ease with a complete stranger. 'He is still rather a shy man who believe he owes a lot to football,' says his wife Verna.

As an All Black, Colin Meads has visited countries he had only read about and met people he would otherwise never meet. He is a Member of the British Empire. He has met the Queen of England several times, been to the Houses of Parliament, drunk champagne

Colin Meads sets up a maul for the 1967 All Blacks against the Barbarians. People say to his son, 'Your father was never injured.' (*S & G Press Agency Ltd.*)

in the casino of Paris. Were it not for his rugby he would have been just another farmer in a nation of sheep farmers.

Since he launched himself in the latest phase of his career he has had to acquire some of the finesse he did not need in earlier days. He still tends to talk in well-worn phrases but he has learned to speak more fully and easily. He rarely turns down journalists who want an interview.

Many rugby followers in Britain and Australia remember Colin Meads for his violence. He knocked out Welshman David Watkins. He hit Jeff Young, breaking Young's jaw, because the Welsh hooker had committed the rugby crime of pulling a jersey. Kenny Catchpole's misfortune was to be caught in a ruck head down, one leg protruding like a ship's mast from amidst the heaving bodies. Meads grabbed it, ripped it as he might a chicken bone, and the Australian's international career had virtually ended.

'I don't think anyone plays for a country as long as I did and remains popular everywhere,' says Meads now when faced with a reminder of his misdeeds. 'You don't play to make yourself popular, do you?'

'But do you have any remorse?' I asked him.

'For some of them you do. The David Watkins episode, for example. We've spoken of it since, so I am not breaking any confidences if I tell you that he toppled over after I hit him. I reckon he was only acting. I'm saying to myself, "Come on, you little bastard," and then everyone starts booing you.'

'And Catchpole?'

'In Australia my name stinks because Catchy was their idol. He had the ball, he was caught in a ruck, and we were trying to get the ball off him so I grabbed one leg to tip him over onto the ground. How was I to know his other leg was stuck? It wasn't my fault the other leg was trapped between two bodies and he virtually did the splits and tore his groin muscles very badly. Catchy and I have spoken to one another since. We toured on Tonga together. There is no malice between us.'

There is no malice between referee Kevin Kelleher and Meads either. At Murrayfield in 1967 when Scotland faced the touring All Blacks, Kelleher sent off the New Zealander for dangerous play. The following Christmas Kelleher sent Meads a Christmas card and one arrives at Te Kuite each Christmas even now.

For a time after being sent off Meads felt nothing but shame, as did Verna, sitting up in bed 12,000 miles away listening to a crackly radio commentary. For the next few days she seemed unable to turn on the television without seeing a reconstruction of the incident. 'If I saw it on television once I saw it fifty million times. It nearly drove me demented.' She was soothed by an outburst of support for her husband from the Prime Minister of New Zealand, from people in Te Kuite and all over the country. One even came from Wales. It was signed, 'From two and a half million Welshmen, bad luck.'

Meads's playing career is over now but his fame survives. Journalists want to interview him and children write from all over the world wanting his autograph. There is a street in Te Kuite named after him, a racehorse called Pine Tree and a house called Meads House in a local reform school.

He knows but does not understand the price of fame and wonders whether his children have even begun to learn to live with it. He worries most about Kelvin, his eldest son, more than Karen, who is the oldest, and Rhonda, Glynn and Shelley. 'It is hard for them to be Colin Meads's children. My sons have to do their own thing. I keep well away from their rugby but they've got to learn to adapt.

Kelvin finds it hard even when he is injured. People say to him 'What the hell is wrong with you? Your father was never injured!'

Life With The Lions. John Hopkins. Stanley Paul.

The British Isles side which vanquished the All Blacks in 1971 was already formidable but in its sixth match it was augmented by the arrival of Gerald Davies who had stayed in Cambridge to complete his examinations. Suddenly there was an extra dimension on the right wing: a weapon which could strike from long range, leaving waves of defenders rolling helplessly on their backs, and could flit through a barely-perceived defensive chink close to the corner-flag. Seven years later hard-skinned Kiwis still went eagerly to Australia to see the little Welshman's final rugby fling and to check that their eyes had not deceived them at Timaru and Blenheim and Napier and Wellington.

A man from Mars watching cricketers in conversation might reasonably conclude that they were dumb folk communicating through sign language. Wrists roll over to signify googlies; first and middle fingers interact conveying seam bowling; stiffened forearms flourish and mimic cover drives, dispatching imaginary balls to the fence. It is as if mere words alone are insufficient to contain the aesthetic of the game.

Very few other sports share this characteristic, certainly not Rugby football in general. Terms like 'power' and 'dynamic' go far towards distilling the essence of Gareth Edwards. David Duckham comes alive if we speak of pounding thighs and blond hair streaming in the wind. The man on the terrace can enjoy a blunt phrase like 'Viet Gwent' to epitomise the Pontypool front row.

Thomas Gerald Reames Davies thus has a certain claim to uniqueness. Just as he leaves tacklers sprawling in his wake, so the literate find themselves floundering in attempts to describe his genius. 'Then Gerald got the ball,' people say. 'He just went – phfft, phfft – to the line.' It seems that future generations enquiring about him will just have to be shown the video tapes.

Of course, you can list his skills. He has always known the fastest, straightest course to the line, as he showed at Murrayfield in 1971 with a late, decisive try. At close range he can turn himself into an eel as he did for the Lions that same summer when squeezing between a defender and the corner flag for a vital Third Test touch-down. This spring, captaining Cardiff in a WRU cup-tie at Pontypool, he

[52]

demonstrated that even at thirty-three he retained the ability and stamina to run in tries from forty and fifty metres, jinking and breaking tackles on the way.

But a bald recitation of the Davies repertoire utterly fails to meter the electric shock experienced by a game of rugby when the ball finally reaches his hands at his outpost close to the touchline. For a few moments the afternoon is supercharged with amps and volts. Crowds jerk to tip-toe with expectancy; the antennae of team-mates vibrate with tension; in the twinkling of an eye a defence can shrivel, blacken and blow a fuse. These are the real reasons why Australia's administrators were so delighted to know that 'Reames' would be with Wales for a final tour fling this summer, and why hard-bitten All Blacks flew to Brisbane and Sydney for a last glimpse of wing play at its greatest.

Australia is chalked on two milestones in the Davies career. It was against John Thornett's Wallabies that he won a first cap in 1966. Then, following a dozen appearances as a centre, came the positional change which lifted him from the ranks of talented also-rans to found his reputation as one of the best wings the game has known.

'Before our Sydney Test of 1969 Wales had three fit centres but only one wing,' he recalls. 'Clive Rowlands, the coach, asked if I would be willing to fill the gap. I agreed, and scored a try in our 19–16 win.

'That, really, was that. I savoured the experience to the full. The ball may reach you less often on the wing, but at least you have room in which to move. It also occurred to me that at eleven-and-a-half stone I was not cut out to play the crash-ball game then beginning to find favour with international centres and coaches. On my return London Welsh, who boasted strong midfield men in Keith Hughes, Jim Shanklin and John Dawes, were happy to go along with my new preference – and I have never looked back.'

The impression is conveyed that Gerald Davies accepted the change only after considerable thought – not a discipline cultivated by all Rugby's great men. But his nursery at Queen Elizabeth Grammar School, Carmarthen, and the finishing schools of Loughborough and Cambridge are all establishments which encourage sportsmen to stand back from the hurly-burly of their game and take time to think. What has Gerald Davies learned?

'Two things,' he declares. 'First that, all other things being equal, Rugby is a game of calculated risks. It disturbs me that many of the

Gerald Davies 'has always known the fastest, straightest course to the line'.
(*Colorsport.*)

rising generation are content with safety-first, stereotyped play. Set
views are accepted at face value. Not enough consideration is given
to exploiting the total potential of the fifteen men who make up a
team.

'Secondly, that the game is for enjoyment.' He grins momentarily:
'On a wet Wednesday night at Pontypool Park I will tell my Cardiff
players that they are there to do a job of work! But seriously, on most
other occasions the message I try to get across in the fifteen minutes
before kick-off is that we are out to enjoy both ourselves and the
game. We are men at play.'

Davies insists that, under John Dawes, Welsh XVs of recent years
have shared this aim. 'It may not have looked like it this year – but
remember, our meetings with England, Ireland and France were
exceptionally hard. They all attacked us remorselessly. Against Scotland we seemed set for a high enjoyment quotient but, sadly and
inexplicably, we lost direction.'

His twenty tries for Wales have given Gerald Davies pleasurable
moments in plenty along the way. So did the quartet he scored at
Pontypool in February. So did his display in the Doble Memorial
match at Moseley, when he took delight in confounding those critics
who claimed that he could not side-step off his left foot. But he asserts

that enjoyment requires more than simply scoring tries and making the crowd roar.

'It's about out-thinking a wing who may be six inches quicker than you,' he says. 'It's about filling an opponent with doubt as to which side you will choose to beat him. It's about keeping the ball alive when you are cornered and enabling a support player to score. For a captain, it's about stamping a recognisable style of play upon his team, as I can claim to have done in my three years as Cardiff's skipper. That is genuine satisfaction.'

Now that he has again accepted the leadership of his club the assumption must be that Gerald Davies will play one more season of first-class Rugby. He may be tempted to turn out for Wales against New Zealand, going on to collect the few caps he would then need to retire with a round half century. He claims that the statistic does not interest him. Why, then, does he keep coming back for more Rugby? As a wing, he must now be ranked a veteran.

The motive is almost certainly extreme disappointment that the Cardiff XV, nurtured by him since 1975, have yet to win the Welsh Rugby Union's Challenge Cup. Beaten by Newport in the 1977 Final they fell at the semi-final stage this year to the eventual winners, Swansea. 'At one stage this winter we were playing the best Rugby in the land,' he says. 'It seemed logical that we should win the Welsh Cup competition, which I regard as the best-conceived in the British Isles. But in the semi-final Swansea were the better side. That was a bitter pill to swallow.'

Such admissions are not made easily by a man who is basically private and introvert. On the field his most histrionic reaction when a half back has kicked away promising possession is to clasp his hands briefly about his head. After scoring a great try he returns briskly to his own half, perhaps venturing an occasional handshake. Refusing to be carried away by the adulation of fans and critics he has more than once chosen to remain with wife Cilla and daughter Emily rather than travel on a lengthy overseas tour.

The book he is writing and the work he would like to do for the media when he finally retires will almost certainly contribute more to the understanding of Rugby than to the ballyhoo about it. Compared with the fire-in-belly make-up of some Welsh 'greats' Davies's approach is self-controlled and cerebral. However, it is open to question whether he has rid his mind of the criticism and disbelief which has greeted his style of skippering Cardiff these last three

Sam Doble in action for Moseley against London Welsh. He punctuated his 1,338 goals with 85 tries – but there was much more to him than records. (*Colorsport.*)

seasons. There are still fans who say that for all his intellect he still cannot 'read' a game; that he has been unable to tame Gareth Edwards's burning instinct for being a tactical law unto himself; that he has remained aloof on his wing when a captain's injection of genius was sorely needed.

These jibes may have penetrated his personal armour. But he is fond of saying that apart from himself, Barry Nelmes and Gareth Edwards, his Blue and Blacks are a team of youngsters. If they can bring Cardiff a first Challenge Cup of modern times, preferably before he retires, then a satisfactory riposte will have been delivered.

He cannot bequeath to posterity the incomparable side-step, the jet-powered acceleration, the perfection of his balanced running, or the electric current that his mere presence can switch on. But victory in the Cup would prove once and for all that the Davies way of playing the game – enjoyment, calculated risks and all – is the right way.

Rugby World, August 1978. David Parry-Jones.

'Gerald' is among a select band of Welsh rugby celebrities whose surname became obsolete over the years. There were 'Gareth', too, and 'Barry'. The English are familiar with the phenomenon in the sphere of politics – 'Ted', 'Jim', 'Maggie' – but in rugby football a 'Sam' is rare indeed. This Sam died all too prematurely.

I never met Sam Doble, but I felt I knew him well. For years he overflowed my bookshelves, a bit like the Suez Canal and Lady Eden's drawing room, though in a much more acceptable way.

Doble certainly caused me more work than anyone else in the sixteen seasons I have been trying to keep club rugby details. But it was work I never grudged – for here, to be sure, was a man making sporting history as goal after goal, with a fair few tries for good measure, filled page after page in my loose-leaf books.

Big Sam entered my life on 4 September 1965, with four conversions and a penalty goal for Moseley v Exeter. His last entry in my records – though not in my cuttings, where there are frequent references to someone 'chasing Doble' – was on 7 January 1976 when he kicked three penalty goals against Llanelli.

Then Moseley dropped him – shame on them! A week or two later he was injured playing in the second XV, and his retirement soon followed. But his memory will live on. If anyone ever totals 3,652 points in his career or 582 points in a season it will be Big Sam Doble's record he's beaten. Peter Butler of Gloucester has subsequently had a 574 and Robin Williams of Pontypool a 560, and though the new differential penalty should slow all challengers down Butler might one day pass that 3,651. Even so, there'll never be another Sam.

For there was so much more to him than records themselves. There was the expectant hush that rippled around every ground when Big Sam picked up his musket for a mighty shot at goal. There was the reputation he helped gain Moseley (who seemed almost moribund in my early days) as Britain's most attractive side ... 'they never seem to mind giving three tries away, confident they can score four themselves; and even if they don't Doble's boot will do the rest,' I wrote once.

Sure, Sam himself sometimes almost clumsily gave some of those tries away – yet with contrasting and surprising deftness for such a big man, he punctuated his 1,338 goals with 85 quite nifty tries of his own.

I myself will retain two particular memories of Big Sam – two that are a little off-beat perhaps, but where would rugby be without a sense of fun?

There was the weekend I expected to announce to the world in my Sunday newspaper that he had clocked up the 3000th point of his career in senior rugby on 29 December 1973. But he beat me to it on the Wednesday, having earlier that season decided to give up midweek rugby! Ah well, it *was* Boxing Day that Wednesday and no doubt Doble too enjoyed a party trick. Even at Christmas, though, it was quite a feat to score twelve points against Coventry ... in those days they seemed to have an injunction against any team getting so many, let alone one man.

My other fondest memory dates back to Rosslyn Park on 19 October 1968, when between kicking six conversions and two penalty goals with his right foot, Big Sam idly snapped up a colleague's knock-on and for the sheer fun of it dropped a hefty goal – which he knew couldn't count– with his LEFT foot.

Yes, he was one of rugby's greats, in stature as well as size. No, there'll never be another Sam Doble.

'When Sam Picked up his Musket'. Michael Nimmo, from *Sam*. Moseley RFC programme.

Clem Thomas, who caused consternation among the top half-back pairings of his day. (*Western Mail & Echo Ltd.*)

R.C.C. Thomas – Clem to his friends and readership – learned the Rugby business at Blundells and Cambridge before covering himself with distinction as a flanker for Swansea, Wales and the British Lions. He caused consternation among the top half-back pairings of his day by his speed around the field and sheer ruthlessness – his great friend Peter Robbins once wrote that Clem, a wholesale butcher, was the only player he could think of who practised his profession on the field!

In later years he became the much-travelled rugby correspondent of the Observer. *Nobody could doubt his passionate Welsh credentials; but in this sympathetic piece about Bill Beaumont's enforced retirement he demonstrates the blood-brotherhood that exists between all top players irrespective of allegiances or nationality.*

William Blackledge Beaumont is a splendid name, but then he is a splendid man. The premature passing of his career will be mourned as much by the Welsh, Irish and Scots as by his own Englishmen, for whom he is the archetypal example of the very best characteristics of his breed.

The injury which finally snuffed out Bill's delightful career was a culmination of three hard blows on the head in a year. The worst of these by far was sustained at Beziers at the start of the current season and the final one came while playing for his beloved Lancashire two weeks ago.

Bill Beaumont wins a ball for the Lions against Western Province. 'His greatest attributes were honesty, integrity and courage ... he contested everything.' (*Colorsport.*)

A computerised brain scan revealed that there were grave risks of permanent injury if he continued to play. Wisely he read the medical evidence correctly and ended one of the most distinguished careers in the history of the Rugby Football Union.

I am not surprised that he acquired so many head injuries, for he was never an instinctive footballer. His greatest attributes were honesty, integrity and courage. He will not be remembered for jumping like a stag in the line-out; instead he was a compressor at the front of the line where his concentration and determination invariably saw him snatch a fair share of the ball.

His principal strength was that, in the idiom of the game over the past decade, he was a marvellous ground player. He would drive fiercely into rucks and mauls, using his head like a battering ram, propelled by what Steve Smith called his outboard motor, which is perhaps the most famous and prominent posterior in the game. His courage in driving into a maelstrom of flying boots and bodies was his danger and eventually his downfall. He contested everything.

Bill will never be forgotten for the charm of his captaincy. He led England a record twenty-one times, winning eleven times and drawing twice. In 1980 he took England to the Grand Slam for the first time snce 1957 when they were led by another Lancastrian, Eric Evans.

If it is a cliché to say that he led by personal example, it is nevertheless entirely true. He had an immense charisma, both on and off the field, and perhaps a reflection of his strength of character was that he was always at his best when things were going badly. In adversity in South Africa in 1980 he could shrug his shoulders and say 'Come on, lads,' and then take ten minutes to get to the coach as he politely signed autographs.

The first major impression he made on me was in 1977 when he arrived in New Zealand as a replacement for Nigel Horton on that difficult, ill-fated tour. I will never forget the Lions meeting him at the airport. Willie Duggan stepped forward to shake his hand and said, 'If I were you, Bill, I would flick off home again on the next plane.' Bill smiled and said, 'Not pygmalion likely.' Immediately he established himself alongside Gordon Brown as an automatic choice for the Tests.

I used to look at Bill Beaumont and wonder what he reminded me of; and finally decided that he was like a St Bernard, a loveable, bulky, gentle old thing possessing great strength under the gracefully floppy exterior, someone who would always come to your rescue.

Yes, Beaumont was everybody's favourite. You see, he always had an advantage over the kind of man who recently broke Geoff Wheel's nose in two places with two punches at the last line-out of the game. It would never have occurred to Bill to act like that. The very idea would be abhorrent because he loved the game, its ethics and its people; and the little man who feels that punching or kicking is part of the game would never morally or physically survive against Beaumont who was a big man in every sense. He may have finished as a player but not as a rugby man and we will, I know, hear and see a lot more of him yet.

Guardian. Clem Thomas.

The expertise of the back-row forward has seldom been better exemplified than by Tony Neary of Broughton Park, England's most-capped player (by just one, from John Pullin). The summation of his talents in Lancashire's centenary publication was succinct and to the point.

Supported by Chris Ralston (left) ball-carrier Tony Neary clearly has no intention of parting with his prize to France's Claude Dourthe or, looming in the background, Gerard Cholley. (*Colorsport.*)

'Nero' was lucky to be born with all the gifts required to make a world-class open-side flanker, for he had consummate ball ability, physical presence and dexterity, mental hardness and vision, and an awareness on the field which caused his decision-making to appear intuitive.

Although he was 6 ft 1 in he always jumped 6 ft 5 in in the lineout with the ability to cup the ball one-handed between palm and wrist – which in itself was an indication that you were in the presence of a player of enormous ball-playing skills. With the ball in his hand he had the almost innate ability to take one or two of the opposition out of the game, be it at a lineout, maul, or in the open, and at the same time make the ball available to a supporting player, whom he would then instinctively support in turn. An illustration of this was a try he scored at Murrayfield a number of years ago when, having received a long flat ball following a penalty from Jan Webster, he ran at a Scottish defender, dipped his right shoulder into his midriff – so committing him fully – and put Andy Ripley through the gap created. Andy then ran approximately fifty metres before being held on the line. On the instant 'Nero' was at his elbow, took the ball, and dived over for a try. A great example of his creative, supporting and finishing ability.

In addition to his ball-playing skills, his mental and physical dedication in the tackle were both resolute and absolute, as was his single-mindedness in digging the ball out of standing tackles and mauls. Summing up, he was the most complete open-side flanker of the modern era, and possibly since the time mental awareness and ball-handling ability became essential ingredients for quality back-row forwards.

'Tony Neary' by Alan Shuker from *Lancashire RFU Centenary Brochure*.

Critics and essayists can have their say in elegant, well-turned prose. In the long run, however, theirs is the mid-distance viewpoint and must be less intimate than the testimony of writers who have run and tackled or shoved and sweated in harness. Affection and respect are the key-notes in Bill Beaumont's recall of fellow Lancastrian Richard Trickey. This is the stuff legends are made of.

At my first Lancashire session I met a player who was to have a profound influence on my philosophy of the sport. Richard Trickey played over a hundred games for Lancashire and a lot of inferior lock forwards have won caps for England. He was the fittest player I ever came across; I found it very hard to credit the masochistic training schedule he eagerly undertook every season in order to perform like a bionic man on the field of action. He really was in perpetual motion. He persuaded me right from the outset that if I wanted to progress I would have to be much fitter than I was. He helped me sort out my priorities and I realised that the ability to time my jump and catch at the line-out was actually only a small part of my overall job as a lock forward. I had also to be fit, strong, fast and perceptive enough to scrummage, ruck, maul, tackle, cover and support flat out for eighty minutes.

Richard was a permanent fixture in the Lancashire team when I took my first tentative steps towards making the grade at county level. As he always packed down on the right-hand side of the scrum, it didn't take me long to work out that I would have to pack down on the left-hand side. I was not accustomed to this scrummaging position, but I would gladly have played hooker if it meant playing for Lancashire so I made light of the temporary inconvenience to which this change of position had subjected me.

Three years after Richard dropped out of the Lancashire side he was recalled for a couple of games in 1980. Even though I had established squatter's rights as the right lock in the scrums, a position I had held for several years for England and that summer for the British Lions, he made it abundantly clear to me at the first scrum that whenever we had played together down through the years he had always been on the right and I had been on the left. He suggested that perhaps it would be tempting fate to change a successful combination at this late stage and bewildered with his logic I obediently moved over to the left to accommodate him.

Our first match together was in 1972 at Fylde against Cumberland and Westmorland just three days after the North West Counties had beaten the All Blacks at Workington. I was especially pleased to play my first game for Lancashire on my own home ground among familiar surroundings. I remember being amazed when a fellow came round dishing out free jerseys and socks before the match. As I unwrapped my jersey and put it on I felt thrilled and terribly proud; even if I achieved nothing else in the next ten years, every time I appeared in our club programme there would be a little asterisk against my name because I was a county player. The game was played at a furious pace and seemed to be over almost before it began, but I did quite well at the line-out and we won 13-nil. However, afterwards I appreciated why Richard Trickey felt the compulsion to be so fit: he played a crucial role in the loose, whereas by the time I arrived at the breakdown, prepared to die for queen, country and John Burgess, the ball was already winging its way to one of the fly halves.

That was the only county game I played that season, but I was determined to win a regular place in 1973. I was aware how difficult this would be with established players like Richard Trickey and Mike Leadbetter as the men in possession, but to my delight and astonishment I was selected with Trickey for the first game against Durham. In retrospect, I think I was lucky to be picked so early in my career; the selectors should have played Mike Leadbetter that season, but Mike accepted that his county days were probably over, and he was the first person to congratulate me and wish me luck. The following year he turned to Rugby League.

My last away trip to that neck of the woods was the bean feast at Percy Park three years earlier, but I had come a long way since then, and now we travelled up the day before and spent the Friday night at a hotel in Durham. I shared a room with Richard Trickey and that was an unforgettable experience. The first thing he did was to turn off the central heating, open all the windows, and announce there was nothing worse than a stuffy hotel room. Who was I to argue, although I thought I was going to freeze to death? We went down to dinner and he proceeded to gorge his way through half a dozen monster courses before dragging me off to a little pub in a quiet side-street where we knocked back a few pints of beer between us.

We returned to the hotel feeling suitably relaxed, and I was ready for bed and a good night's sleep. Wrong again. Richard ordered a mountain of sandwiches which he demolished during the next couple of hours while watching the midnight movie on television. I managed to slot in a few hours' sleep before he woke me up at the crack of dawn to drag me down to the restaurant for a huge cooked breakfast.

After breakfast he put on his old brown duffle coat, which had seen a fair bit of service in the cause of rugby, and took me off on a brisk walk to Durham Cathedral. We climbed to the top of the spire to witness the magnificent panoramic view and then went for a long walk in the grounds. He had carried out this ritual every time he played in Durham and for the next eight years I did likewise. It was

[65]

exhilarating and refreshing. By eleven o'clock, however, Richard's stomach began rumbling ominously and we rushed back to the hotel so that he could consume even more food. To be fair, between us we ate exactly the amount two fifteen-stone rugby players with healthy appetites would be expected to eat. The fact was, though, that I ate exactly nothing and he went right through the menu. I was rather surprised at half time during the match that he was prepared to make do with a piece of orange. But enough of the eating habits of the Trickey beast – he was one helluva player and I learned a lot playing alongside him.

His advice before that match was forthright and sound. 'Whatever you do, don't try anything fancy. No side-stepping or selling dummies or trying to drop a goal – just stick your head up the prop's backside and shove like a lunatic and contest every line-out no matter where the ball is meant to be thrown. We've plenty of prima donnas in the backs to provide the tricks as long as we provide the ball. Just remember you are a donkey, and behave like one.'

Thanks to Rugby. Bill Beaumont. Stanley Paul.

HISTORY

Rugby Football in the Making

William Webb Ellis and Rugby School represent a watershed beyond which the historians are content not to search too diligently. Knappan is acknowledged; likewise Harpastum; but before the nineteenth century, detail is conspicuous by its absence and the idea is subtly transmitted that Rugby Football came into being in its pristine, well-ordered state. Webb Ellis 'with a fine disregard for the rules of football as played in his time first took the ball in his arms and ran with it'; but it must be doubtful whether he founded the Game. Rather, he perhaps forced the codification of the Laws – something at which the Victorians were very accomplished.

It is more fun to go back towards an earlier improvisation for the start of this section on the Game's history.

Legend has it that the first ball used by the natives of Cheshire was the head of a Dane. After being captured at Chester he was slain and the population then 'kicked his head about for sport'.

This partiality in Cheshire for kicking heads obviously continued, for in the Ledger Book of Vale Royal Abbey there is an order dated 20 October 1320 directing the Justiciar of Chester 'to hold an enquiry on the oath of honest and lawful men as to who were the malefactors ... who villainously slew John de Boddeworth, a servant of our well-beloved in Christ the Abbot of Vale Royale at Darnehale, and afterwards cut off his head and carried it away with them and kicked that head with their feet like a ball and made their sport therewith.'

The History Of Cheshire RFU Brochure.

Thirty-nine years after the Webb Ellis aberration clubs were busy trying to standardise regulations for play. Bearing in mind the difficulties of interpretation which bedevil the modern game despite sophisticated aids to communication and comprehension, the mind boggles at the obstacles to be overcome in early club fixtures. Here are reproduced the regulations of Blackheath RFC in 1862, but one wonders what happened when the visiting team turned up with a rule-book of its own . . .

RULES OF THE BLACKHEATH FOOTBALL CLUB

1   That the ball be started from the centre of the ground, by a place-kick.

2   A fair catch is a catch direct from the foot, or a knock-on from the hand of one of the opposite side; when the catcher may either run with the ball or make his mark by inserting his heel in the ground on the spot where he catches it; in which case he is entitled to a fair kick.

3   It is not lawful to take the ball off the ground, except in touch, for any purpose whatever.

4   A ball in touch is dead; and the first man who touches it down must kick it out straight, from the place where it entered touch.

5   A catch out of touch is not a fair catch; but may be run off.

6   Running is allowed to any player, on his side, if the ball be caught or taken off the first bound.

7   Any player holding the ball unless he has made his mark after a fair catch, may be hacked; and running is not allowed after the mark is made.

8   No player may be hacked and held at the same time; and hacking above the knee, or from behind, is unfair.

9   No player can be held or hacked, unless he has the ball in his hands.

10   Though it is lawful to hold any player in a scrimmage, this does not include attempts to throttle or strangle, which are totally opposed to the principles of the game.

11   A player whilst running or being held, may hand the ball to one of his own side, who may continue to run with it; but after the ball is grounded it must be hacked, not thrown or lifted.

12   If the ball goes behind the goal, it must be kicked out by the party to whom the goal belongs, from in a line with the goals; but a catch off a kick from behind goal is not a fair catch, but may be run off.

13   No player to get before the ball on the side farthest from his own goal; but if he does, must not touch the ball as it passes him, until touched by one of the opposite side; he being off-side.

14   A goal must be a kick through, or over, and between the poles;

and if touched by the hands of one of the opposite side, before or whilst going through, is no goal.

15   No one wearing projecting nails, iron plates or gutta percha on the soles or heels of his boots be allowed to play.

Uniform: Dark blue trousers, black and scarlet striped jerseys and socks.

Blackheath RFC Rules: 1862.

Rules Seven, Eight and Nine make it clear that at this early stage in their history Blackheath were committed to 'hacking', that is, kicking an opponent's shins or tripping him. It becomes clear in the short passage that follows what a profound effect the hacking issue had upon organised sport in Britain and the evolution of competing football codes.

Although some authorities are prepared to argue the claims of Guy's Hospital, it is generally conceded that Blackheath are the oldest of all organised Rugby Clubs. Formed in 1858 by former pupils of the Blackheath Preparatory School, the club broke away from an association of clubs which had appointed themselves the governing body of Football in London. This was in 1863, and the issue involved was that of 'hacking' (Blackheath objected to a proposed ban on it), so Blackheath's defection was in effect the final cleavage between the existing game and the new one of Rugby Football. In the same year came the first encounter with their greatest rivals Richmond, which took place on Richardson's Field, Blackheath. In 1866 the club joined Richmond in a move to abolish hacking, and were among the founder members of the Rugby Union in 1871. In 1882 they took over the tenancy of the Rectory Field, which has remained their home ever since.

The Encyclopaedia Of Rugby Football compiled by J.R. Jones. Robert Hale.

Just as conduct during games was slowly being sorted out, so were the accoutrements of play. Boots became the accepted footwear, though it was a long time before bars, sprigs and studs were fitted. By about 1890 a majority of players had discarded breeches in favour of shorts. Match balls were being standardised thanks to the growth of specialist manufacturers. By the mid-nineteenth century the days of pigs' bladders, which had been kicked around by

countless generations of young men at play, were numbered, as emerges in this
excerpt from a paper by a member of the famous Gilbert family of ball makers.

These unsavoury articles were put into the leather cases in their
'green' state, the stem of a clay pipe was fastened to the opening of
the bladders and they were then inflated. The balls were then hung
up until they were wanted. You never see a pig's bladder being
kicked about now, but when I was a small boy you very often during
the winter used to see a pig's bladder being kicked about some side
street.

The substitution of rubber for the pig's bladder for inflating rugby
balls took place about 1870. Mr Lindon of Rugby first hit upon the
idea of making a bladder of rubber and also invented a pump for
inflating it, and so the far from salubrious task of inflating pigs'
bladders came to an end. Messrs Chas Macintosh & Co Ltd were
the first people to manufacture rubber bladders, and now all the big
rubber firms make them.

In 1892 the Rugby ball was standardised and now has to be as
near as possible certain measurements and weight.

The shape of the modern ball varies somewhat from the ball made
in 1892. When new it is not so rounded at the ends and measures
slightly less in the width circumference, that is, it is not so fat. Some
slight variations in the ball to suit the ideas of the various Unions
and the requirements of the modern game exist. New Zealand, for
instance, favours a ball measuring half an inch less in the width
circumference than the ball used at home, and we have been asked
on several occasions to make balls for South African customers with
even a narrower width circumference.

Four-panel balls – that is, balls made by stitching four pieces of
leather together, as in the early days – are still the most popular.
There is no mention in the Rules as to the number of panels or seams
there should be, and South Africa uses nothing else but eight-panel
balls.

The qualities demanded of a Rugby ball today are that it shall be
so far as possible the correct shape and weight, be able to stand up
to hard play, and retain its shape. All these qualities depend on the
leather case. The ball should weigh between $13\frac{1}{2}$ and 15 oz and to
obtain this the thickness of the case cannot be more than about
2 mm. The leather must be therefore of the best quality and be
thoroughly stretched or the ball will go out of shape quickly. Cowhide

is the leather used, and for the best balls only the middle of the hide is used, that is, the butt. The belly part of a hide is not much use to football manufacturers as it stretches too much. The shoulder part of the hide is used for making cheaper quality balls.

The manufacture of football leather is a specialised job, and its production is in the hands of a comparatively few tanners, firms with many years of experience behind them. There is no leather more suitable than English hides; they have the advantage of being tight in the fibre and strong in the grain as compared with other kinds of hides. It is interesting to note that the annual peace-time consumption of English hides for Rugby and Association footballs just before the war was 16,000.

Rugby Footballs In The Making. James Gilbert.

Many people might imagine that floodlit rugby belongs to the second half of the twentieth century – a game between Bristol and Cardiff at White City in 1954 is thought to have been the first staged under lights in southern Britain. But in the north, where daylight is severely abbreviated in winter, experiments were taking place more than a hundred years ago. The first recorded match under lights was that between Broughton and Swinton in October 1878. North of the Border it was Hawick who pioneered the trend with a match against Melrose in 1879. The verdict of one eye-witness was scarcely favourable!

Heavy snow, followed by severe frost, had rendered ground conditions nightmarish; but the game had to be played. Spectators had travelled from Gala, Melrose, Selkirk and other places of greater or lesser renown to see a match played by electric light.

Two dynamo machines, supplying a total of 3200 candle power, provided the light for this historic evening match. Takings amounted £63 which, at sixpence a go, wasn't bad, but it was reckoned that had every spectator paid, the gate money would have at least doubled. Three or four times the gate was rushed and forced open and many gained entrance to the Park without having to put their hands in their pockets. The wee soul whose duty it was to collect the tanners, aided by 'a chair with a kitchen table in front of him, whereon was set a small lamp and ordinary delf bowl' had sadly underestimated the probable attendance and paid for his lack of foresight by being cast 'table, chair, lamp and bowl in one confused heap'.

The game itself was farcical. Players tackled shadows, fell over

[71]

each other, and hacked at balls which were either non-existent or disappeared into patches of gloom having made but fleeting appearances. Somehow Hawick managed to retain possession long enough to score a goal, a feat which Melrose could not emulate. The vast crowd had been attracted by the use of the electric light, not the prospect of seeing rugby as it should have been. Entertainment was provided; Rugby certainly was not.

To add a final theatrical touch to the proceedings the little man who was working the lights betrayed a gruesome Aberdonian streak in his make-up by switching off immediately play stopped, leaving a crowd of between 4000 and 6000 in total darkness – a state in which many maintained they had spent the match, lights or no. How so many people managed on that night to avoid the chill embrace of the nearby River Cheviot is a point worth pondering.

Hawick Club Archives.

In days when tours are ten a penny and players hop the hemispheres in jumbo-jet comfort it is worth sparing a thought for the very first tourists to come to Great Britain. For the New Zealanders of 1888 their visit was akin to a modern-day moon voyage, and lasted a great deal longer. The fact that they undertook it emphasises that the desire for the widest possible sporting contacts has been a powerful motivator of young men down the years.

The Natives beat Ireland before losing to England and Wales, but their durability was what makes them memorable.

Imagine a player telling his family and employers, 'I've been chosen for a rugby tour. I'll be away for a year and two months.' It sounds ridiculous. But this is just what happened when the New Zealand Native Football Representatives set off on their mammoth programme of 107 games in 1888–9. They were nick-named the Maoris, though four of them were white and a number were only part-Maori. Joe Warbrick, their captain, was a half-caste, who played for Wellington against the 1888 British team in New Zealand and assumed a major role in making possible this first tour of Britain.

The British team of 1888, captained first by R.L. Seddon, who was drowned whole rowing in Australia, and then by Andrew Stoddart, startled New Zealand rugby with their revolutionary heeling and combined passing from set scrums. The New Zealand practice had been to drive through in the scrums by sheer force, as used to be the

Wing Robert Kururangi attempts to step inside Cardiff full-back Paul Rees during the 1982 Maoris' 17–10 win at the Arms Park. The tourists played seven games – but their predecessors of 1888 took the field 107 times! (*Western Mail & Echo Ltd.*)

tactics in Britain. But the game had developed into a science of back play in the United Kingdom, making it far more attractive to play and watch. It opened undreamed of horizons for New Zealand backs. Joe Warbrick was one of them.

He had been a full back who switched to three quarter and saw the opportunities the new style provided. He was eager to learn more of these methods – and what better way than a reciprocal tour? With the interest and help of Tom Eyton, an Englishman who had settled in New Zealand, Joe gathered a touring party. He had an encouraging start to this task because three of his four brothers were leading players including William, a full back, who was to become the star of the tour.

William was a flamboyant attacker as well as an expert in the prime essentials of catching and kicking, and this exciting player emerged as the first of a long line of great full backs from the Land of the Silver Fern. He was to be followed by W.J. 'Carbine' Wallace, brilliant in any position; another great Maori player, George Nepia; the imperturbable Mike Gilbert, the one and only Bob Scott; the deadly accurate Don Clarke and the record-breaking Fergus McCormick. Though styles differed, all these New Zealand full backs go down in rugby history for their contributions to the game and especially to their country.

[73]

Joe Warbrick intended his team to be composed of entirely Maori or part-Maori players; however, he was advised to strengthen the party and four whites, or Pakehas as they are called, were invited to join them. They were New Zealand-born colonists, of whom Pat Keogh proved a superb half back and the most daring of the attackers as he scored 34 tries in Britain. In 1891 he was declared a professional by the New Zealand Rugby Union. The other white players were W. 'Mother' Elliott, an experienced half back, G.A. Williams, a powerfully-built six footer, and E.M. Causland, an excellent goal kicker.

Unfortunately for Joe Warbrick he was injured in a match in New Zealand, where the Maoris played a number of fixtures to help raise funds before setting off. The injury proved a handicap and he was seldom at his best in Britain, where he is remembered as a man who enjoyed a verbal battle with referees. A tragic death was in store for this great pioneer of New Zealand tours when, while he was guiding a party at Waimangu Geyser in Rotorua the geyser blew unexpectedly.

The tour, which began on 23 June 1888, lasted until 24 August 1889 and of the 107 matches the Natives won 78, drew six and lost 23, scoring 772 points with 305 against. They won 14 of their 17 games in New Zealand and all 16 in Australia. They completed their 74 games in Britain in less than six months, won 49, drew five and lost 20. It must have been the most exhausting programme any team has undertaken; but they had to play so frequently to pay their way in days when profits were far from rewarding.

On one occasion they played on three successive days. Yet the party consisted of only 26 players. Not surprisingly, what with injuries and illness, backs often played in the pack while forwards were pressed into service as backs. At least they must have developed a fine understanding of team play. W. Nehua saw duty as full back, three quarter and forward, while Davey Gage, dubbed the 'iron man' though he was only 11 stones, played in 68 of the 74 matches in Britain.

Most of the fixtures were played in the industrial north of England, where attendances were larger. The Maoris proved a novelty on the football field as they demonstrated their pre-match Haka wearing native head-dresses and mats, chanting 'Ake, Ake, Kia, Kaha,' which means 'For ever be strong and bold.' The legend that the Maoris played without boots was denied by the tourists, who explained that this practice had died out after the early years of the game in New

Zealand. Anyway, it had been adopted in purely Maori communities, and then because boots were unobtainable.

Unfortunately the tourists were inclined to a physical approach against the rugged North Country packs, who certainly did not begrudge an exchange of bruises. As well as this tendency to rough play, the New Zealanders were often guilty of arguing with referees. Had the 'ten yards further on' ruling for objecting to penalty kicks been in vogue in those days the Maoris might have played the bulk of their rugby deep in their own 25! It is reported that the worst offender in debate with referees was skipper Joe, who seems to have set his team a poor example in this direction.

Against England at Blackheath the tourists were upset by the 'erroneous and depressing decisions' of referee Rowland Hill, who was secretary of the Rugby Football Union, and five of the Maoris walked off the field in disgust. What they said before they went is not recorded, but the RFU extracted an apology from the management for this act. Neutral referees were in control for the next tour in Britain when the 1905 All Blacks played their International matches.

All Blacks In Wales. John Billot. Ron Jones Publications.

Like participation itself many of the rewards of playing the Rugby game are intangible. There is no trophy for winning the Five Nations' title (indeed, there is no officially-designated Championship). The 'Triple Crown' exists only in the minds of patriots and statisticians. But the Calcutta Cup, for which England and Scotland compete each year, is very real — and elegant. It has three snake handles and a cover on which stands an elephant with which the lid is lifted. It was fashioned by Indian craftsmen out of silver rupees.

To account for its existence we need do no more than reproduce the sad letter which one day reached the RFU.

H.J. Graham Esq	5 Bankhall St
Hony Secy & Treasurer	CALCUTTA
Rugby Football Union (Wimbledon)	20 Dec 1877

Dear Sir,

I regret to say that the Calcutta Football Club has ceased to exist, it being now found quite impossible to get sufficient men together to play even a scratch game, this is the result of a variety of causes, but chiefly from the fact that some of the old members who started the Club in 1872 and kept it going, have been dispersed over India or gone home, etc. and there has never been enough new blood to supply the loss; then the great and rapid development of Polo has proved a fatal blow to Football here, it being considered (as it requires no training or condition) so much more suitable for this climate; lastly the loss of the 'Buffs' who were undoubtedly a mainstay of Football in Calcutta. This being the case I proposed at a Meeting of the few remaining Members of the Club held on Tuesday last the 18th inst. as the best means of doing some lasting good for the Cause of Rugby Football as a slight memento of the Calcutta Club that the Funds remaining to the credit of the Club should be devoted to the purpose of a *Challenge Cup* and presented to the Rugby Union to be competed for annually in the same way as the Association Cup or in any other way the Committee of the R. Union may consider best for the encouragement of Rugby Football.

This proposition was carried unanimously and I now write to beg you to place the matter before the Committee of the Rugby Union and beg their kind acceptance of a Cup and also to enquire if the Committee would prefer one of Indian workmanship, or the money remitted for the purchase of a Cup at home?

The sum of money at my disposal at the present rate of Exchange is about £60 sterling.

Hoping to be favoured with an early reply and with every good wish for the success of Rugby Football, I remain, dear sir,

Yours ffy,

G.A. James Rothney

Capt. Hony Secy & Treasurer of the late CFC.

The thrift of Scotland's selectors in days gone by is well attested, particularly by notables such as the late 'Jock' Wemyss who won his first two caps in 1914.

After a six-year cessation of fixtures during the Great War Wemyss again won a place in the Scottish XV to play England in 1920. On his arrival in the changing room, he noted that the fourteen new Scottish players' jerseys were hanging neatly on their pegs, but there was none to be seen beside his bag.

'Where's my jersey?' he enquired of the senior selector.

'Ah, well now, Wemyss, you'll be remembering that you were given a jersey in 1914,' came the terse reply.

However, in the last decades of the nineteenth century a lobby grew up which felt that there should be, if not cash rewards for playing rugby, at least something more than mere Cups and mythical titles for amateurs who had surrendered wage-earning activity to take part in a match. As the game spread from the public school and professional classes to embrace all strata of society, including hourly-paid workers, the 'broken time' issue loomed larger and larger, and was brought to a head by the northern faction within the Rugby Union at a heavily-attended meeting in London. The rift in Rugby Football's ranks has never been healed.

The historic General Meeting took place at the Westminster Palace Hotel on 20 September, 1893. J.A. Millar and M. Newsome (both members of the Rugby Union and Yorkshire committees) proposed and seconded respectively that players be:
    'allowed compensation for *bona fide* loss of time.'
    Against this W. Cail (President) proposed, and G. Rowland Hill (Hon. Sec.) seconded:
    'That this meeting, believing that the above principle is contrary to the true interest of the Game and its spirit, declines to sanction the same.'
    The amendment was carried by 282 votes to 136.
    The northerners came down in two special trains, to make sure of maximum possible representation, but some of them got lost in the metropolis as country bumpkins used to do even in those days. But they were up against the brilliant organising genius of H.E. Steed (Lennox FC), who saw to it that there was a full poll of all the clubs who were to oppose the motion, and found proxies for 120 of those who for various reasons could not attend the meeting. His plans were ready days beforehand, and were certain to succeed. The Northern Union subsequently said that instead of Oxford and Cambridge Universities having a single vote each, the individual colleges from both Universities voted.
    The 418 votes cast constituted a record attendance, and the 120 proxies were probably decisive. At the opening there was a strange and uncanny silence which often comes before the settlement of great issues by ordeal of battle. Everybody now knew that a decisive engagement was at hand. No possibility of compromise obscured the prospect of a fight to the finish. Feelings ran higher than ever before or after. When the chairman announced the result there was a loud, contrasting burst of applause.

[77]

Thus was laid the spectre of professionalism in the Rugby Union game, and a special General Meeting of the Union was held immediately after the close of the main one, when careful and significant revision was made of some of the bye-laws, altering the system of election of Members to the Committee and officers of the Union, and laying down new lines of procedure for general meetings. These were carefully prepared and served their immediate purpose – 'to crush any attempt to establish professional cells within the Government machine'.

That famous occasion saved the Union, but it remained to drive out professionals, so the Committee prepared a draft of proposed new laws against professionalism, which contained exceedingly wide definitions and drastic punitive clauses. These were introduced and passed at a general meeting on 19 September 1895, and at the same time the revised bye-laws were adopted which tightened the Union's hold upon leagues.

These happenings produced exactly the result expected and desired by the Committee. On 29 August 1895 (only three weeks before the General Meeting of the Rugby Union) there was a meeting of twenty-two clubs at the Mitre Hotel, Leeds, at which it was decided to form what was then described as a 'Northern Football Union,' to be established 'on the principle of payment for *bona fide* broken time'. Following this meeting all the clubs involved resigned from the Rugby Union.

Centenary History Of The Rugby Football Union. U.A. Titley and Ross McWhirter.
Reprinted by kind permission of the RFU.

It is curious that while the Home Countries adopted symbols such as the rose and thistle at an early stage in their history they continued to be known by their national names and do not possess nick-names; even in the case of France there is something forced about the use of 'Cockerels' or 'Tricolours'. On the other hand the great southern hemisphere nations have used 'All Blacks' and 'Springboks' as alternative nomenclature from their first sorties as national fifteens.

The following newspaper comment on the first Australian party to visit Britain in 1908 indicates that the selection of a nick-name was not lightly undertaken and required tact and diplomacy.

There was some little difficulty at first in deciding by what name these latest Rugby visitors to our shores should be handed down to

[78]

posterity. The obvious name was 'Kangaroos', but a Northern Union professional Rugby team from Australia had already annexed this title. At a banquet given to the tourists before they started 'Rabbits' was suggested as a possible name, but this was quite tabooed by the players themselves who looked on it as a term of contempt.

Finally the list of possible names was cut down to three – 'Wallabies', the name of a small species of kangaroo; 'Waratahs', a red flower peculiar to New South Wales; and 'Wallaroos'. At a meeting called by Captain McMahon, the manager of the team, it was decided to christen the team 'Wallabies', which would embrace all the players, some of whom were not from New South Wales.

Already they have won golden opinions wherever they have stayed. They are the most unaffected, 'unsidy' team of tourists that has ever visited England. And they are thorough sportsmen. They love the game, they play it cleanly and wholeheartedly, and they study it seriously and work out their tactics brainfully. For instance, while on tour the first, second and third row forwards are room-mates; likewise the halves and three quarters: consequently they can always discuss their plans together and work out their methods of attack and defence.

The Wallabies, moreover, are certainly the most picturesque team to visit England, and are sure to win golden opinions from the feminine portion of the spectators owing to their artistic turn-out. They wear exceedingly pretty light-blue jerseys with the Waratah worked on the left breast, dark blue knickers, and dark blue stockings with light blue tops. In addition to looking smart, the light blue jerseys show off the physique of the Wallabies to great advantage and without doubt they are a wonderfully fine body of men. In fact, they are perfect athletes, since they look far bigger and more powerful in their tight-fitting jerseys than they do in their ordinary clothes, a true test of well-trained men.

The Welsh think back fondly to the first years of the twentieth century as a Golden Era for their game, with Grand Slams, Triple Crowns and Championship titles galore. But the game at large prospered, too, sustained evidence of its powerful attraction being provided by the waves of exotic tourists who arrived to take on the Home Countries. New Zealand, South Africa – twice – and Australia all came before World War I and France came into the annual

Championship as the Fifth Nation in 1910, having served a satisfactory apprenticeship. There seemed few clouds hovering over rugby's future.

Then came the orgy of war. For six years rugby was a dead letter. Followers of the sport rushed to the colours in thousands and Scotland was left with nothing but schoolboys to carry on the game. This is one of the saddest and, withal, one of the most glorious chapters in the history of the sport. No field game was more thoroughly represented in France, Gallipoli and Mesopotamia, to say nothing of the high seas, than Rugby Football, but the toll exacted for patriotism was a heavy one. J. Aikman Smith, the Honorary Secretary of the Union, issued a notice in September of 1914 asking that Rugby Football should not be played. He was too late. The players had already gone. Rugby had automatically ceased. The losses sustained in the war were enormous and there is no doubt that it will be a long time before we completely recover from the severe toll which was levied on our best men. Scotland lost no less than thirty-one International players.

In 1920 the game was renewed, but the selectors in a sense were groping in the dark, and yet Scotland were victorious in their International engagements with France, Wales and Ireland, but were beaten by England. We are in a state of transition, and the losses sustained in the war have not been made good, nor will they be made good for several years.

'The Game in Scotland' by C.D. Stuart from *Rugby Football Up To Date* by E.H.D. Sewell. Hodder & Stoughton.

War took the lives of men from all nations at random. Scarcely, however, had the clamour of battle died away than Wales had another grim reaper at the door, this time Depression. Contraction in the coal industry, with a disastrous loss of custom as the world's big ships began burning oil, meant a halving of the number of miners at work between 1920 and 1933 – and the wage bill plummeted from £65 million to £14 million.

In a pithy essay Gareth Williams correlates Welsh economic confidence and success with victories on the rugby field. In the first 'Golden Era' southern Wales was boom country. Undeniably the twenties with their Depression were a lack-lustre decade in which Welsh performances and results were the poorest on record. Consider the impact made by the slump.

As money coming into Wales dwindled to a trickle, and as the numbers of people going out rose to a flood (the Rhondda lost 20 per cent of its population between 1921 and 1931, while a thousand people left Merthyr every year on average between 1921 and 1937), the social fabric and cultural vitality of south Wales began to crumble. Its institutions, politically, industrially and socially, were savaged.

Both religion and recreation were mauled. The Rhondda suffered a 70 per cent reduction in chapel membership between 1921 and 1935. There were nine chapels in Cwmavon in 1930 without a minister; the total debt of the nonconformist churches of South Wales in 1937 was near half a million pounds. The monopoly that the great mixed and male choirs of the Rhondda and Dowlais had exerted on the choral competitions of the National Eisteddfod was broken by Ystalyfera and Morriston from the less hard-hit Swansea Valley.

Many rugby clubs, especially in east Wales, were not merely less in evidence, but in danger of actual extinction. In the season 1926–7 the Welsh Rugby union, whose own takings halved during the decade, was inundated by requests from clubs like Ebbw Vale, Cross Keys, Blaenavon, Pontypool, Pontypridd and Skewen for financial assistance. Their pleas were both poignant and persistent: 'We are forced to appeal to you to again kindly consider granting us financial assistance to enable us to carry on,' wrote the Cross Keys club to the Union late in 1926; 'please ask your Committee to be good enough to give the matter their serious consideration to see if something cannot be done for us.' In May 1927 the secretary of the Glamorgan Leaguè wrote from Treorchy to the WRU appealing for a cup competition to be launched to revive interest and gates, since 'the season 1926–7 has been disastrous for all clubs'. The evidence was all around. Treherbert RFC had been in financial trouble since 1924; by 1928 the rent charged by the Great Western Railway, which owned the club's playing field, was consistently higher than the gate-takings. In March of that year the GWR announced that 'the club was in a state of hopeless insolvency [and] could be forced into disbandment ... local distress has seriously affected the club's receipts'. In December 1929 Treherbert RFC was forced to disband. That year, in the Llynfi valley in mid Glamorgan, Nantyfyllon RFC also disbanded. Around the same time Pencoed RFC was decimated when nine of the first XV left in one particular fortnight for the Midlands and London.

[81]

In the valleys of Monmouthshire the outlook was no less gloomy. Machen had already had to withdraw from the WRU in 1926. Cwmbran, or Pontnewydd RFC as it was then called, collapsed in 1927. By the end of the decade Pontypool was hovering near bankruptcy with an overdraft of £2000. The closing of the Works at Tredegar between 1924 and 1926 led to the closure of Tredegar itself in 1929. That year steel-making ceased at Ebbw Vale, putting 10,000 out of work. Disaster stared the local rugby club in the face. Within a year, even with admission reduced to 4d, a gate of £4 was handsome. By 1932 the receipts seldom reached £1, despite a catchment area of 40,000, and the club resorted to public subscriptions.

Nor were the coastal clubs unaffected. The ports, dependent on their hinterland as they were, lay stranded like beached whales. Cardiff and its environs had a 25.3 per cent unemployment figure by 1930 despite a diversified labour force in port services and distribution trades. Penarth RFC fell into £1000 debt which was eventually brought within manageable limits by the tireless efforts of its renowned secretary Lot Thorne in organising countless bazaars, raffles and – this being Penarth – fetes. Rugby at Barry had already come to a halt in 1925; Pembroke Dock Quins was reduced to five members by 1927; Haverfordwest RFC struggled and went under between 1926 and 1929....

... The buoyant, bustling pre-war world of spectacular industrial and urban expansion, of immigration, investment and innovation, was turned upside down as far as south Wales rugby was concerned. From the 1890s, when the thousands tumbling into south Wales began to win for it industrial renown, the other football unions had looked on enviously and muttered darkly about Englishmen, working and playing in Wales, achieving honours in the scarlet jersey. In the inter-war period that process was sharply reversed.

From Grand Slam To Great Slump: Economy, Society and Rugby Football in Wales during the Depression. Gareth Williams. The Welsh History Review.

The enervating effect of the slump between the Wars not only drained the Valleys of manpower and sinew; it seemed to inhibit and dampen even the normal evolution of the game in Wales. For the Welsh Rugby Union's centenary publication Fields of Praise *Gareth Williams joined forces with another historian with a passion for Rugby Football, David Smith.*

Welsh packs of the twenties were strong but not skilled in their strength, for they were unable to control the decisive ball-winning areas of the contemporary game, the tightly-bound scrum and the loose heel. There was an abundance of powerful individual forwards like Steve Morris, Whitfield, Sid Lawrence of Bridgend, and a clutch of faster 'winging' forwards like Hiddlestone, Tom Jones of Newport, and Ivor Jones of Llanelli, but to expect the Welsh Match Committee to find the appropriate blend between them was like asking them to contemplate the mysteries of Einstein's physics. The selectors resumed their activities after the War with the aim of fielding a heavy pack of pushers. This unimaginative scheme came unstuck in the 18–3 defeat at Twickenham in 1921, so it was partially jettisoned in the belief that younger, faster men would supply the required vim and dash. This compounded the weakness, for the real deficiency was the refusal to recognise the significance of specialist skills. As late as 1935 Horace Lyne would be telling his members that 'specialist forwards distressed him for they were spoiling football in all the countries'. No particular importance was attached to the role of hooker: the best hooker in Wales in the 1920s was Llanelli's Idris Jones, but the selectors either ignored him or put him in the second row, as they did against Scotland in 1925. It was not entirely true that the obsolete axiom of 'first up, first down' still prevailed, for most Welsh clubs had two acknowledged 'front rankers', but bizarre national selection often forced bigger second-rank men into the front row, front-rankers to the back-row, and left recognised hookers in limbo. This perversity sometimes took quite grotesque forms, such as against Ireland in 1929, when Cecil Pritchard was flanked in the front row by the tallest man in the pack, Tom Arthur, on the one side, and by Arthur Bowdler, who was the shortest, on the other. After Watcyn Thomas dared take his role as captain seriously by rectifying one particular selectorial lunacy in the team selected to meet Ireland in 1933, he never again appeared in the scarlet jersey. It was not until the end of the twenties that Wales once more began picking a specialist hooker like Pritchard; until then the captaincy, which went around like an unpacked parcel, theoretically on senior-ity but in practice virtually out of a hat, decided the disposition of the selected forwards. When Rowe Harding met the team he was to captain the following day against Ireland in 1926, he had to call them together and allocate them their positions in the scrum. But line-out play was changing too. Before the War, when the scrum half threw the ball in, quick line-outs prevailed. In the twenties, play in this quarter became more specialised, but until the arrival of expert maulers like Tom Arthur and E.M. Jenkins, and the two-handed technician Watcyn Thomas, Welsh line-out play was haphazard, marking was untidy, covering was unco-ordinated, and any chance of a quick heel from a loose maul was sacrificed on the altar of the eternal foot-rush.

While the search for 'blend' went on among the forwards, the men behind were neglected. Only two backs of the nondescript team beaten by England at Swansea in January 1924 travelled to Scotland in February. Half-back was a problem, and for many years the selectors had a pious horror of playing club partners. This, again, is a trifle puzzling. It almost suggests that the dislocated economic world in which South Wales was now struggling to stay afloat had induced collective, or at least selectorial, rugby amnesia, since much of this policy was in contradiction of the lessons already learned before the War. Against England, the half backs had been Albert Owen of Swansea and the diminutive Neath terrier, Eddie Watkins. Owen, hounded by the English back-row, had had an uncomfortable time; few were given a second chance in those days. The selectors, like many others, had been impressed by the many original touches in the play of Vincent Griffiths of Newport. The natural combination would have been Griffiths with his club partner, the evergreen Jack Wetter, or the coupling of Neath fly-half Eddie Williams with his club link, Eddie Watkins. Unhelpfully, the selectors paired Griffiths and Watkins. Three new caps were chosen at three quarter, to face the famous all-Oxford University back line of Smith, McPherson, Aitken and Wallace. Few supporters were tempted north to Inverleith by the rail excursion fare of £1 3s. 0d., and those who did were outnumbered by the committee. The Scots thought they might win by a large margin, and they did. By half-time they were 22–0 up, and eventually ran in a total of eight tries, four from the wings. This highlighted another weakness: Wales had no answer to three quarters who ran straight, drawing their men and passing swiftly, and in these years, apart from the exceptional heroic performance like Rowe Harding's in Belfast in 1926, the defence on the wings was lamentable, with no flanking coverers in support. Ian Smith, the Scottish patrician with the speed and leg strength of an ostrich, capitalised on a timetable service from Phil McPherson at centre, to score seven tries against Wales in 1924 and 1925. In 1924 he made life so

[84]

miserable for his opposite number, the hapless Harold Davies of Newport, that later in the evening Davies gamely asked to be introduced to him since he had not seen him on the field. He was able to deepen the acquaintance later that year as Davies was one of the four Welshmen – Smith was one of the ten Scots – who toured South Africa with a British Lions party managed by Harry Packer, the Welsh union member and former International. On the Sunday following the 35–10 rout the Welsh team went on the traditional ride to see the Forth Bridge. 'Take a good look at it, boys,' urged T.D. Schofield of Bridgend; 'It's the last time any of you will see it at the expense of the Welsh Union.'

This defeat accelerated demands for reform in the administration of the WRU, and of its selection methods in particular. As early as 1921, *The Field* had condemned the Welsh Match Committee as 'an obsolete selecting force', and proposed replacing it by five former Internationals, as in England: Gabe, Nicholls, Hodges, Boots and Trew. Of these, Nicholls alone would become a selector. In March 1923, after Wales had lost to the other three Home Countries for the first time in over thirty years, 'Old Stager', who had been writing in the *South Wales Daily News* since the 1890s and, unique among pressmen of the time, used binoculars 'to distinguish pushers from non-pushers', began a campaign to change the nature of the selection committee. 'We would suggest,' he editorialized, 'that the WRU should seriously consider whether the present method of selecting players cannot be improved by reducing the number of persons on the match committee ... the Union cannot be unaware that there is a considerable body of opinion which fears that some of the selectors are too much influenced by the members of clubs to which they owe their position.' For the next twelve months, as further defeats followed, 'Old Stager' never missed an opportunity to argue the case for a selection committee of five, irrespective of club or area interests, as Ireland had since 1894 and England since 1920. When the proposal that five members only of the Match Committee should act as selectors was put to the 1923 AGM, however, it was defeated overwhelmingly.

Fields of Praise. David Smith and Gareth Williams. University of Wales Press.

Cliff Jones, later to become President of the Welsh Rugby Union, was one of a crop of gifted players whose careers were interrupted by the War against

Hitler. Looking back on nearly six years of hostilities and loss of life he was able to highlight an ironic bonus that accrued to the amateur game.

Obviously during the War it was only by great efforts of perseverance and courage that the game was kept alive throughout the Home Countries, particularly in Scotland and Northern Ireland. With most of the pre-War players away in the services, and under such trying conditions of labour, transport, and materials, no praise is too high for those club enthusiasts throughout the British Isles who kept the torch alight until the War ended and normality reigned once more. Looking back, it seems almost a miracle that the game was kept alive at all during those fateful six years and one can be grateful that the only real effect that they had on the game was an inevitable lowering of the standard *pro tem* which each succeeding post-War year seems to bring nearer back to normal. The resumption of full-scale Internationals is a good indication that the leeway has been bridged for the greater part and that only a few more playing seasons will see the standard back to its former full glory.

In one respect the War had a most salutary effect on the game in that its advent, apart from heralding the return of France to the fold, enabled Rugby League players to mix freely with Union players and each to benefit from the other's differing styles of play. Will anyone who was fortunate enough to see wartime service Internationals ever

forget the unique spectacle of Haydn Tanner (the greatest of Union scrum halves) passing the ball out to Gus Risman (one of the greatest of League outside-halves) or Horace Foster's amazing forward displays, or yet the thrill of seeing so many star-studded League and Union players combining to produce some of the most scintillating and glorious football ever seen in Wales? What a pity that this temporary war-time rugby amnesty which gave all

Cliff Jones as seen on a pre-War cigarette-card.

genuine Rugby lovers so much pleasure and food for thought could not be continued with suitable modifications and safeguards, of course, in time of peace.

Rugby Football. Cliff Jones. Pitman.

Another bonus to emerge from World War II is noted by Tim Auty in his work on Headingley RFC prepared for the club's Centenary. The passage that follows is also worth consideration as a reminder of 'austerity': the regime that existed after hostilities had ceased when the British were no longer threatened by an enemy just across the Channel but when, nonetheless, life's little luxuries – or even basic necessities – were hard to come by.

During the Second World War the Club, of course, put up its shutters in the playing sense but, as in the earlier war, players kept in touch with senior members and when home on leave often got a game with other local sides. The grounds at Kirkstall were let to the Army and in this way a certain amount of income continued to come in and, what was more important, the playing area was kept in condition so that in the summer of 1945 after the Armistice it became possible to think of a partial resumption.

For the first season there were very few of the pre-war players available. Many of them were not demobilised until the following year. Many others were in no fit state for football after service overseas or periods of detention as prisoners of war. We won only twelve out of the twenty-nine games played that season.

The two succeeding seasons were little better from the point of view of results, not surprisingly with the tremendous difficulties to be faced. The fuel shortage meant that hot water could not always be guaranteed. Jerseys were impossible to obtain. An appeal to old players relieved the situation, but the club had to retain the jerseys to be cleaned and re-issued each week. Soap could not be supplied, footballs were as scarce as gold bars, petrol rationing made travelling difficult and, above all, promising young players were called up into the services.

However, as after 1918, some good came out of it all. Because of the many domestic difficulties the help of some of the lady members and relatives of members was enlisted to repair old jerseys. From this beginning it was a natural step to ask them to provide food after training and Saturday games. With food rationing still in force something to eat at any time was welcome, and the ladies began to provide limited refreshments. As the work gradually developed it became too much of a burden for the few. Accordingly in 1947 there came into being the first properly constituted ladies' committee with duly elected officials.

Headingly Centenary Brochure. Timothy Auty.

Since World War II, Rugby Football has not demonstrated the radicalism of earlier years. The latest decades have shown it modifying a Law here and a custom there; bowing to political imperatives in one case, defying Government elsewhere; coming to terms with the media and sponsorship, while remaining obdurate about its regulations protecting the amateur ethic.

If anyone were to suppose, however, that the game had remained and will remain static he has only to consider this brilliant essay written in 1980 by a member of the staff of L'Equipe. *Its theme is creeping – some might say galloping – evolution. Spurred – inevitably – by individual players.*

Last season in Toulouse the French XV met a completely unknown team, that of the USSR. And this match, which seemed to be of only anecdotal interest, in reality opened our eyes to everything which inhibits and obstructs the pure expression of the game.

On the face of it, one did not give the novice Soviets any more chance of beating the French at Rugby football than one would have given them of beating the West Indies at cricket. It takes a long time to reach another planet, and still more time to conquer it. So imagine our surprise when we saw the Russians playing as if they had already played France a hundred times; as if they had spent the last fifty years perfecting the best ways of stopping the French from playing.

For more than an hour the Russian forwards exerted a well-planned and methodical pressure on every ball which reached the hands of the French half-backs. It was only in the final minutes of the match that the French were able to establish running as the basis of their attacks, and this culminated in two tries for the wings Guy Noves and Daniel Bustaffa. In the meantime, though, the USSR had even found time to score a try themselves. It was produced by an 85-yard run, initiated by the Russian full back, who intercepted when the French were attacking in his 25.

On the day, the French forwards did not have a good match. Quite frankly the French pack was dominated in the rucks and mauls, partly because it was still suffering from the fatigue of a tour to Japan and Canada, but above all because it had underestimated the capability of its opponents. The fact is that the USSR XV, in its first match at this level, gave the impression of knowing more about the basics of the game than France did after thirty years in the International Championship, which was at about the time that another Russian, Prince Obolensky, caused something of a surprise on the green sward at Twickenham.

It is possible today for Soviet beginners to learn more about Rugby in a few months than the French did in thirty years of heroic exploration, and quite simply they can do it because of the development of modern means of disseminating information which make it possible to examine the strengths and tactics of the opposition in great detail and which make that information available to the whole world. It is not difficult then to make a most detailed match plan as a counter. The Russians probably played their first match against France a hundred times before they actually went onto the pitch. All they needed was a good video-tape recorder to replay the most recent games played by France.

I do not know if this machine will allow us to reverse the history of the world until, for example, we can eliminate the surprise from such events as Trafalgar and Waterloo, but what I do know is that with it the French XV would not have had to wait until 1958 and the advent of Lucien Mias to discover the indispensable virtues of well-organised forward play – virtues which had to be explored in the heat of battle and not in the cool and well-ordered study of film evidence. Until then the French had learned their Rugby back to front. They had neglected what might be called the bricks and mortar, and here I am thinking of scrummaging, and instead had poured the whole of their talent into Rugby football's equivalent of the decoration, by which I mean the great handling code. They enchanted the public, but they were very badly marked indeed by the examiners.

Today, a good session with a video replaces a century of patience, of sweat, and of tradition. The French game was no stranger to the Russians; they already knew it and all its culture, just as Armstrong knew exactly what he was doing when he stepped onto the moon. But if one transposes this phenomenon to the level of the countries who are members of the International Rugby Football Board, one quickly understands why Rugby has fallen into the hands of the counter-espionage service. World-wide television has reduced the entire world of Rugby to the dimensions of a village where everyone knows everyone else's business. The Rugby field is a sky swept by all the radars of the squad system; a new ploy by the centre three quarters represents a surprise as big as an Unidentified Flying Object.

Nowadays one can no longer imagine an army like the one of Lucien Mias storming the beaches of South Africa to the stupefaction of the whole country. But the progress in question is not evolution in the best sense. It has only driven the rules of the game into a state of almost total blockage on the chessboard of the pitch, because such scientific study of the strengths of the opposition is only carried out with the object of destroying them. How can one talk of progress when the fundamental concept of carrying the ball is in such decline?

From 1971 until 1978 one team dominated the French club Championship, and it did so by bringing to perfection the understanding of the small print of the law. The team was Beziers, and it was unequalled in swallowing and digesting the ball in the mauls, hiding it for eighty minutes from the view and the appetite of the opposition. It is actually true that in the course of a recent match between Beziers and Auch, an Argentine forward freshly enrolled in the Auch pack ended by crying out, 'What has happened to the ball?'

This cry of despair made his captain almost die laughing. The captain in question was none other than Jacques Fouroux, but in that phrase was summed up the dilemma of the true Rugby game. Jacques Fouroux made light of it and, with his team in opposition to Beziers, put up with everything that the French XV, of which he was then captain, was making others endure. I cannot recall that the pack of mastodons driven by Fouroux earned much in the way of sympathy. It even encountered a lot of hostility, exactly the same hostility that Beziers encountered in France. This proved simply that Rugby which is brought to this degree of organisation, strength and rigidity cuts itself off completely from its origins. It must therefore discover another freshness to make its faithful sing.

In this situation the French team have often been accused of sins which are not theirs, because after all the French were the last of the great Rugby nations to realise that one could win a match without scoring a single try and without attacking once through the three-quarters. One morning in 1968 on our way back from New Zealand I was in an Australian television studio surrounded by a pack of interviewers, who fired questions at me off the cuff as surprising as the following: 'Why do French players kick their opponents in the guts?' 'Why does General de Gaulle pay the French International players?'

That was a bit like asking me, 'When did you stop beating your wife?' and I must admit, my breath was taken away by it all. Only the players could make the correct responses to questions like those and they did it on the turf of Sydney Cricket Ground. They did it beautifully, too, with all the gallantry and style associated with players like Villepreux, Maso, Trillo, Cester and Spanghero. Mind you, this did not prevent other players in the French team from being drowned under a shower of penalties for kicks in the guts, even if those kicks did miss.

Similarly, only the players can answer the problems of Rugby today, despite the calculations of the generals of the video. Only the players can dig out the ball buried in the tomb of the mauls. They have to go beyond the knowledge which is now public property and explore again the originality and folly that William Webb Ellis displayed when he found himself confronted by the same problem of blocked play and a buried ball.

I confess that I have great hopes that our own JPR, Jean-Pierre Rives, will turn out to be the revolutionary, generous and slightly mad sportsman who will provide this positive approach that we need so badly. One evening at the beginning of last season, in a street in Tokyo, our JPR said to me, 'It is said that everything has happened before, but I believe that the most important things will happen last.' He was speaking as a simple soldier, as a simple amateur, as sensitive to the wafts of the old-fashioned spirit of the game which blew over our meetings with the best players in Hong Kong and British Columbia. Fate without doubt has had a most felicitous hand in recently giving us Rives first as an improvised captain and now as a most thoroughly deserved appointment. Against Wales last season he breathed new life into his team and into the Championship. In him you see France, newly elected to the International Board, and poised to give back to Rugby football everything which Rugby football has given to France in the last eighty years.

An Hour With A Video Is Worth A Century Of Sweat. Denis Lalanne. Wales–France match programme 1980. Programme Publications Ltd.

THE SKILLS OF RUGBY FOOTBALL

Blood, Thunder and Tactics

Rugby Football contains so much blood and thunder – or thud and blunder as someone once wrote – that it is not always easy for uninformed onlookers to perceive, let alone appreciate, the level of skill being deployed. There is also a generation gap, whereby the moderns in any generation find it hard to conceive of thought being given to tactical considerations by their predecessors. The section that follows gives the lie to such beliefs.

The 1912–13 South Africans registered a magnificent five-Test Grand Slam and were clearly an outstanding side. However, applied cunning by the London XV, and in particular its pack, tipped the balance against the tourists.

The only game lost by the South Africans in England 1912–13 was their second match, against London, who had six Blackheath forwards in the pack. Both London tries were scored by a forward.

The South African pack was at least a stone and a half heavier per man, but not quite so fast.

The backs were well matched.

The South African pack in previous games had carried all before them, and had made a practice of pushing their opponents right off the ball. By half time they generally had their opponents well beaten forward and could win as they pleased. Their pack was otherwise slow at heeling and never bothered to wheel when it was so easy to walk straight ahead. They were also slow at breaking up.

Our forwards had an unofficial meeting before the game and our tactics were discussed and agreed on. (Owing to local jealousies the committee had failed to appoint a captain, or scrum leader, until a few minutes before the kick-off!) Our scrum tactics succeeded perfectly and were as follows:

When the scrum formed up (but before the ball was in) the South African pack began to shove and we made no attempt to hold them, but promptly gave way five or ten yards. The referee then blew his whistle and the scrum re-formed. After this had happened five or six times, the South African forwards were hot and angry, and ours cool and fresh. The South Africans also realised that it was no use putting their weight on till the ball went in, as there was nothing to shove against. Consequently when the ball came in the two packs were balanced and stationary. We could just hold them for the second or two necessary to hook and heel. We had to heel like lightning in one motion from the hooker to the half, or we should have been pushed off the ball, but we were better hookers than they were, thanks to G.R. Hind and F. le S. Stone, and generally got the ball. If they got it, our front row fought a gallant rearguard action, making a rampart of their bodies, whilst the rest of the pack broke at once and smothered their halves; or if our opponents kept the ball and pushed straight ahead, we began a furious attack in flank on their scrum which always broke it up. Both our tries were scored by our wing forwards from scrums in which the South Africans had secured the ball, but could not get it away.

The first try was typical of the 'double wing forward play' which I have tried to outline above. For London C.H. Pillman was 'field side wing forward', and I was 'blind side wing forward'. From a scrum the South Africans had secured and heeled slowly. Pillman was on the right of our scrum and kicked the ball from the half's hands and dribbled to the three quarter line – incidentally drawing the opposing full back over to that side. He knew that I was 'in support' on his left and, when opposed by the South African three quarter line, he drove a long Soccer foot pass behind them, diagonally to his left, which I had no difficulty in 'trapping' (to use a Soccer expression), steering it some ten yards to the goal line and falling on it. The other London try was exactly similar except that two of our backs also had a hand in it.

'Modern Forward Play' by Lt-Col W.S.D. Craven from *Rugby Football Up To Date* by E.H.D. Sewell. Reproduced by permission of Hodder & Stoughton Ltd.

'Feet, Scotland, feet!' is a slogan with which rugby fans have become familiar, though many would admit that they have never actually heard it shouted. Indeed, to the cynic it smacks of muddy, ill-kempt fields; mis-shapen balls which in years gone by were easy to steer along the ground; and players disinclined to play the handling game.

Here, however (from a Welsh stronghold; W.J.T. Collins was 'Dromio' of the South Wales Argus, Newport, *for many years), is evidence that dribbling was a real, formidable way of pressing home an attack – and that the Scots were pretty good at it.*

Great forward play has always been, over any considerable period, the outstanding feature of Scottish Rugby. In some seasons since 1894 (the Scottish Union were then persuaded by the logic of events to adopt the four three-quarter system) the brilliance of their halves and three quarters, and the skill and rhythm of their combination, outshone the play of the pack; but usually first thought has been given to the selection of forwards who carried on the national tradition, with the natural result that the play of the forwards had usually seemed the most impressive contribution the Scots made to any game in which they were engaged.

Elsewhere I have said that differences in the forward play of the four countries have persisted. Some qualities are demanded of all forwards, and all great forwards have had them in some degree: they are matters of mind, heart and technique. But the one aspect of play in which Scottish forwards have excelled is scientific dribbling. They have been more consistently clever in ball control than the forwards of any other country, though there have been days when they were beaten at their own game.

It was this special skill in footwork which first impressed me when I saw R.G. MacMillan playing for the London Scottish in 1889–91. The same clever dribbling was the marked feature of Scottish play in the epoch-making game with Wales at Raeburn Place in 1893. I would not be misunderstood: the great Scottish forwards have had 'all the gifts', but 'this in them was the peculiar grace'; and, that it might have full play and effective scope, Scottish packs studied and perfected the arts of wheeling and breaking up the scrummage.

The earliest Scottish forwards to make an impression on my mind were R.G. MacMillan and F.W.J. Goodhue (London Scottish and Cambridge). I never saw the latter in an International game (he played in all Scotland's games in 1890–92); but he gave unmistakeable signs of greatness in club matches just as his Irish contemporary, V.C. Le Fanu, did playing for Richmond.

But MacMillan in 1893 was as great in the International game as he had seemed to me playing for his club. He and H.T.O. Leggatt (Watsonians) were particularly brilliant dribblers – I can see them as I write as I saw them that day, shoulder to shoulder, keeping the ball close to their feet, and giving the Welsh defence the greatest test it had during a desperately contested match. These two men were not only the best dribblers on the field, they were also the most prominent men in the two packs, and that is saying a lot seeing who the Welsh forwards were. Yet in making comparisons we have to remember that the Welsh pack were there primarily to feed their backs, while the Scottish policy was to trust to the forwards and allow them to dominate the game – if they could.

Rugby Recollections. W.J.T. Collins. Johns of Newport.

The commonplace scrummage formation of three men in the front row, four in the second, with a single 'number eight' forward at the rear is today taken for granted, though occasionally a flanker will drop back to bind against a second row forward ready for a wheel or back row attacking ploy. But it was not until the 1950–51 South African tour that the British accepted that they might have to re-think their allegiance to the three-two-three formation. Once they did, forwards gradually realised that they felt more comfortable and more able to push their weight.

Here, Vivian Jenkins harks back to the time when the change of mind was in the process of taking place. How would the 1955 Lions (managed by Jack Siggins) pack down against the Springboks?

There had been much controversy in the previous British season on the relative values of the 3-2-3 and 3-4-1 scrummage formations. Scotland, at the instigation of their President, Mr J.M. Bannerman, (holder of the record number of Scottish caps, thirty-seven), had reverted to 3-2-3, with not unsatisfactory results. There were four Scottish forwards included in the British team, and one wondered what effect this was likely to have on the scrummage formation when the team reached South Africa. Mr Siggins left the matter in no doubt. 'I am all in favour of 3-4-1,' he said, 'and unless the other members of the selection committee have very definite views to the contrary we shall adopt it.' Finally the team used the 3-4-1 formation on almost every occasion, unless they were packing 3-4, or even 3-2-1, owing to injuries!

One point always made in favour of the 3-2-3 formation is that only thus can the wheel be effectively brought into play. This assumes that a pack must adhere to a rigid formation throughout a game, but there is nothing to prevent a 3-4-1 pack reverting to 3-2-3 in the middle of a game if they wish to heel. As for the question of the arrowhead formation, with a 3-2-1 push directed on to the hooker in the 3-2-3 formation, the snag is that it puts a disproportionate strain on the two props. With a 3-4-1 formation against them, their opposite numbers are supported from behind by two men pushing directly, instead of one. If the front row breaks up, what use then is the 'arrowhead'?

Many people think that the main advantage of the 3-4-1 formation is that it enables the flank-forwards and number eight to break away more quickly towards the fly-half or that it makes for a quicker heel. But altogether more important, in my experience, is that it has proved to be a fundamentally better scrummaging formation *qua* weight applied. The inward thrust of the two flank-forwards makes for a more compact front row with the two props securely bound on their hooker. Thus the push from the second row is securely held and not allowed to go through owing to the front row breaking up. A 3-2-1 arrowhead push on the hooker is of no avail if there is no solid front row in front of it. The second row forwards merely push through into the empty gaps. On the other hand I have spoken to experienced international hookers who say they prefer 3-4-1 with a heavier pack behind them, but 3-2-3 if outweighted. I am for 3-4-1 if a choice must be made.

Lions Rampant. Vivian Jenkins. Cassell.

Like Irish fire, the deviousness of the men in green on the rugby field is well known and documented.

The story is told how Dr Karl Mullen found himself marking another fine hooker, Ronnie Dawson, in a provincial cup-tie. At the first line-out, without ado, he proceeded to give his rival an unmerciful hack on the knee-bone.

Then, immediately, he hurled himself backwards to the ground shouting out, 'I'm all right, lads – don't retaliate.'

Are tacklers born or made? The main ingredient in their make-up would appear to be courage or 'bottle'. Certainly the great defenders – the J.P.R. Williamses, Fergie McCormicks and Hennie Mullers – have always taken fiendish delight in putting opponents down in all sorts of circumstances and from every angle. From their heights of excellence and bravery the degree of commitment and enthusiasm shown for tackling diminishes steadily through the merely adequate and the takers of evasive action, as far as practitioners of shadow tackling which, in fairness, is a skill in itself: the more gifted among their number can make their approach appear very convincing. (There is also a special category of players whose attitude to tackling is completely dismissive and can be roughly summed up as, 'I believe that I am more use to my team on my feet.')

So personal make-up may well dictate a man's skill in the tackle. But there are technical guidelines, too, which can be pointed out and which do not date – as shown in this piece by H.L.V. Day (Leicester and England) written in 1954.

Most players if asked what gave them most enjoyment in a game of Rugby would probably think at once of running with the ball, making dazzling cuts and scoring tries. This is only natural because tries stick in the memory long after other incidents have been forgotten. But scoring tries is only one side, important though it may be; there are others.

There can be few more agreeable actions to a player than to bring an opponent down good and hard, nor one which stimulates spectators to such enthusiasm as to see a certain try prevented by a glorious tackle.

It is, too, a safety valve to your feelings. Tempers do sometimes become a little jagged. But instead of allowing them to affect the spirit in which you want to play the game, why not relieve them by going harder, legitimately, at the next tackle?

TIMING THE TACKLE

Opinions differ on whether to watch an opponent's eyes or knees. The eyes are said to be the key to the mind; but a man cannot give a dummy with his knees. I am all for watching the knees. Don't wait for your man. If you stand still you give him time and space in which to manoeuvre and he will leave you clutching at his shadow. Go towards him and try to shepherd him in one direction, preferably between yourself and the touch line. To approach him thus diagonally tends to limit his chances of escape.

[97]

Choose *your* time for tackling; don't let him dictate to you. Go into him without delay. But a full back must use his discretion when confronted by a player running at speed. If he makes his tackle too soon he may be caught off balance and easily by-passed with swerve or side-step.

Above all go for the man with the ball. Despite all the fanciful modern theories on defence which, for backs at any rate, encourage this pernicious shadow tackling, to go for the man with the ball remains the only sound method. I have seen two Internationals and one county Championship match, as well as a host of other games, thrown away by disregarding this ancient but sensible rule. On the supposition that a fly half breaking through the centre will be tackled by the full back or the wing forwards, the defending centres must not go for him. Could anything be more ridiculous! Every second's delay means nine or ten yards' advance. And who is to know whether one or other of the attacking centres is not fast enough to beat his shadower for the scoring pass, or the fly half has speed and resource to outwit the back?

In theory, of course, no try should ever be scored because every square yard of the playing area is bound to be policed by a given player, and no-one ever buys a dummy. Well, well! Half a dozen short, sharp passes soon expose the futility of shadow defence, as the Springboks did against Scotland.

Play Better Rugby. H.L.V. Day. Frederick Muller.

The urbane Godfrey Smith once paid a visit, in his capacity of English rugby buff, to Llanelli where he was guest speaker at a local club's annual dinner. His introducer told the audience that as a young man Mr Smith had been President of the Oxford Union, in which office he had taken over from Sir Robin Day and given way to Jeremy Thorpe.

There was a moment's pause while the audience digested this information, wondering whether to be impressed or not.

The laughter dam burst when a voice from the back enquired, 'Sort of reverse pass, like, was it?'

The obsolete term 'loose scrum' not only sounds loose but was indeed employed to describe a feature of the game that was aimless and scrappy. Rugby Football is forever in debt to New Zealand for evolving the ruck – which occurs 'when the ball is on the ground and at least two players, one from each side, are around the ball on their feet and attempting to push'.

New Zealand, it appears, also coined the word 'ruck' itself which, curiously enough, was still not appearing in prestigious dictionaries in the eighties, though 'serve', for example, and 'penalty' are accorded their sporting connotations. Undoubtedly, however, both the word and the skill date back to the post-War years when Victor Cavanagh was coaching Otago and, even if he did not invent rucking, certainly developed it to a high degree. By 1966 the British were encountering it on tour and a member of the Lions pack of that year could observe, drolly and memorably, that 'seeing one of our backs being rucked by the opposition was like watching clothes going round in a tumble drier'.

So let a leading figure in New Zealand's administration and coaching shine some daylight on the ruck.

Movements from this important attacking platform not only make for good rugby but can also produce valuable points.

The first essential is for the pack to get to the loose ball, tackled player, or whatever has precipitated the ruck, as rapidly as possible. Players naturally find this easier if they are going forward to the ball, and consequently the rucks most likely to produce advantages are those occurring behind their opponents' advantage line. But players should also be ready to go backwards to the ruck situation, and should practise for this eventuality. Flankers should be fit, fast and ball-hungry.

The ideal ruck must be based on the 3-4-1 scrum formation – three players in the front row, four in the middle row. A solid platform must be created by the first people to the breakdown. There is an obvious correlation between good rucking and good scrumming, and all of the forwards in the pack must be able to operate effectively in any one of the scrum positions when the scrum forms. It's unimportant which one of them arrives first at the breakdown point; whoever it is must become the basis of the three-man front row, with the others making up the composite unit as they arrive on the scene. (Formation of this type can be essential to winning the ruck.)

The essence of good rucking is the players' body position. This should be low, with the back horizontal and the feet in a pushing stance, not too wide apart, with weight on the toes. Though arriving players should join the ruck with speed and vigour, they should not in their enthusiasm bind too high up on their team mates and start pushing on a point above the hip rather than below it.

If the position is correct the ruck can drive forward towards the opponents' goal-line, can contain all the opposition forwards and control the ball. At the start of the ruck the ball should be covered as soon as possible. Any player who can arrive at the break-down and secure possession of the ball, maintaining it at the pick-up point, has made a major contribution towards winning the ruck. If forward movement is maintained, even if your side does not win the ball it gets the ensuing scrum put-in.

As mentioned earlier every forward in the pack should be drilled so that each person can act confidently in any of the scrum positions when a ruck forms – so that the number eight, say, can act as a hooker, or the prop go down as lock. It is fatal for a loose forward who is in an ideal position to become a front row man in a ruck to be expected to hang back because some other forward had been nominated for that role in a set scrum. This used to happen too often in New Zealand. Many will recall how the Lions in 1971 won the Third Test at Athletic Park, Wellington, by a morale-boosting try after they had pushed back an unready All Black pack slow to the ruck.

On the other hand speed and decisiveness in getting to the ruck should not degenerate from what should be a controlled set-piece into an indecent mêlée. Each arriving forward should assess the situation and place himself into the appropriate vacant position and stay on his feet and drive. Players who clamber on top of their team mates in the mistaken notion they are doing something constructive only ensure the collapse of a ruck and the loss of a chance to control the ball.

Forwards should always remember that they need a clear channel to hook or control the ball. Their body position on the tackled ball is very important in creating a clear channel in the early formation of a ruck. They can achieve this by being consciously aware that they must run in the tackle as they are brought down.

In any ruck the role of the half back is, of course, critical. His is the decision whether to hook quickly or to hold the ball in the ruck, and he must learn to make a quick assessment of the possibilities arising from each ruck and to call for the ball when the opposition is disorganised or at a disadvantage.

To perfect the 'hook' or 'hold' possession won from rucks is a drill requiring a great deal of practice, but it is absolutely vital to enlarge the opportunities for varying play and to create – if possible – demoralising uncertainty in the opposing team.

New Zealand rugby, both in the All Blacks and at provincial level, has always been blessed with strong, powerful forwards to whom the 3-4-1 formation in the ruck has become second nature. This has contributed greatly to the effectiveness of our forward play and the success of our teams. But it must be remembered that this rucking capability was gained only through constant drilling on the practice field and in the gymnasium. The key to this is the ability of the forwards to play every position in the ruck, and to turn on this drill in any area of the playing field.

Pattern and controlled rucked balls constitute gilt-edged possession.

'The Ruck' by Ivan Vodanovich from *New Zealand Rugby Skills and Tactics.*
Lansdowne Press, Auckland.

'Coaching' is one of the least attractive words in the language. It seems inescapably smeared with artificial excellence – small cricketers being taught to play forward immaculately to wides or classroom duffers receiving a fix just sufficient to propel them through vital examinations. When coaching for rugby received the blessing of the various Home Countries near the end of the sixties, and schools, clubs and national XVs began to be run by coaches, it met strident opposition from the old guard, whose angry noises reverberate down the decades.

Yet the coaching function is surely useful and important and belongs in our section on Skills. Most players are or were taught the game by someone, often a schoolmaster; and any meaningful training session must be directed or organised. The best and most attractive touring sides to visit Britain in the last quarter of a century have been coached – F.R. Allen's All Blacks of 1967 and the Wallabies of 1984, under Alan Jones, for example.

What critics of coaching fear is that the initiative and imagination which they say ought to characterise good rugby are being left on the sidelines, ousted by programmed 'moves' devised by the coaches. To which the latter reply, 'There is no bad coaching – only bad coaches.' The argument is a live one.

Much evidence exists that coaches themselves agonise over their role – though perhaps few have thought it through so thoroughly as did the authors of the piece that follows.

The closest parallel to the rugby coach that we can think of lies outside sport altogether. If it helps to make the role of the coach easier to comprehend, the digression should be worthwhile. One key figure from the world of the theatre is the director of a play. He has been an actor in his time and understands from the inside the doubts, the fears, the ambitions and the problems that confront the actors out there on the stage. By organising and planning rehearsals, by ensuring that each and every player knows his lines and understands both his own role and that of the other players, he can build up a performance of the play. He instils a sense of self-discipline into every member of the cast to make sure that no-one over-acts to hog the limelight, winning cheap applause to the detriment of both his fellow players and the play. He makes sure that the individual performances are based on sound technique but does not neglect the value of improvisation. He can use the new ideas that the actors will bring to their parts. He will have the organising ability to plan the six weeks' preparations so that when the curtain goes up the cast are all right on the night. He is the involved yet detached spectator who can sit in the stalls and see what no-one on the stage can – the overall picture.

To us this is exactly what the coach should be striving for. He has his fifteen players; he knows their roles; he knows their abilities and their potential; he can help them give their best performance as a team at the right time. He has built up their confidence and concentration to the point where they know their lines and can perform them with the panache born of self-discipline. Again, he is the one man who can see the overall picture.

Even to mention the term 'military' is calculated to raise eye-brows and to get the immediate reaction of 'Yes, I knew it – these blokes who coach rugby teams are frustrated sergeant-majors. They treat training fields like parade grounds and get a sadistic pleasure from ordering people about.' We think it is more subtle. One is not thinking of a reluctant squad of national servicemen ripped untimely and unwillingly from their families. One is thinking of a band of men, all for their individual reasons, who have volunteered for one of the top-line combat forces, say the commandos or the paratroopers. They are willing to put themselves under a rigid discipline which in its turn breeds a self-discipline, a confidence and a pride to the extent that they can act efficiently even in battle conditions.

The military manuals were not written by idiots, and they lay great store on operating at the outside edge of the possible. Every man in the unit is pushed continually beyond what he would hitherto have regarded as his limit. Gradually, his self-imposed limits become extended. His self-confidence grows, he begins to develop a pride in his own ability and he is undaunted by obstacles he would a few months before have regarded as insurmountable. After a time, nothing seems impossible.

One remarkably effective and simple example is the sort of no-limit route march. A squad of men will be marched out of camp for about nine or ten miles and then marched all the way back. As the camp gets nearer and nearer the marchers begin to think, 'Great, thank goodness that's over.' Instead the squad is taken right through the middle of the camp and off in the opposite direction. Suddenly the squad does not know how far it will have to march. Crucially, instead of this lowering a man's morale, it begins to enhance it and the feeling grows that it does not matter how far it is, he is going to finish on his feet. He is beginning to withstand hardship and come out on top. Training for rugby can successfully be run on broadly the same no-limit principles.

If a rugby coach can win the respect of the players he will develop the sort of authority that an officer can command. This authority, unlike an officer's with the full weight of the army behind him, is vested in him by the players. It lasts as long as they, and all of them are volunteers, are prepared to subjugate themselves to his discipline because they believe in him and because they believe that what they are doing is for their benefit. He cannot order; he can only cajole, persuade and even drive so long as they allow him to. If they respect him enough to follow his kind of discipline, they can begin to extend their limits on and off the field. Even after seventy minutes of a hard-fought game they will have the necessary self-discipline and confidence to force themselves to even greater efforts than they thought possible. When the crunch of battle comes, faint hearts begin to flutter and faint hearts have no place in rugby. The necessary courage comes from discipline and morale, and starts not on the field but on the training ground. If one cannot do something in training one will never do it in the course of a match.

Rugby Under Pressure. Brian Jones and Ian McJennett with Brian Dobbs.
Faber and Faber.

Carwyn James believed that players should be challenged to think about the game in a lively coaching session. (*Colorsport.*)

Among the greatest British coaches, if not the greatest, in the history of Rugby Football was Carwyn James, whose tragically early death in 1983 left a great void in the game. Shortly before he died on holiday in Amsterdam he completed an important work on his attitude to rugby which was checked, edited and published by loyal colleagues.

In this passage Carwyn is musing and allowing his mind free rein. Above the desk, no doubt, hangs a pall of blue tobacco smoke; the midnight oil burns, ever so quietly.

Rugby football is a thinking game. The word 'think' and the imperative of the verb should be heard often in a lively coaching session. The players should be challenged to think about the game, to think and to memorise and to recall in the correct order the exercises they may have done in a skill sequence.

During a line-out session, as a brief interlude, the thickest forward may be asked to reveal the line-out signals of the opposition. A laugh or chuckle may shorten the agony, and a slight digression on signals is permissible.

Any kind of ambiguity should be avoided. A word sign beginning with the letter 'p' was the call for the forwards to go right. When Gareth Edwards, typically, called 'psychology', half the forwards went left! The Welsh team, incidentally, use the Welsh language though most of them are ignorant of it as a daily means of communication.

I was quite amused, probably because in Wales we never use the pronoun 'thee', to observe that Ray French in his characteristically down-to-earth dissertation 'Running Rugby' uses the 'me to thee, thee to me' call for the scrum half and the number eight. Acceptable and less ambiguous for the lads of Cowley and the north of England than other parts, I'm sure. The least ambiguous and the most surreptitious sign I ever encountered was by Arthur Summons, the Wallaby fly half, who pointed the toe of his right foot in the direction that mattered.

Calling signals or decoding them should keep players alert. Another wakey-wakey contribution is the use of the whistle: two blasts and all the players must fall flat on their faces, three means six press-ups, and four is to stand again. I'm a great believer in constantly reminding players orally and by practice how important it is to get off the ground immediately.

It isn't easy for a twelve-stone scrum half to get up quickly following a dive-pass. Imagine the effort for an eighteen-stone forward!

It is a skill and should be taught as a skill. For a perceptive thinker I would offer the subject: 'The undiscovered skills and the forgotten arts of all football games' for a post-graduate degree, probably a doctorate.

Incidentally, in case you are asking the question, I reserve the one blast on the whistle during the action for a deficiency in technique. Play carries on, but the point has been made. More about this later when I discuss my Italian experience to make coaching points. This was an invaluable experience, really, because it made me re-think my philosophy and approach following a longish connection with top-class material at Llanelli and with the British Lions.

It was almost like teaching youngsters in the junior school again with the accent on the basics, the fundamentals, the skills and the habits; and forgetting, more or less, that there were forwards and there were backs. They all had to learn the individual skills. An awareness of this simple fact could be the salvation of the game in the eighties. Players need to be shown the way, but above all they need to be encouraged into action.

I have a feeling that coaches generally tend to talk too much. Talk provokes talk and too much of it can lead to indiscipline.

In my first week as a schoolmaster I learned that silence is golden. Chattering children hate a silent teacher. Silence suggests strength. Silence, I have found, provokes silence and obedience.

I shall never forget my first training session at Rovigo in northern Italy. I knew no Italian. Most of the players knew no English. Fortunately the hooker, Paolo Ferracin, spoke English quite well and I gave my instructions through him. I first asked him if the boys always talked so much in a training session. He laughed and said that they were Italian! If you want to be heard in Italy you have to speak louder than the next guy.

My first instruction, naturally, was that no-one should speak. Imagine their disbelief. Like naughty children two of them tried me out and for their curiosity they spent the next twenty minutes in almost solitary confinement, fifty yards apart, running around the adjoining pitch while in the blissful silence I gave quiet voice to the falling eventide and the encircling gloom, which bewildered my Italian friends even more.

What a joy, once they had learned the value of silence, to see them working hard in training and to observe their discipline in matches against garrulous opponents who inevitably quarrelled amongst themselves when things began to go wrong. Their silence and their disciplined approval easily won for them the championship of the first division and a private audience with the Holy father, John Paul II, at the Vatican. The following day Sanson Rovigo played inspired rugby against Frascati, the home of my favourite *vino bianco secco*.

With or without wine, the tongues of too many coaches are loose. They will insist on delivering lecturettes during a coaching session. My advice to any aspiring coach is to cut the chat to a minimum.

One of the worst examples I ever witnessed of a coach who loved to hear his own voice was in Villa Dose, a small village in northern Italy. I had been asked to assess him. It was a bitterly cold night, the kind of night when I cursed my luck and yearned to be beside a coal fire. The coach, an Argentinian who prided himself on his Italian, dominated the session with words and more words while the players were hanging around getting more and more miserable in the freezing conditions.

I soon relegated him to the touchline and took over to conduct a short, sharp session full of running and passing and amusement. Even the elephants in attendance chirped and twittered as if they had swallowed nightingales, while the Argentinian cuckoo moved on to another nest.

He was replaced by Alex Penciu, a Rumanian exile, who had played brilliantly for Locomotiva against Clem Thomas's All Whites in 1954 and again as a full back against R.H. Williams's Scarlets in Moscow in 1957. I spent hours discussing those matches with Alex, and also the coaching methods of Vogel, now exiled in Buenos Aires.

Another type I can't abide is the immaculately tracksuit-clad coach who, although past it, turns the clock back and leads the field to set the pace for the running-around-the-paddock bit. I would hope that my players could set and maintain a faster pace than I could.

This type of coach, too, will insist on demonstrating particular skills badly. A coach should never demonstrate unless he has perfected the art. Choose the best performer in the squad and let him demonstrate. Use the expertise that you have around you, comment briefly on the points to look for in the skill, and let the lads practise. The better coaches will accept the fact that certain players may have a more specialist acquaintance with a particular aspect of play than the coach has, that other players may be able to demonstrate better, and that they should all be fitter than he is. It is bad psychology to reveal the shortcomings of a player in front of others. Equally bad at the end of a hard session, when most of us are gasping for a fag, to see our 'fitter than thou' coach setting off on another round-the-field jogging trip in full view of the dressing room.

A coach should be able to diagnose what is wrong with his team. If he is unsure, then he must look for expert opinion in much the same way that a family doctor calls for the help of a consultant. Once the ill or ills are diagnosed the coach must set up a clinic to provide the correct treatment. . . .

. . . I don't think rugby suffers too much from over-coaching, rather from poor coaching – coaches who don't think enough. Content with their certificate and their badge, they go through the motions of what they were told to do on the coaching course. There is a basic sameness and a boredom in their sessions.

Units and teams are essentially boring. Individuals are interesting. Coaching, like teaching, is about helping the individual. If his skills are good and improving the sum total will be so much better.

Focus On Rugby. Carwyn James. Stanley Paul.

Whether it is an art or a science or a craft, captaincy is certainly a skill even if today the gibe is often heard that the captain is no more than the coach's on-field arm.

Certainly in bygone days far more was expected of the skipper than has been the case in the later decades of the twentieth century. He undertook many of the tasks coaches carry out today; and at International level had to inspire and direct fifteens which, though they might have played a Trial match together, were in essence little more than scratch sides.

John Gwilliam became one of the great captains. Under him the Welsh recorded two Grand Slams in 1950 and 1952, their first since the early years of the century. His vignette harks back to a more happy-go-lucky era in the game when far more was evidently left to chance.

My experience as an International captain began almost by accident. Bleddyn Williams had been chosen as captain of the Welsh team to play against England at Twickenham in 1950, but on the journey to Paddington he reported unfit and when we arrived at the London Welsh ground for an eve-of-match practice no captain had been appointed in his place. In the changing-room one of the selectors approached me and said quietly: 'We'd like you to captain the side tomorrow. Don't use any of those long wild passes, don't flip the ball back from the line out, don't hold the ball in the back of the scrum. Otherwise play your own game'!

During the run-out it was clear that there were some lively players among the newcomers and fortunately some wise heads among the older members. At outside half W.B. Cleaver gave us a feeling of great solidarity and confidence while in the front row we had in Cliff Davies, of Cardiff, a born humorist as well as one of the most able forwards Wales has produced.

On the Friday evening we had an interesting discussion about the game; and two points emphasised were that the standard of football would not be any higher than that of a good club match, and that if we were a yard faster on the ball than our opponents we would win. Trying to imagine ourselves in the enemy's position we decided that as our full back was only seventeen years old and was appearing in his first International the English policy would be to play on him. Apart from instructing the blind side wing to drop back in defence and exhorting the forwards to dominate the game there was little we could do about this.

Our anxiety on his behalf was unnecessary. In the game the full back in question, Lewis Jones, not only dealt calmly with everything and anybody that came his way but also produced an amazing zig-zag run in which he must have loped deceptively round most of the opposition before sending Cliff Davies over for a try. This gave us heart to fight back after an early English try and incidentally must have been worth about £5000 to Lewis Jones in terms of Rugby League offers. It also made clear that the full back's role had changed.

Generally the duty of a full back had been to tackle hard, fall bravely and find a safe touch. Nowadays a weak defender is still a liability, but he is called upon to do much less tackling, and can be well covered by the forwards and the blind side wing three quarter. Instead he is now expected to instigate attacking movements and produce the change of direction which can deceive the most well-laid plans of the modern theorist.

Apart from this remarkable performance by Lewis Jones there were other encouraging signs for the Welsh rugby follower. A lanky second row forward named Roy John showed that he had the gift of handling the ball expertly, leaping high in the line out and also doing his share of work in the tight. At practice I used to make a point of jumping to touch the cross-bar, first with one hand, and then the other; and given the normal height of 10 ft 6 ins for the bar this is a useful jump. Imagine my surprise when Roy John stood underneath the cross-bar and, springing up nonchalantly, tapped the wood with both hands together – I was grateful that he was on our side.

About ten minutes after the beginning of the game I found that my voice had disappeared and my only means of communication was a whisper. The game went on at a fast pace and no-one seemed to worry about my lack of exhortation (anyway players rarely listen to long harangues from a leader of the forwards). However, I did my best to encourage them – and then two tackles in particular by R.T. Evans and Ray Cale, the wing forwards, raised such a roar of approbation from the Welsh section of the crowd that further encouragement from me was unnecessary.

Twickenham has always been an interesting ground for me. Welshmen find it has a dark, forbidding atmosphere, and for the players it is dominated by the proximity of the two clocks. In no game which I played there can I remember extra time being allowed although play had been held up for injuries and the referee had power to extend the game if he wished.

Twickenham is also memorable as I was once locked out of it before a game. At 1.30pm on the afternoon of the match I went out of the dressing room and through the gates, intending to give a stand ticket to my father, who was coming up for the game. There was no sign of him and as it was getting late I left the ticket with a friend and made back for the ground.

But the gate had just been shut as the ground was full. The gate-keeper was not impressed when I told him I was a player; and I felt like Sydney Howard making his celebrated entry to the Cup Final, first as a reporter for *Old Moore's Almanack* and then, with his bowler hat pressed under his coat, as a ball boy. After a few minutes the situation began to be alarming, until eventually a plain clothes policeman of Welsh ancestry was persuaded that my claim was genuine.

To be unrecognised by gate-men, policemen and disappointed spectators was a salutary reminder that perhaps Welsh captains – and especially if they are second row forwards – rival the newly-commissioned second lieutenant as the lowest form of animal life.

'Leading the Welsh Pack with a Whisper' by John Gwilliam from *Try! An Anthology To Celebrate The WRU Centenary 1881–1981.*

By the seventies and eighties captains of Test sides, particularly those in the southern hemisphere, more frequently than not found themselves saddled with a round-the-year job. Graham Mourie, for example, spent much of every summer leading a team abroad from the time he captained the New Zealand Juniors in the Argentine to the 1981 All Black visit to Romania and France. Small wonder that his thoughts on tour discipline are so carefully articulated, with man-management qualifying as a skill.

The major part of a tour is concerned not with rugby but with touring. Selectors have the main say in determining the composition of a touring team and intelligent selection was always the biggest help in ensuring the balance of a side. But once on tour it was the responsibility of the management to ensure that the side remained happy in each other's company – that there were no rifts, no cliques, no adverse inside or outside influences. I always promoted the philosophy that the most important aspect of a tour was the personal achievement of a balance between rugby and the touring life, the sweet life: the finding of a tour rhythm which permitted the player to gain the most enjoyment from the tour while enabling him to produce the best rugby of which he was capable. Each found his balance in different ways. Ian Stevens, the Wellington half back, would train and play hard and set aside a particular day for relaxation ... to have a few jugs. If that relaxing day began as soon after sunrise as possible, he was happy. But he'd be out training the next day, retaining his balance. For Bill Osborne the balance was a steady diet of fruit juice and the occasional glass of good wine when he was in the mood. Most of the players with whom I have been associated have a great respect for their physical well-being – if amateurs in fact and by Victorian decree, they are professional sportsmen in application and dedication. The sippers of soft drinks at team sessions often equalled those partaking of what, in gentler times, were known as alcoholic beverages.

Bryan Williams, the tourist of all tourists, often spoke up about an insidious syndrome that afflicts new All Blacks: the Gee Whizz disease, the desire of first-time travellers to spend so much time trying to absorb the sights of a world much bigger than them that they don't notice the world of rugby passing them by.

Balance is the key. 'Have you got your balance?' That was the question.

Other things were important, like the rooming arrangements at hotels, the music to be played on interminable bus-rides, the dress to be worn on a particular occasion. Andy Dalton was usually the man in charge of who would share rooms with whom. He was always alert to any symptom of incompatibility among players which could have flared into discontent should they need to share the crowded rooms which sheltered the homeless. As Andy was in charge of rooms, others would be delegated their particular functions, all aimed at the smooth, harmonious running of the tour. The man mostly in charge of 'gimmees' – an English-origin word the players use for hand-outs by local unions or factories or breweries visited – was Andy Haden, who always displayed profound ability to find these things and ensure they were shared equally by all team members. The accounting and ticket distribution was another job shared, usually delegated to someone who could add or subtract, but seldom for some reason entrusted to the front row. There was always that emphasis on participation, on having as much involvement as possible within the club. Trying, striving to develop off the field a sense of togetherness, of commitment to the aim, striving to achieve and usually obtaining a professional dedication to game and country.

The example of those who proved that they had obtained the balance was important to me – the members of the club, whose example and leadership was crucial in the training of those who were merely candidates. Men such as Stu Wilson, Bruce Robertson, Bryan Williams, Frank Oliver, Dave Loveridge, Brad Johnstone ... I could continue for a page with a list of those who set the example, assisting in any way they could to develop the team to a plateau of success which their own standards and those of their predecessors had enabled them to achieve.

With that balance, that touring confidence, the players were able to achieve a similar sense of confidence in themselves in the other two facets of touring life, the training and the matches.

Graham Mourie: Captain. An autobiography with Ron Palenski. Arthur Barker.

Elsewhere in this book there is an essay by Michael Gibson in a light vein. In 1971, at the peak of his career, he was a member of the British Isles side which won in New Zealand, and at that time was rated by many good judges as the best all-round back in the world. Like a number of other Lions, on his return he contributed to a volume on the tourists' success edited by Terry O'Connor. Here, then, is some straight-from-the-shoulder writing about midfield play.

Too often players of talent are permitted to acquire and develop faults. These faults are common to the game, regardless of the level, be it coarse or International rugby.

For example, study any fly-half. Note his positional play, remembering his role as the initiator of almost all the movements. If his team is under pressure you will frequently see him moving behind the set-piece instead of holding his correct position. This is simply self-protection. The fly-half may gain comfort by directing the play but such positioning reduces the possibilities open to his side. Once he adopts such a position he is compelled to run across the field and the rest of the backs have no option but to follow.

Another defect concerns his state of mind. A fly-half can become so self-important that he considers he must do something as an individual with each ball he receives. He then neglects his role as a link and so neglects his side. To succeed at the highest level the fly-half also requires absolute concentration. Once his mind wanders or he becomes determined to achieve individual supremacy over a wing forward or his opposite number, his appreciation of any situation wanes, and he becomes less alert to new possibilities.

The faults of a fly-half are easy to see and often have a greater effect than errors made by his fellow backs, but the principles involved when discussing a fly-half's defects apply equally to the backs as a whole. Watch a centre in action. Often he feels he *must* make a break, and even makes it *before* the ball arrives. This is stupid play; it is better to go through an entire match without a clean break than to waste possession with a futile attempt to force a break. Proper centre play involves rapid appreciation of the options on receipt of the ball, but too often a centre will expose his mental limitations by simply stampeding at the opposition, allegedly setting up a 'risk situation'. This method can sometimes work, but recently it has become the standard play of the centre who is heavy – both physically and mentally!

With that style it means the centre can retain his place in a side *ad nauseam*, as nothing drastic can happen provided he holds onto the ball having set up the risk. The finger of blame can often be pointed at the coach, with his overwhelming desire to cross the gain line at the earliest possible opportunity. Also, a centre must resist the temptation to measure his contribution to a match by adding up the number of occasions on which he had the better of his opposite number. To become involved in a duel within a match results in wasted possession, with a centre running across the field in an attempt to create a break and tucking the ball under one arm, so advertising his intention of making an individual sortie.

A centre should master the simple arts of rugby and recognise his role as a supporter of movement. He should be willing, in other words, to do more running in support than in possession. Compare rugby with the world of commerce. No business could provide a better return for investment than rugby. The rewards are the product of the effort.

'The Three Quarter's Skills' by Mike Gibson from *How The Lions Won*, edited by Terry O'Connor. Collins.

The colours worn by the oldest established members of the International Board were adopted at a very early stage in each Union's history. For example, England's white uniform with its red rose was worn for their very first match in 1871 at the decree of the self-appointed selection committee which had issued invitations to play. The contribution that follows argues that the styles and prime skills of countries, as demonstrated by their back divisions, are as different as their colours.

Are the styles of back play indigenous? Do they reflect, for instance, national characteristics? It is popularly held that Welsh backs are born brilliant, that French backs become brilliant and, from time to time, the others have brilliance thrust upon them. In my view generalisations are dangerous, especially when you consider Scotland. They have raced from the ponderous to the precocious almost overnight.

Still, there are enough historical trends to lend a fairly reliable identity to the patterns and attitudes of the various countries. English back play has always been associated with forthrightness, physical presence and no little valour. The archetypal English three quarter is tall, and if there is no tradition of great pace – with the exceptions of Keith Fielding, who was the fastest man I ever played with or against, and before him J.R.C. Young – he usually has a decent stride on him, considerable velocity and a sense of directness. He is a lancebearer, with little time for subtle skirmishing.

Some stand out from the common herd – Jeff Butterfield, for

instance. A touch player supreme; one of the best timers of a pass the game has ever known. And there is many an Englishman who will stop at Butterfield and W.P.C. Davies when the roll of great centre partnerships is called; a potent combination of cleverness, opportunism and sheer verve.

Davies was out of the classical English armoury: all thrust and finish. And think of some of the men who have followed him – Chris Wardlow, Jeremy Janion, Tony Bond, Peter Warfield, to name just a few. There was considerable height and weight when John Spencer and I played in the middle and the wings have usually been big men. Think of Ted Woodward, Rodney Webb and Peter Thompson whom I remember the late Bert Toft describing as 'a rare hybrid of tank and gazelle'.

It follows that when size is your ally, manoeuvrability becomes a lesser consideration. English backs, therefore, have tended to be swervers rather than jinkers like, for example, the Welsh. Because of the English backs' obsession with size and physical impact they have lacked not just overall pace, but acceleration – though from that generalisation I will exempt the Coventry pair Peter Preece and Geoff Evans who were genuinely capable of making the outside break. Who can forget that match at Twickenham in 1973 when they sliced the French defence to shreds to make both of England's tries?

If Preece and Evans are exceptions in the matter of sprinting, there are very few odd men out when it comes to defending. Few who have played for England could not present a sound defence.

I will move on to Welsh back play next because it provides the biggest contrast. The lasting impression of the Welsh is of profound cunning and a passionate belief in their ability to beat a man with the ball in hand. I see them as dark and devious and usually not very big, invariably very swift, and with an apparently divine ability to run in two directions at the same time.

The typical Welsh fly half is a darter. Invariably on the small side, he flicks out jinks and side-steps with the speed, and often the numbing effect, of the cobra's tongue. Think of Cliff Morgan, David Watkins, Alan Rees, Phil Bennett and Gareth Davies. Each had his own hallmark, but they came from the same factory. Then there was Barry John. He did not stun you; he was all stealth, and crept up and poisoned you when you were not looking. A superb lineage, unmatched by any other country in the world. And it goes without saying that every one of those players was an outstanding kicker.

Welsh backs have an inborn knack of linking extreme acceleration with elusiveness, and the jink is a paralysing weapon however it is used. Some, like Ken (D.K.) Jones used it early, a savage stab off one foot or the other and then a surge of pace. Others, like Gerald Davies, left it very late, coming right up to the defender, then murmuring the side-step without noticeable loss of speed or line. There is great pride in back play in the Principality, and it shows.

The French are also highly distinctive, and if you have seen a wide variety of expressiveness and skill I doubt very much that you have ever seen a slow French back. Some, and I think back to Jean-Marie Bonal, are quite indecently rapid. He and another speed merchant, Jean-François Gourdon, were also pretty sizeable specimens, but in that sense they were exceptions.

Like the Welsh, French backs tend to be neat and wieldy and they exude artistry. Jo Maso was a magician of a centre; Jean-Pierre Lux a marvel of economy and effectiveness. The French have this very special gift of not committing themselves too soon, of keeping their options open longer than anyone else. Their centres stand deeper than most, they run at three quarter pace plotting all the while, and when the decision is made there seems to be an extra gear to shift up into. And they are masters of the switch, of the one-handed flick. Jacques Cantoni epitomised the sheer panache of the French game. He was incredibly sharp, had a lightning change of direction and was so light on his feet that he never seemed to be touching the ground.

Class is what the French game is all about and when I use that word I think of Pierre Villepreux, the most complete full back I ever saw. And beyond the elegance to which the French backs aspire there is a remarkable versatility. So many of them can play in so many positions; and while they are great individualists they are also great team players. Their support play is a revelation; they are totally unselfish.

It is very difficult to pin specific labels on to the Scottish game. In the years when I played against them they were a rather dour collection, some quite embarrassingly cumbersome. But the Scots have usually tried to be creative at full back, and that is a tradition that I suspect was laid down by Ken Scotland, one of the most enlightened footballers of his day. Indeed I would go so far as to say that Ken was in advance of his day; perhaps the precursor of the running full back who followed universally when the touch-kicking laws were altered.

In my experience the Scots were poor readers of a game and they were not good exploiters of situations. They had indifferent unit skills and, to a man, they hung onto the ball too long. Perhaps their sources were too diverse for they took their players from distinct pockets of clubs – the Anglos, the Borders and the North. It always struck me as a paradox that a country which gave the world the seven-a-side game should show so little of the natural sevens dexterity when it came to fifteen-a-side. Billy Steele was the most liberated Scottish back of my time. He was very light-footed and extremely tricky.

Now, of course, the emphasis has changed dramatically. The Scots have become almost frantically mobile. Whether this is the result of power failure in their forward supply lines, evolution or revolution, I would not care to say; but coinciding with an exceptionally weak series of packs is an almost convulsive shift of attitude behind the scrums. Scotland now run everything and while this makes for marvellous entertainment and must make the game great fun to play – and there must be a lot in that – they leave themselves pathetically vulnerable and there is nothing in their results to suggest that they are on the right lines to success. Andy Irvine, John Rutherford, David Johnston and Jim Renwick have emerged to give substance to the Scottish dream but they are a long way from consistently winning matches.

For a very long time Irish back play could be summed up in two words – Michael Gibson. Over a span of sixteen years the man's remarkable talents were applied to his country's cause, first at fly half, then centre, and finally wing. Gibson covered an awful lot of cracks.

While he was in office Ireland never really developed a style. Gibson simply gave them whatever they needed on the day. Other great backs have emerged in Ireland, and who can forget the young Tony O'Reilly? But none has done so much on his own as Gibson.

He has left the international scene now and it will be interesting to see how the Irish develop their game without him. They are generously endowed at half back, which must be encouraging, and perhaps we shall see a clear pattern of play from now on. I have always felt that they lacked corporate method when going forward, which is surprising when you consider the length of time some of their players were in the side, but they nearly always put up a high quality defence. And there is a burning competitiveness in their approach.

Venturing further out into the ever-widening world of rugby football, what of New Zealand? I have to be very careful here.

The enduring impression of All Black play is based on their forwards. Until very recently – and this is probably only a passing deficiency – they have succeeded one titanic pack of forwards with another and in this country, although the image is fading, we still tend to regard them as ten-foot-tall supermen. With forwards like theirs, who needs backs?

Some will say, however, that New Zealand are the non-three-quarters side of all time. Their concentration on forward strength in the past precluded any chance of their three quarters developing as runners. Individual skill and flair did not exist. There were runners-in, and there were battering-ram midfield men like Ian McRae to set up the second phase, but this desperately stereotyped outlook was never exposed because, in general, the other sides could not get ball with which to run at them.

Then in 1971 the British Lions achieved parity with them up front and what followed from there resulted in New Zealand back play being held in contempt. They were exposed, cruelly at times, as players without vision or initiative. To their credit they were able to see the reflections in the mirror that the Lions held and there was a radical shift in emphasis. Their backs were invited to play.

I will not be so unfriendly as to say, though many will, that New Zealand were forced to change their ways because of the abrupt decline in the quality of the forwards who followed Colin Meads, Brian Lochore, Ian Kirkpatrick and the rest. Brian Williams was a world-class wing before 1971 and there followed players of the calibre of Bruce Robertson to parade high-grade midfield skills. New Zealand could play a decent game a decent distance from their forwards.

And yet at the first sign of danger, whenever they were under serious pressure they still tended to revert to type. They would clam up in an instant and I do not think that to this day, despite the brief spell of expansiveness first under Fred Allen in the 1960s and later under Jack Gleason in the 1970s, that New Zealand back play has found its ideal context. It remains to be seen how long they keep trying.

Where do South Africa fit into the picture? Competence has been

English backs have tended to be swervers rather than jinkers, according to David Duckham. He modestly overlooks his own extravagant side-step with which he wrong-footed so many able defenders. (*Colorsport*)

their achievement above everything else because that seems to be the way of things almost everywhere that forward power prevails. There have been some quite stupendous Springbok packs and such a wealth of back row talent that the need for invention elsewhere has never really arisen. Their backs are big men who have been bred to believe that actually beating a man is one of the game's more trifling irrelevancies.

Traditionally, though, Springbok backs are enormously powerful in the tackle. Solidity is the mark of a South African back division, and coupled with that a constant attention to the needs of the team. They are great team players.

The transience of talent in Australia, where rugby has to compete

[119]

with so many other sports, notably Rugby League, makes it difficult to pin the Wallabies down to a lasting style. But what has always struck me about Australian back play is its almost vulgar vitality. The Aussies are so overtly athletic, every one of their players looking as though he has just stepped off Bondi Beach into that gold and green uniform. With their natural aggressiveness the Australians ought to beat the world but rugby, alas, is small beer to them as a nation.

Every now and then, though, a player of towering ability emerges and stays; and the name that will spring to everyone's lips is Ken Catchpole, a genius of a scrum half who was perhaps the fastest passer the modern game has known. To see Catchpole go in after the rubbish ball his forwards so often provided and turn it, in a flash, into a pearl was one of the truly exhilarating experiences in rugby football.

Rugby Union Back Play. David Duckham. Pelham Books.

Besides skills, rugby contains thuggery. No doubt in days before the Laws were formalized, a game between different towns or villages or even schools was seen by the more violent members of society as a licence to wreak legitimate physical havoc on heaven-sent victims. And if idealists had imagined that the simple drawing-up of rules by fair-minded folk would persuade such men to keep their temper, they had another think coming. In 1889 the Laws had to be amended to deal with foul play or conduct that might 'bring the game into disrepute'.

Today, warfare on the pitch still causes onlookers to wring their hands and deplore the damage being done to the game's standing and image. Rugby's nature, however, means that in order to win, a team actually needs to play as close to the limit of permissible violence as it possibly can. 'Tackle him hard!' means 'Let him feel your physical presence!' That is, make your opponent less keen to try and beat you next time – because you hurt *him.*

Play is always likely to trespass on the wrong side of the acceptable. It does not follow that rugby is somehow doomed or should be banned. There is an understanding that penalties, final warnings, sendings-off, bans and trenchant readings of the riot act are an inevitable accompaniment to a macho, physical contact sport.

All of which does not mean that the kind of conduct which figures in the next few excerpts is condoned or excused. Beginning with a Test incident involving Australia and South Africa in 1937, here is a short parade of anti-skills.

From the moment Pierre de Villiers was crumpled into uncon-
sciousness with a blatant kick and had to be carried off the field by
Boy Louw 'like a father removing the body of his child from the
scene of an accident', as one writer put it, the game became a bar-
room brawl. Brave little Pierre returned after a while, but George
van Reenen was hurt so badly that he could not resume. Fights broke
out all over the place with the Springboks so incensed that they
virtually forgot all about the ball and allowed the Wallabies to notch
11 points without reply.

Harry ('Kalfie') Martin and the Australian eighth-man Aubrey
Hodgson flew into each other on one occasion and stood exchanging
punches like two boxers. More than thirty years after the incident
Martin, then the recently-retired Chief of Staff in the South African
Air Force, but only a lieutenant in his Springbok days, talked about
that infamous incident:

'De Villiers was laid out completely. He was in a terrible state, his
eyes were rolling and his tongue was hanging out. It really upset us.'

Springbok Saga. Chris Greyvenstein. Nelson and Toyota.

*Punches thrown on the rugby field are often un-targeted haymakers designed to
warn rather than injure and to let off steam rather than eliminate an opponent.
Thus when 'victims' have time to assume horror-stricken expressions, hold their
hands to their faces and stagger around for a few paces, there has to be general
doubt that a blow actually struck them.*

However, there is another breed of puncher, thankfully rare.

Steve Finnane, the Auststralian prop whom British players came up
against several times, did a great deal of propping but a hell of a
lot of punching too. The quality of his propping was low for an
International player, for he rarely caused any of his opponents much
bother in the scrum. The quality and quantity of his punching,
however, has rarely been equalled: when Steve Finnane hit you, you
stayed hit. He was a phantom puncher, in that he would hit people
from behind and then blend in with the scenery when the concussed
victim staggered to his feet trying to find out who had delivered the
blow. I had very little respect for much of Steve Finnane's efforts on

the field on either side of the Laws. My critics can say that those who live by the sword can expect the old Wilkinson straight through the heart themselves, but even in the jungle there are laws.

Returning to Finnane's technical skills: he was usually struggling. Tight heads like Ray McLoughlin, Robert Paparemborde or Fran Cotton would have had him for breakfast and still had room for their kippers. It was probably the ascendancy which Graham Price had over him in the infamous tests against Wales in 1978 which caused the Australian to boil over and break Price's jaw with a blow from behind: the rugby equivalent of shooting the sheriff in the back as he walks away into the sunset. Finnane was workmanlike but not formidable, and the smokescreen thrown up by his misdeeds obscured his lack of class. . . .

. . . The amazing thing about the man is that he was educated and intelligent. He was a barrister, of all things, and I often used to contemplate whether the Australian legal system allows a lawyer to defend himself in their higher courts. Despite the fact that he wasn't in the highest class as a prop he won more column inches than the McLauchlans, Cottons, Carmichaels and Prices put together, and rarely seemed to show much in the way of public remorse for his actions. At least I can see *some* of the errors of my ways, looking back!

Never Stay Down. Mike Burton. Queen Anne Press.

Sometimes thunderclouds gather inexorably over a big game before ever it gets under way. Provocative statements by participants – 'So and so has got it coming to him' or 'Our opponents are rubbish' or 'X shouldn't have been picked: he plays it dirty' – can generate pre-match tension which develops into a storm at the kick-off.

Such a game took place at Twickenham in 1980 between England and Wales, before which doubts had been cast on the fairness of Welsh techniques at the ruck. The media appeared to have made up their minds that it was bound to be an ugly affair; and sure enough the visitors' flank forward Paul Ringer got his marching orders after fifteen minutes.

There is no suggestion of false heroics in these reflections by an England forward.

The battle began in the first scrum as both packs smacked into each other. From that point it was just a matter of time before someone was sent off, or carried off, or both, which in fact was the case. Even before Paul Ringer was sent off by David Burnett in the fifteenth minute there were several outbursts and the referee had already issued a general warning. Paul Ringer's late tackle was indicative of the climate and mood of the game, but he had chanced his arm – this time into John Horton's face – once too often. That we applauded the referee and slow-handclapped Paul Ringer off the field says all you need to know about what we thought of his behaviour. Even before the John Horton late tackle he had been up to his tricks. Dusty went to collect a high ball and was bowled over by David Richards and Steve Fenwick; the ball went loose and Paul Ringer came charging through to put his knee into the small of Dusty's back. The John Horton affray was not nearly so bad, but Paul Ringer took no notice of his pre-match trial or the referee's general warning and carried on as a law unto himself.

If you expected his dismissal to ease the tension, then you were wrong. From the sending-off position Dusty put us ahead, but Wales countered immediately when the English scrum lost control near its line and Jeff Squire beat Steve Smith to the touch-down.

Well, we had had one sent off . . . . who was going to be carried off? It turned out to be me! Nearing half-time I went back to gather a rolling ball and, as I gathered, I remembered the golden rule of keeping my back to the opposition to protect the ball and me. Suddenly everything went black as I thought my head was on its way between the posts. I realised that I had received a vicious kick to the head and, as I groggily got to my feet, I could feel the rough edge of flesh where my nose had been split open. There was blood everywhere.

The referee looked a bit horrified and Tony came over to me and said, 'Christ!' Off I went with Don Gatherer to the touchline where my regular escort, Doctor Leo, was waiting. Mike Davis came down to the medical room, and after he also had looked aghast, I decided to have a look in the mirror at this horror. It wasn't a pretty sight and now I know what being battle-scarred means. Leo stitched up the wound; the skin was stretched tight and the whole area felt very tender. Mike asked if I wanted to go back. Stupidly for a moment I thought about it before common sense prevailed and I said no. Mike Rafter came on at half time to replace me.

Go back to play in that? You must be joking! Scared? Too right. That first forty minutes had knocked the stuffing right out of me.

[123]

Coming off the field to take a detached view for a few minutes made the whole affair look like a brawl. There was very little rugby in that crazy game; everybody was at each other's throats and growling instead of watching the ball. People were giving 'verbal', being niggly, pushing and generally taking the fun out of rugby. The ball seemed the last concern.

Pride In England. Roger Uttley with David Norrie. Stanley Paul.

Japan's 'Mr Rugby', Shiggy Konno, tells a story against himself.

It seems that during World War II he trained to be one of his country's 'kamikaze', or suicide, pilots. These airmen flew fighters whose noses were loaded war-heads, and crashed them like flying bombs onto Allied shipping in the Pacific theatre, thereby honouring the Emperor and bringing great glory on themselves.

Shiggy, however, was never selected for a mission and finally, with the War near its close, he secured an interview with his commanding officer at which he complained bitterly that he had not been allowed to die for Nippon like his fellow pilots.

'Well, Konno,' came the reply. 'We have your flying record constantly under review. The fact is that, even if your target was the largest warship in the American fleet, you would be unlikely to hit it.'

Dirty play is unlikely to be described dispassionately and clinically – unless the victim happens to be a doctor. In this case the great full back John Williams, himself a medical specialist, describes being done over while playing for his club, Bridgend, against an All Black touring side.

No major touring side had ever graced the Brewery Field. Our only misfortune was the terrible weather conditions. It had rained continuously for five days and all pitches in South Wales were turned into quagmires. Our field is usually very good, but even this was under water on the day of the game. Our team had been picked on the previous Sunday and we had a full day's squad training as our final preparation. The weather was a bitter blow to us, as we intended to throw the ball around and run it. But we still felt we were in with a fair chance, as we were at least a club side and a very good one at that. I remember running onto the field and being so excited to see seventeen thousand spectators packed into our 'modest' ground. In spite of the rain the stands and surroundings looked superb.

We started off tremendously, but then unfortunately missed an easy goal kick which would have been very important to us psychologically. I asked Steve Fenwick to take it, knowing his big match temperament, but our outside half wanted to take it instead and Steve felt he should be allowed to do so. I now feel in retrospect I should have insisted on Steve taking it.

Then it happened.

I was involved on the edge of a ruck on the All Blacks' twenty-five-yard line when they won the ball on the opposite side from where I was lying pinned down with my head out of the ruck. I was about five yards or so away from the ball when I felt a kick in my face. The first one didn't do much damage but when the second one came I knew it was bad. I could feel the studs near my right eye, then my cheek bone clunked. As I had broken this previously it was stronger than normal and held firm. Then the studs moved down to my upper jaw which was protected by my gum shield. This flew out but my teeth were intact. Something had to give and I was left with an horrendous hole in my cheek all the way through to my tongue. I knew I had to go off the field, as blood was pouring out at a terrific rate. One of the branches of the facial artery was severed and I think I lost about two pints of blood before the stitches were completed. My father was there immediately, along with a dentist, inserting stitches inside my mouth, and together they patched me up quickly. My brothers had also rushed down to the medical room to help and tried to dissuade me from returning to the field. But they knew, as my father knew, that it was impossible to stop me. Unfortunately during this time the All Blacks had scored seven points against our fourteen men and this, in the end, was to prove vital to the result. I probably shouldn't have returned, but I knew how much my players relied on me and this was shown on my return. We came back to 10–6 at half time and were in with a real chance. Unluckily the wind blew up in the second half and even though we tried hard we found it difficult to get out of our half. With a silly try near the end we lost 17–6 but felt nonetheless that we were the 'real' winners, as we came off with far more glory than did the All Blacks.

Not having seen the incident I was kind to the New Zealanders in my speech that evening and once again congratulated them on their form. But I was hurt that nobody had come to apologise or ask how my face was. Still, it must have been an accident, I thought.

When I saw it on television the following day I was nearly sick. My assailant raked me once and then came back for a second go when he saw who it was. It corresponded with my recollection but I was amazed to see the referee so near. The evidence was irrefutable and I needed to say nothing – it was plain to see. In spite of pressure from everyone I wanted the incident to be closed; I didn't feel prolonging it could do anyone any good.

JPR – An Autobiography. J.P.R. Williams. Collins.

And finally let us put the boot on the other foot: Association Football players have for long known how it feels to cease playing and become temporary spectators, viewing the attempts of police to quell mayhem on the terraces.

Though this has mercifully been rare in rugby, there were occasions in 1970 when the Sixth Springboks could only stand and stare at the antics of onlookers. During the sixties demonstrations had established themselves as a means of making graphic political points, especially when television cameras were at hand to capture the scenes for a wider audience. Thus, on what was to be their last official rugby tour of Britain the South Africans caught the full brunt of anti-apartheid demonstrations, often disruptive, often violent, often both.

Whatever their private views on South Africa's system of government, however, it became clear that the rugby lobby disliked the demonstrators and their tactics even more. Nowhere was this more clearly shown than when the Springboks met Swansea.

The breakthrough of demonstrators onto the pitch came just a few minutes after the start of the second half and looked as though it had been a well-planned operation. Some trouble that broke out in one part of the terraces caused police in the cordon around the pitch to converge there, thus leaving an unguarded gap. It appeared that this had been a diversion created by design, for demonstrators to pour through the gap and on to the pitch. But demonstrators after- wards said that it was purely fortuitous. It did, however, provide a good lesson for the police as far as the following matches were concerned. After all, this was merely the fourth game of the tour and the police were at the stage of evolving the best techniques for dealing with the trouble-makers. After Swansea the cordon around other pitches stayed at their stations and outbreaks of trouble were dealt with by a mobile task-force.

But at the St Helen's ground on this afternoon when the hole appeared in the ring of police it was an invitation to the demonstrators. Two girls led the onrush from the west terrace. Screaming and waving their arms they could have been a couple of teenagers running to greet a pop singer, had they not looked so militant. Other demonstrators dashed onto the field behind them and this was the cue for an onslaught from the other end of the ground, where demonstrators ran at full tilt across the open space of the cricket pitch and came at the police with such speed that they could not help but break through them.

Suddenly the whole field was a confusion of people running around, yelling and fighting, accompanied by the non-combatants in the grandstand screaming out the most bloodthirsty, vicious advice to those who had to cope with the demonstrators. The mêlée on field had three components. The players, the only inactive ones, standing in a cluster looking bewildered, uneasy for their personal safety. The police, who the Chief Constable afterwards said 'were met with force and had to retaliate'. And the stewards, with orange armbands on their sleeves and hatred of the 'long-haired twits' in their hearts, who needed no such provocation. Demonstrators were bashed, kicked, dragged by the hair in the five-minute battle of clearing the pitch.

When fighting broke out on the terrace at the Mumbles end and a mobile TV camera crew started running along the touchline towards the trouble, spectators in the stand shouted, 'Don't photograph them! Don't give them the publicity!' The TV men paused for a moment and then, no doubt telling themselves it was their job, carried on. The result was some of the most gruesome shots of the tour, including a most grisly one of a demonstrator who had got onto the field being bundled back over the fence of metal railings on to the terrace, for him to be impaled momentarily on the small of his back on top of the railings.

People on the terrace edged away from those who were fighting, which meant that the antagonists could be seen clearly in this opened up section of the terracing. It was a snarling, brutal fight. The ardent Welsh rugby fan, like the official stewards, was having his keenly-awaited go at the long-hairs. Skinheads were prominent, their heavy

[127]

boots ideal for use against those pinned down on the concrete steps.

Immediately the match was over the irate Chief Constable of the South Wales Constabulary, Mr Melbourne Thomas, let it be known that he was holding a Press conference. The newsmen gathered in the crummy improvised tea-room under the stand which serves for committee entertaining and were told by Mr Thomas: 'Five constables were taken to hospital. One sergeant was severely injured in the chest and abdomen from blows with a sharp instrument.'

What had been used to inflict the wounds had been a broken-off bit of one of the sticks to which the anti-apartheid banners had been attached. There were piles of these broken poster poles to be seen on the pavement among burnt out smoke bombs and torn-up placards as one came away from the match with home-going spectators making the comment that they had witnessed what were the worst scenes that had ever taken place at a rugby match.

There Was Also Some Rugby. Wallace Reyburn. Stanley Paul.

HUMOUR

Game for a Laugh

Rugby players in conversation prefer humour to hype. For eighty minutes – and eighty minutes only – the contest is the thing; for the other six days and twenty-three hours of the week straight faces are out. It is enough for the game to be taken seriously by media pundits and coaches and treasurers and selectors and committttee-men. And referees.

It seems unlikely, however, that this basic truth was grasped by authors, certainly in the Home Countries, for at least three quarters of a century of the game's formal history. Writing about it up to 1960 tended to be strait-laced and in serious vein. P.G. Wodehouse may have created buffoon-like figures like Walkinshaw, the acting football captain in Tales of St Austin's: *'a well-meaning idiot. There was no doubt about his being well-meaning. Also, there was no doubt about his being an idiot'; but these were ludicrous creatures who simply happened to get involved in Rugby Football. It would have amounted almost to sacrilege to go into print suggesting that there could be anything intrinsically funny or absurd about the game or the people who played it.*

Thus Michael Green's book on Coarse Rugby represented something of a watershed – as if his readership was being invited to 'come out', as the saying goes, and acknowledge the mean tricks and subterfuges and hoary stratagems with which third-rate players can play out their private first-class fantasies. It may not have been suitable reading for empire-builders, moulders of character or aspiring alickadoes – but it was an instant best-seller. Here is the re-commended build-up for a vital Coarse Rugby match.

Every possible preparation has been made and the team takes the field. Yet still more can be done before play starts.

First, *do not indulge in a warm-up.*

Countless games have been lost because of this foolish habit. It is impossible to exaggerate the boost the other side receive from seeing their opponents throwing the ball to each other and dropping it, taking kicks at goal and missing by miles, or doing all-out sprints at about 5 mph.

Instead of warming up, concentrate on depressing the opponents. The best kicker in the side should take a series of shots at goal from in front of the posts and about twenty yards out. As even a Coarse Rugby player should get about 25 per cent of these over, the other side will be scared of giving away penalty kicks.

The forwards should stand still, glaring towards the other side with curling lips and snarling faces. If the enemy kick the ball in their direction, let them come and fetch it themselves. Spit occasionally.

The backs should pretend to be planning fantastic tactical moves. It is best if they gather round the fly-half, who can use his hands expressively, like an RAF pilot shooting a line. Wave the hands to indicate men criss-crossing each other, jinking sideways and bursting through. The other backs should nod sagely and jig up and down eagerly as if they can't wait to put these moves into operation. As a final gesture the fly-half does an imitation of a savage hand-off with the heel of the hand, and everyone nods and looks fierce.

Meanwhile the referee, if any, will be asking the captains how long they want to play. In this connection I must protest against an appeal made by the then President of the Rugby Union some years ago for games to last forty minutes each way. This is a typical rugger move, based on the fallacy that the game is played by fit supermen with energy to burn, leading lives of monk-like celibacy and temperance.

But to expect the sort of person who plays Coarse Rugby, perhaps an undersized youth or a flabby clerk, to play forty minutes each way is not only cruel, it is dangerous. An ideal period would be twenty minutes each way with an interval of fifteen minutes in which drinks are served, but as tradition seems against this it is the duty of every captain to bargain with the referee for the shortest possible playing period.

Occasionally a referee who has strayed from a higher sphere will hopefully suggest to the captains, 'Forty minutes each way?'

This should be met by a howl of derisive laughter and a counter-suggestion is made of twenty-five minutes each way with ten minutes' break at half time. This is purely a bargaining suggestion, like the initial price asked when selling a car. Although it is meant seriously, the referee won't take it that way. It is up to him to make his bid now, which is invariably thirty-five minutes.

The home captain points out that it gets dark around here very early and that if they go on too long there won't be any tea left because the other teams will have scoffed it. This leaves the gate open for possible negotiations at half time (which is nowhere near the middle of the game) The referee makes a mental note to play only thirty minutes, but for the sake of appearances sticks at thirty-five.

A captain who wins the toss should always play with the wind or slope in his favour for the first half, as the first half is invariably longer than the second. This because of the late kick-off, but is also caused by the unfitness of the average coarse referee, who's had enough long before the end and is glad to finish it all. On an average I should say that the first half of a coarse game lasts thirty-one minutes and the second half twenty-six minutes, so you gain five minutes' advantage.

Whether wind or slope is a bigger help is a problem. Personally I always favour the slope, because touch-kicking is at such a low ebb that a team never make proper use of the wind, whereas the slope is kind to ageing limbs and gives an illusion of vigour to the unfit (i.e. everyone in the team).

One captain always chose ends so that in the second half his team defended the end nearer the dressing room. This was one of those ghastly grounds shared by twelve teams and it was the only way to ensure that the bath-water was hot. Probably that's as good a reason as any for making a choice, and a good deal better than some.

If the toss is lost, it is important to pretend that the opponents' choice suits your team. The captain should call out clearly, 'OK, chaps, they've played right into our hands. That's just what we wanted. We've a great chance this half,' and give the thumbs up sign. With luck, the enemy will feel their skipper has bunked the whole affair, and a sense of defeat will spread.

In fact anything that can be done either before or during a game to cause a split between their captain and his team should be done. A quiet word at half time or during a break for an injury can do untold damage. Just a remark like 'Right-ho, chaps, they've made a fatal mistake switching those centres, the plan has worked perfectly' can send doubt and distrust sweeping through the enemy,

One should also directly attack the captain in his capacity as a player and suggest that he is the weak link in the other team (he probably is, anyway). For instance, if their skipper is fly-half, shout 'Don't bother about the fly-half, chaps, go for the centres. The fly-half won't score, don't worry about him.' It is a strong man who can stand up to that sort of stuff. His game will probably go to pieces.

The wheeze can be used to attack an individual player on the other side. Select one who is obviously slightly off form and hammer him mercilessly. Roar with laughter when he drops a pass, groan when he muffs a kick, loudly tell the team not to bother to mark him, ask him if he feels ill, or would he like to leave the field? In short, *shatter him.*

It is surprising how strong the herd instinct is in rugby. If you persevere long enough at one man, his own side will eventually turn on him and start blaming him for all their troubles. They will be heard bickering as they line up for a conversion. And when a team starts doing that, all is lost.

The Art Of Coarse Rugby. Michael Green. Hutchinson.

A prop with a Home Counties club went in for body-building, and had a physique that bulged with muscles. After one match as he eyed himself with satisfaction in the changing room mirror a team mate said caustically, 'Look – Adonis.'

'What do you mean, Adonis?' came the fast retort. 'The Donis!'

Though it took a long time for Rugby Football itself to become a target for the satirist, that is far from saying that humorists were non-existent, or that they lacked opportunism – witness the following essay written in 1907 and preserved in the Cardiff RFC archives but unfortunately unattributed. (The writer ought to have been around in 1984 to write a sequel, when Cardiff went on tour to Bangkok and left their kit at Heathrow.)

Baskets would never have been suspected of being important items in the paraphernalia of football teams; but the experience of the Cardiff team at Bristol on Saturday opened everybody's eyes to the potentiality of a basket when it contains the sartorial outfits of the players. All went well until Ashley Hill station was reached, all who were bound for the Bristol County ground, where the match was to be played, de-training in perfect order and in excellent good humour. Most of the Cardiff players and officials had crossed the bridge, and the train was on the point of steaming out of the station, when the cry was raised, 'What about the basket?' It was the voice of Nash, the Cardiff trainer, whose face was a study. The train was now moving, slowly but surely, out of the station amid wild, appealing cries for the basket; but they were heeded not and President W.T. Morgan looked at secretary C.S. Arthur in blank amazement and wonder. The silence on that platform for some minutes was oppressive, and it was only broken when someone made the practical suggestion that a wire should be sent to Bristol requesting that the basket should be sent back immediately in a cab. This had the desired effect, but not without involving the loss of an hour's time at a period of the day when light was a valuable asset. The mistake which led to the delay was the very simple and natural one of labelling the now celebrated basket to Bristol instead of Ashley Hill. And to Bristol it went.

While the Cardiff players were anxiously waiting for the return of their togs two junior teams who were playing on an adjoining pitch suspended play and very kindly offered their boots to the Cardiff men. The offer was a particularly welcome one at the moment and everyone looked happy. But the joy was short-lived. The biggest boots in the thirty pairs could not be coaxed to cover more than the toes of John Brown's pedal extremities, and the good-natured International had to submit to endless chaff. There were others, too, who could not be fitted and the boots had to be returned to the juniors, who promptly slipped into them and resumed their game.

One could not help pitying the poor bandsmen 'working overtime' in the centre of the enclosure. Two or three of them who had to blow into the big instruments were showing signs of exhaustion, and the volume of sound became fainter and fainter as time went on. The trombone man surrendered at last, and stood aside to watch the valiant struggles of his colleagues. Others dropped out of the ring one by one until the poor cornet player realised the futility of playing solos all 'on his own' and he, too, retired to the touch-line. Exasperated by their long wait the five or six thousand spectators did not seem in the mood to appreciate the humour of the situation. Their gloomy silence was ominous of the coming storm and when, a few minutes before four o'clock, the Cardiff players made their appearance in white jerseys the storm broke and the only welcome they got was 'Boo, boo, boo-oo-oo' from all parts of the field.

Who Lost The Basket? Cardiff's Novel Experience at Bristol by 'Forward'. 1907.

Down the decades the referee has been the man Rugby Footballers love to hate. This luckless character is on a hiding to nothing. Since to referee well is to spend eighty minutes virtually unnoticed, few but the most perceptive onlookers pay him compliments after the final whistle. Poor refereeing, however, blunts the enjoyment of players and spectators alike and will draw their fire throughout a match.

Even so, sustained invective like the one handed out by a Daily Mail *writer covering the 1905 All Blacks' tour has been rare. The tongue may be in the cheek but it still administers a fearful lashing.*

Probably the greatest Rugby football farce in the history of the game was enacted yesterday at Richmond, where the New Zealanders beat the Surrey Fifteen by 11 points to nil.

In face of lowering clouds, which threatened every minute to burst – and which did eventually drench the great majority of the spectators – over 10,000 people, many of them ladies, made their way from various parts of the metropolis to see the 'All Blacks' that everyone is talking about. They expected to see some wonderful football, but they had reckoned without one factor – the referee. This gentleman – a Londoner and a member of the Rugby Union Committee – was evidently under the impression that everybody had come to hear him perform on the whistle, and as he was in charge of the stage, so to speak, he was enabled to indulge his fancy to his heart's content. The finest artists are said to shut their eyes when whistling their hardest and, judged on that hypothesis, the referee must have had his eyes closed on and off for the greater part of the game.

The fantasia commenced in the first minute, and continued with brief intervals for respiration throughout the game. As one of the rules of Rugby is that you may not kick or handle the ball while the whistle is blowing, it is obvious that there was very little actual football. Directly someone got the ball, and there was a prospect of a bit of play worth seeing, the referee would recommence his fascinating solo. A Scottish young lady, whose first football match this was, and evidently with literary recollections of the efficacy of the pibroch in clan warfare, asked her escort after one particularly dangerous 'All Black' movement had been stopped at the referee's musical behest, 'Why aren't the New Zealanders allowed a man to whistle for them too?'

The rain came down in torrents, and between the bars of the

[134]

referee's interminable selection the players flipped and flopped about the slippery ground like seals on an ice-floe. A confused, entangled mass of legs and arms, and black and red and white jerseys danced in rhythm to the referee in various corners of the field. But there was no football.

'When are they going to begin?' enquired a 'Soccer' enthusiast who had come many miles because a Rugby friend had assured him that he would see something in the way of football he would remember all his life. It was then closely approaching half-time.

Twenty-five minutes from the start, however, the referee showed signs of fatigue whereupon the 'All Blacks', quickly seizing their opportunity and the ball, crossed the Surrey line and kicked a goal. Several explanations were advanced for the referee's extraordinary lapse, but the two most generally accepted were that he had either dropped his whistle or that the pea in it had stuck. Unabashed by his temporary eclipse, however, he blew harder than ever and for the remainder of the first half football was again out of the question.

During the interval the referee was the recipient of many congratulations from musical friends on his magnificently sustained effort, though fears were expressed that the severe exertions he had undergone would tell on him in the second half. And this proved to be only too true. His whistle failed him on at least two other occasions. The line was crossed twice more.

To their credit be it said, the crowd had by this time realised the mistake they had made in supposing that the affair would be an athletic display. Some, stung to emulation, whistled obligatos to the shrill music that rose from the middle of the field. Others, with their sodden coats over their ears and their dripping umbrellas in front of their faces, beat time to the pulsating notes that indicated the whereabouts of the referee's triumphant march. 'What an awful day for an open-air concert,' shivered a young lady in the grandstand as she gathered up her skirts to depart.

As for the game – there was no game. It was an exposition of the power of music to tame even the New Zealand Rugby footballer.

Though unnoticed by the crowd there were some highly interesting interludes to some of the referee's most brilliant flights. The 'All Black' captain, who evidently has no ear for music, desired enlightenment on more than one, to him, discordant passage. He is still pondering the answers. It is understood that Mr Dixon, the New Zealand manager, is also dubious as to the correctness of many of the notes and that he intends to take the earliest opportunity of interviewing the President of the English Musical Union on the matter.

Everybody went away whistling except the New Zealanders. 'No wonder it rained,' they said.

At the end of these games there is usually a rush for the jersey of the man who has scored, so that it may be kept as a trophy. Yesterday there was a scramble for the referee's whistle.

Daily Mail. 1905.

The evolution of match programmes is a fascinating study in itself. The earliest ones were no more than plain cards with printed team lists and little other information. By 1933 spectators at England's match with Wales could invest 2d (about 1p) in a folded sheet whose cover featured an aerial photograph of Twickenham – courtesy of the RAF– with useful directions superimposed, for example, 'turnstiles', 'motors'. Inside are the teams; and the fourth page carries an 'Important Warning to Spectators: The Rugby Football Union Committee wish to draw the attention of spectators to the dangerous practice in the past of throwing cushions about after a match. If spectators do not refrain from this dangerous practice it will be necessary to withdraw the privilege of providing cushions.' So there.

By the post-war years programme editors had applied themselves to the business of providing good reading for spectators waiting for the kick-off, and it became standard practice for International Board match programmes to contain essays in a variety of moods, thoughtfully and carefully constructed. What a pity, however, that such a contribution to an Ireland–Scotland programme, for instance, goes unappreciated by the mass of supporters in the other nations. Thanks to the kindness of the publishers, therefore, several of these pieces can appear in this anthology and hopefully reach a wider readership.

For the first time ever, the Brother and meself arrived *very* early at Lansdowne Road, a good hour before kick-off. I could tell you the year if I had the energy to look up the newspaper files but I haven't so I can't. But it was in or around twenty years ago (and as sure as God some crank will write in after this and argue, 'Yer man is *wrong* – that match was in so-and-so and *not* such-and-such. . .').

Anyway, there we were, at the bottom step of the Lansdowne Road terrace to watch Scotland play Ireland. We were, as befitted

FORTHCOMING MATCH.

SATURDAY, 11th FEBRUARY at 2.45 p.m.

England *v.* Ireland

Stand Tickets, 10/-; Ring Tickets, 6/-

Tickets for this Match are obtainable at the official Agents:

ALFRED HAYS, Ltd., 26 Old Bond Street, W.1,

74 Cornhill, E.C.3, and 62 Strand, W.C.2,

if early application is made.

WALKER & CO. (PRINTERS) LTD., 38 HEATH ROAD, TWICKENHAM.

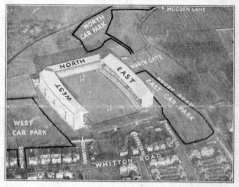

Royal Air Force, Official.   Crown Copyright reserved.

ENGLAND *v.* WALES

SATURDAY, 21st JANUARY, 1933,
Kick-off - 2.30 p.m.

OFFICIAL PROGRAMME

ENGLAND (White)	REFEREE: Mr. T. BELL (Ireland)	WALES (Red)
No.		*No.*
15 *T. W. BROWN ... ... Bristol	Full Back	A V. G. J. JENKINS ... Bridgend & Oxford Univ.
	Three-Quarters	
14 L. A. BOOTH ... ... Headingley	R. Wing L. Wing	E A. H. JONES ... ... Cardiff
13 *D. W. BURLAND ... ... Bristol	R. Centre L. Centre	C W. WOOLLER ... Rydal School & Sale
12 *R. A. GERRARD ... ... Bath	L. Centre R. Centre	B *CLAUDE DAVEY ... ... Swansea & Sale
11 *C. D. AARVOLD (Captain) ... Blackheath	L. Wing R. Wing	D *R. BOON ... ... Cardiff
10 *W. ELLIOTT Royal Navy & U.S., Portsmouth	Stand-off Half	G *H. M. BOWCOTT ... London Welsh & Cardiff
9 *A. KEY ... ... Old Cranleighans	Scrum Half	F M. J. TURNBULL ... ... Cardiff
8 *A. VAUGHAN-JONES The Army & U.S., Portsm'th		H *BRYN EVANS ... ... Llanelly
7 *B. H. BLACK ... ... Blackheath		I EDGAR JONES ... ... Llanelly
6 R. BOLTON Wakefield & Univ. Coll. Hosp'l		J *A. SKYM ... ... Cardiff
5 A. S. RONCORONI ... ... Richmond		K R. B. JONES Cambridge University & Waterloo
4 *C. WEBB ... Royal Navy & Devonport Services	Forwards	L *D. THOMAS ... ... Swansea
3 *N. L. EVANS Royal Navy & U.S., Portsmouth		M *WATCYN THOMAS (Captain) Swansea & Waterloo
2 *G. G. GREGORY ... ... Bristol		N *T. ARTHUR ... ... Neath
1 *R. J. LONGLAND ... ... Northampton		O I. ISAAC ... ... Cardiff
©International		*International

2d (1p) was the charge in the between-the-wars years for match programmes, which contained only rudimentary information – plus, at Twickenham, occasional stern warnings to spectators!

[137]

the time and place, well fortified in mind and spirits, particularly the latter and more particularly the Brother, whose devotion to the native brew accelerates sharply on International days like a Richard Sharp knife through an Irish defence.

Now the Brother, cheerfully ignoring the fact that he has never in his life kicked a rugby ball and who to this day couldn't tell you the difference between a maul and a ruck (and he's not alone there, I can tell you), fancies himself as an Expert. He has, I'll admit, all the attributes of one – total disagreement with everyone else, especially with selectors; a constant readiness to voice his opinion whether asked or not; a voice like a maddened elephant both in support and denigration; and all of this bound together with a fervent wish to see the opposition drop dead.

The Brother, let me tell you, has more often than not been an embarrassment to me at a rugby match, both as player and spectator. My own rugby was fixed firmly in those dark regions known politely as 'coarse'; in that class the numbers of spectators are, well, limited. Not quite one man and his dog but definitely no more than two men and sometimes two dogs. And maybe an odd cat now and then.

But the Brother was always a great supporter for me. We happened to work in the same Dublin business house which at one time in the dim past had a rugby team and a dedicated and enthusiastic following of dolly-bird secretaries, led even more enthusiastically by the Brother. He used to organise cheer-leading activities from the side-line, conducting with his rolled umbrella. It wouldn't do at Lansdowne Road, perhaps, but on the back pitch at Guinness or in the outer vastness of Terenure it went down a treat.

Came the day when we played a rival business house somewhere on the lower foothills of the Dublin mountains. Bitter indeed was the rivalry, the other team having beaten the tar out of us some weeks before to the tune of sixteen–nil. We set off like men demented and in a great hurry to finish the thing off and get down to the pub; in no time at all we were leading 29–nil and the referee was having a job writing down the scores in his little blue book and keeping up with play at the same time.

We had twin brothers on our team (the identification of whom today would cause great guffaws among those who, not knowing that at one time they played rugby in their slimline days, are acquaintances of these two roly-poly gentlemen). And that was the cause of what happened at the beginning of the second half. One of the opposition (we only found this out afterwards) was what we Irish like to call 'a bit soft in the head, like'; and, frustrated by his side's dismal condition, went even softer in the head.

I was lying peacefully on the ground on our 25 taking a bit of a breather while the play was some fifty yards away and I saw the whole thing clearly. One of the twins, who even then was giving hints of his coming corpulence, was puffing up towards the play when your man (the soft-in-the-head lad) took a flying leap onto his back and began to belabour him about the head.

The twin's terrified roars nearly split the hills; his brother turned round, saw what was happening and raced down the field to help his nearest and dearest. 'You hit my brother, you hit my brother,' he yelled and took another flying leap onto the backs of both struggling combatants, who both fell deeper into the muck under this extra avoirdupois. Before you could shout 'penalty', any players from both sides who were fit enough to make it as far as the fray were rucking and mauling in one vast swarm of muddied flesh. Except that it wasn't the ball they were after. Sundry shouts shot forth from this whirling vortex like sparks from a cartwheel: 'Take that, ya b——s' and 'Jasus, I'm on your team, whatya hittin' *me* for?'; and all the time the frenzied roars of the twins kept up a constant cacophony.

It was now that the Brother took a hand. He had been busy during the first half conducting with the umbrella, and both he and the dolly-birds were hoarse with shouting and screaming at every try we scored. But the honour and glory of our firm had been smirched by this wanton descent into open barbarism. That wouldn't do at all. So he leaped onto the field, darted over to the heaving, swarming mass of combatants and began to beat it freely with the umbrella.

This was too much for the referee, who during the scrap had hovered about the edge of the mêlée uttering timid entreaties such as 'Now, now boys – what about a bit of sportsmanship.' He took one terrified look at the clattering umbrella, decided that the cause was lost beyond redemption, and took off for his car (there being no such commodity as a pavilion) with all the speed of a flying wing, abandoning the match there and then.

The Brother, after we had patched up a few wounds and adjourned to wash the mud from our throats, was unrepentant at his intrusion onto the field of play. It was, he argued, part of the role of the involved spectator to look after the interest of his team. You can't argue with that sort of warped logic. And from then on, the Brother became an Expert. Rugby grounds throughout Dublin grew to quiver at the gravelly voice from the touchline; players shrank into oblivion before his penetrating exhortations. And now here he was, all set to embarrass me even further, at Lansdowne Road for the big game.

He was, moreover, not alone on that day. There were forty thousand other Experts also in the ground, none of them in the slightest persuading all the other Experts that they were wrong. We're all, after all, entitled to our own opinion.

Lansdowne Road is best savoured in the hour or so before kick-off. Indeed, more usually happens of interest during that time than during the actual game. There's always some eejit dodging about, full of stout and athletic ambition, scoring dazzling tries with leeks or thistles or crowing cocks under the posts, sidestepping embarrassed stewards, handing off puffing policemen with abandoned insouci-ance, and swerving skilfully past equally drunken Irish supporters.

Then there's the band, always fair game. 'Give us a tootle on your flootle,' bawls the Brother at some raw recruit of a garda fresh from the pastures of Poulpeasty, squinting shyly at his music disintegrating softly in the inevitable rain. 'Hey, you,' yells the Brother at a vast figure behind the big drum and whose red face and stout build denote your true son of the soil: 'Hey you, Fatso! Didya eat your bacon and cabbage today?'

Now all of this, eminently permissible in the coarser element that demeans the terraces, would be very embarrassing indeed in the sheepskin-coat sanctuary of the West Stand (*never* the East Stand, you fool – the sun will shine in your eye right through the second half, especially when Ireland score the winning try, of which you see not a thing). In the West Stand are sited the exclusive reserves for wives and mistresses (mostly the latter, since all the wives are busy at home washing the dirty knicks from last Saturday's match or making Irish stew for the ten kids) and it is here that these delicate and pampered creatures assemble on International days only to discuss with each other the affaires of the day, thus depriving hard-ened Alickadoos of stand tickets. Within these cultured circles the voice of derision and vituperation is heard but rarely and then only from some ageing scrum half who's feeling out of things because *his* mistress is at home washing the dirty knicks . . .

Down in the Gods, though, things is different. Yes indeed. You can say what you like when you like to whom you like. No-one, not even the Brother, is averse to a contrary opinion or the hard word. Indeed, it's in places like these that the Brother finds his cultural home.

'Who'll we barrack today?' says he to me. Before I can answer, a roar from the crowd, half submerged by boos, whistles and catcalls, signals the arrival on the field of fifteen Scotsmen, all about seven feet high and weighing just under the ton a man.

'Who's yer man with the bald head?' queries the Brother.

I peer at the programme. 'Robson,' says I.

'Right,' says the Brother. 'He'll do.' He lets an unmerciful roar out of him. 'Hey, Robson, you baldy bastard,' he bawls.

Now he had picked that instant in time when the roar for the Scots had died into the hushed moment when everyone was saving their breath for the big roar when the home lads would trot out 'in a hape of form like Sonny Sutton's greyhound'. Into this lull of sound the Brother's bellow shot like an arrow. Robson, the balding target of the shout, turned a menacing glare in our direction and all around disapproving looks were bent on us.

'Merciful Jasus,' say I to the Brother, who's about to open his mouth for further insult; 'that bloody pack of forwards will come down here and eat us alive.'

But then Ireland trot out and the Brother is forgotten. There are the presentations, the little ceremonies, the national anthem; the players run to their places and line up as the ball is kicked off. And the game is on. And Robson, that tough little flanker, plays a blinder.

Like all, or nearly all, matches between the two countries, the spirit of enterprise runs through this one. Like all Internationals it has its own distinctiveness. With the Scots, we are determined to prove something and like them we forget what it is in the heat of battle. Celt against Celt, like against like, man against man and heaven help the weaker; a match like this, full of boiling fury, is full too of the characteristics of such contests. Both sides make appalling errors and brilliant runs in such succession as to make you wonder if this is a schoolboy match or a top-flight International. In some curious way the players themselves play out of character and cohesion; and if all this is confusing and frustrating, it does lead to an open-ness and an excitement that makes this match one of the best of each season.

As for the Brother, he'll be there today, perusing his programme for a suitable target to barrack. Perhaps also it will be the emblem of the thistle, as a red rag to an Irish bull; or the bandsman who misses a note; or the over-pompous steward who will merit the sharp reprimand. All of them are part and parcel of this occasion; and sure, isn't it all in fun?

The Brother And Meself. Niall Fallon. Ireland *v* Scotland match programme 1980.
John Rattigan Ltd.

Cross Keys RFC's ground lies beside the fast-flowing River Ebbw, and a gusting south-westerly would always ensure down the years that a fair proportion of touch-finders finished up in the river. Hence the importance of their canine club-member – he really was! – at the beginning of the century. He was remembered in the club's centenary publication.

Many a story is told of the football fame of the Hicks family, but what about 'Tiger'? 'Tiger' Hicks was a black retriever owned by the family in Bright Street. The Keys then changed at the Cross Keys Hotel and with only the Tredegar Arms entrance at that time, it necessitated a walk of some 800 yards or more, but the teams were always headed by the Cross Keys Silver Band. As soon as the band struck up Tiger would head for the procession. After walking with the teams to the park he would then take up a post at the river, and the claims are that Tiger never let a ball get away. In the fast-moving water Tiger could control the ball with his head to get his teeth into the loop provided by the leather lace. The rugby club bought his licence each year and when Tiger was laid to rest he was honoured with a spot in the in-goal area just in front of the boys' club in a moving ceremony.

100 Years In Black And White. Horace Jefferies. Cross Keys Rugby Football Club.

Not too many authoritative writers on rugby can let their hair down and indulge themselves with out-and-out colour pieces when the occasion demands it. One of New Zealand's most respected and outspoken critics, Terry McLean, got it just right after the 1971 British Lions had thrashed Wellington in their build-up to the Test campaign. His wry reflection on the calibre of the All Blacks' opponents contains just the right amount of shell-shock.

It fair shakes you to come into Wellington Airport, bouncing around as you always do, and walk along to where a band is about to play a welcome-to-Wellington tune when a Friendship about 15 yards away starts warming up. That puts the kybosh on that little lot, but you ain't seen nuthin' yet. Wait till you get inside the dump proper and Gorsaveus, what do you see? Thousands of small boys rushing about wearing yellow-and-black paper caps and T-shirts, black, with 'I'm mad about Wellington' in yellow across their chests. It's a manifestation, some smart guy says, this is the first sign of the Wellington Supporters' Club – Dick Evans's outfit. Jeez, you say, what's the poor old game going to suffer next? You'd never guess. They dump the team in an old London bus and trundle it all the way to the St George, making maybe six miles an hour, maybe eight, while outside lots of other kinds caper and say to each other, 'Hey, cop that gut, willya? That must be Duggie Smith.' And Willie Evans, not long out from Wales, he says, 'I heard Barry John say to Gareth Edwards in Welsh, Barry said, "Things was never like this in Cef-neithin, man," and Gareth answered back and he said, "Some fellow come up to me and he shook me by the hand and he said, he said to me, man, he said, "Heroes may come and heroes may go, but Lions go on forever." This place is raving, man.'

Well, like I say, all this was pretty heady going, but you oughtta seen Willis Street that Saturday morning. You know Willis Street on a Saturday, if they didn't have that TAB it'd be a dead ringer for a morgue. Well, *this* morning, it's chocker, there's thousands there, and they're laughing off their heads because Dick Evans is coming down the street leading the supporters' club band in a suit of yellow and black vertical stripes, imagine it, and blowing his ruddy trumpet, and up there on the verandah of the old Grand 'Scotty' McCarthy is making cracks into the microphone about Dick and Jack and Tom and Harry, whoever the hell Jack and Tom and Harry are, and I'm telling you, Willis Street ain't no bleeding morgue, it's a madhouse. Oh, I forgot to tell you there's still thousands of them kids rushing round say they're mad about Wellington.

Jeez, that weren't nothing, that place was just a quiet country churchyard, not that I've seen many quiet country churchyards, compared with Athletic Park that afternoon when these jokers, the Lions, were waltzing around. Jever see Graham Williams looking like he'd been smacked on the kisser by Rocky Marciano, blown up the backside by Ngauruhoe, and hit right in the bread-basket by the *Queen Mary*, all at the same time? Well that was Graham when he'd run out there and started to work out which way that Barry John was going to go. Jever see greased lightning wearing a No. 12 jersey? Well, that was the joker Gibson. And then there was that bloke, Bevan, on the wing – I reckon he was breaking Olympic records every time he took the pill and set off, you know, with his socks way down around his ankles and his sleeves rolled up. Not for me, trying to stop that lightning bolt.

Jeez, I seen a few things in me time, mate, I knew little Eric of Berhampore well, he was an old mate of mine and I can remember old·Cliff and Mark and Jack Shearer and they was pretty good teams in them days, but I'm telling you, you ain't seen nothing on this park compared with this Lions' outfit. Forty-seven points to nine! Imagine it! They tell me Billy Wallace sitting up there in the stand, ninety-two years they say he is, I'd still say you'd have to call him the greatest there ever was, they say old Bill said it didn't hurt too much because he can't see too good no more. Well, he was lucky there, you ain't never seen non-tackling done proper till you've seen this Wellington mob, but getting back to old Bill, I'd still say he must of suffered because he's still got his hearing and he must of heard the whole mob.of us groaning. We was to ashamed to yell, we just groaned and every time that flaming Gibson, he must be about the greatest there ever was, or John or Bevan started belting up the field, we just groaned some more. I'm telling you, we was mad about Wellington, all right. The first kid I seen I give a cuff over the ear and I says, Sonny, get your priorities right, we ain't got a show in the Tests, we're done, these bastards'll beat the world.

Lions Rampant. Terry McLean. A.H. & A.W. Reed.

From beyond the pale, or certainly the dead-ball line, there has always been a lobby sniping away at Rugby Football. Its amateur ethic, its tolerant politics, its happy certainties have always been a big, easy target for those who enjoy ruffling feathers.

Here is a typically ingenuous piece by a thoroughly seasoned correspondent affecting unfamiliarity with the game. It rates its place in this 'Humour' section by virtue of the 'snob-appeal' cliché loosely tossed in.

Incidentally, the game the writer went to see in 1955 turned out to be something of a classic.

They do say that Rugby is a hooligan's game played by gentlemen and Soccer is a gentleman's game played by hooligans. So I shall try out the old false or true test this afternoon and take myself down to Twickenham to watch Oxford engaging Cambridge.

Mark you, there may be a lot in the above observation but you must admit it is the Soccer hooligans who make the crowds pay large amounts of money for the privilege of seeing them.

Put a couple of class sides out at Richmond and you are lucky to have an audience of 5000. It will be slightly different this afternoon for the young gentlemen will come down from the Varsities and the older gentlemen will abandon their City offices to urge the chaps of Oxford and Cambridge to get jolly well mobile.

The congregation should be around 50,000. And the England *v* Wales affair next January was sold out two months ago.

But the ordinary bloke is suspicious about this game, and I have heard it said that Rugby is 'just a bunch of snobs larking about with a mis-shapen ball'. The ordinary bloke may be partly right. For there is undoubtedly a snob appeal to this game of Rugby (pronounced 'Ruggah').

The Soccer-loving schoolmasters are protesting that it is the snob tag that is turning so many of the new secondary modern schools to Rugby. From Devon comes the lament: 'In twenty years' time Soccer will be listed as a bygone British pastime. So many headmasters taking over loftily opine that playing Soccer is a bad show. "Must have 'Ruggah', old boy."'

The Rugby defence is that more boys can play the game and you can have five Rugby pitches where you can only have four Soccer pitches.

Away from the snob angle this game of Rugby breeds much tougher characters than Soccer – I mean, of course, the hired athletes who play for professional clubs. If these Soccer slaves took some of the knocks and tumbles endured with no more than a shake of the battered head they would be howling for trainers, stretchers and nurses.

But here is Douglas Baker, one of those keen-fanged British Lions who toured so gloriously in South Africa, observing that although Rugby may look a tougher game it is much easier to be hurt in Soccer.

Our Rugby commentator, colleague Pat Marshall, helps out in the problem: Why does the normal club Rugby lack crowd appeal? He says, 'Soccer is the better game to watch if you have only a sketchy idea of the rules of both games. But for the expert there is only one game, Rugby.'

I shall have my own view this afternoon when these Soccer-schooled eyes take in the Oxford-Cambridge match. I only hope that the eternal nuisance who seems to haunt the football stands is not behind me howling, 'Get rid of it.' Although I am told by Pat Marshall that a Rugby fan in full voice could give the Billingsgate fish porters several words' start.

Daily Express. Desmond Hackett.

International referee Mike Titcomb tells of refereeing an early-season pipe-opener between one of the first-class West Country clubs, including a rather prematurely pompous England International, and a local junior side. To make sure that the score did not become embarrassingly high it was agreed that thirty-five minutes each way should be played.

When the referee blew for the interval the International player observed loudly as the teams changed ends, 'That felt like a short half to me. We must have a second-class chap in charge.'

Early in the second half one of the junior team put in a Garryowen which descended towards the International player, who had ample time to catch the ball and call a good mark. There was no whistle-blast, however, and the attacking side followed up at top speed, flattened the catcher, knocked the ball from his grasp and rushed through to score a try.

As Mr Titcomb hurried past the winded, groaning figure prone on the turf he called out cheerfully, 'Sorry, mate – second-class decision.'

Consider now the generation gap, brilliantly bridged by one of the 'Old Brigade' at a centenary banquet.

Look up at the Committee Box, or seats adjacent, and what do you see? 'You behold a range of exhausted volcanoes. Not a flame flickers on a single pallid crest. But the situation is still dangerous. There are occasional earthquakes, and ever and anon the dark rumblings of the sea.'

Disraeli used his celebrated smile in a different connection; but I daresay there are young players about today arrogant and insensitive enough to find the description not inapposite to the older members of the Club. To any such whippersnappers I wish to address a few words of kindly and quite unprejudiced sexagenarian warning. Humble yourselves, cultivate a proper respect for seniority. Above all, before passing judgement on that row of grizzled veterans up there, consider how you yourself down below in the playing area, in your ridiculous little panties and your flimsy football pumps, must appear in the eyes of men who played in sensible boots and wore warm shorts terminating just above the knee and cut most becomingly (in my own case, at any rate) with a flare at the sides after the manner of riding breeches. If you think the team photographs of the nineteen-twenties look odd, wait till the hundred and fiftieth anniversary of the club comes round and then take a shuddering glance at your own lot.

Deference to older members, desirable at all times, is obligatory during centenary seasons. Their recollections of the twenties, conceivably even of 1905, however apt to clear the bar in normal years, must now be eagerly sought after and recorded by compilers of club histories and brochures. The man who was once patted on the head by Bush or can recall R.T. Gabe dropping a pass against Scotland in 1902 becomes (or should become) metamorphosed from an old spuffler into a symbol of continuity, a repository of the glorious past, the very spirit and essence of tradition. He may even be asked to reply to a toast.

> Ah, did you once see Shelley plain,
> And did he stop and speak to you,
> And did you speak to him again?
> How strange it seems and new?

For Shelley read Nichols (E.G.) – Shelley, for all his gifts, not being a Cardiff man. And though strange, not necessarily perhaps 'new'. I mean, the fact may have been mentioned before. The old brigade sometimes repeat themselves, not out of forgetfulness (is it likely that a man who remembers so clearly the initials of every forward who played for the club between 1912 and 1932 would forget what he said, at considerable length, the day before yesterday?) but out of pure kindness; they are aware, you see, that fresh faces are constantly joining and they don't want the newcomers to miss anything.

I have myself repeated at some ten or eleven club dinners, and perhaps once or twice in print, an account of a trifling incident at Twickenham, but have no hesitation in telling it again here, if only to show that repetition is no proof of senility. Gather round, then, and let me assure you in advance that this is *not* a description of the running of Poulton-Palmer (who was before my time) nor even of the thunderous silence that wrapped around poor Cyril Brownlie as he left the field in 1925 (which I saw with my own eyes, or heard rather, or didn't hear, but am reserving for the Centenary Year of New Zealand tours to Britain, 2005) but relates to very recent times, when even some of you who are listening to me with such restless attention were old enough to start growing side-whiskers.

Well, there I was, pushing my way past endless knees in search of my seat before the start of a Calcutta Cup match and, naturally, wishing to know how much further I had to go on this stumbling journey. I referred to the number on the ticket in my hand and said, more or less at large, 'Let me see, I'm ninety-four.' Whereupon some women in the row behind called out, 'Are you sure you were wise to come?' – an impertinence which raised, I am sorry to say, the heartiest laughter I have heard at Twickenham since a referee was knocked stone cold there one afternoon and had to be revived by that little scudding figure with the watering pot.

Passing lightly over an occasion in New York some years ago when, on emerging from a club (social, not Rugby football) known as the Century Association, I was stopped in the street by a total stranger and asked 'Say, do you have to be over a hundred to belong to that lot?', I am reminded of an even more – and I shall be obliged if you young men will kindly take that glazed look off your faces and pay attention; the time will come when you too will have interesting reminiscences to impart – I am reminded of an even more inexcusable question put to me by a French reporter during the William Webb Ellis Centenary Commemoration match at Menton in February 1972. It is true that I may have been looking a little strained that morning, for the hospitality on the previous evening had been French to a degree; but when this young woman came up, notebook in hand, and said, '*Vous êtes le fils de Viliam Vebb, n'êtes-vous pas, Monsieur Ellis?*' I was strongly moved to reply, 'Mademoiselle, if this were the centenary of the *birth* of William Webb your question might be permissible. On the centenary of his *death* it is downright tactless.' What I actually said, not knowing the French for 'tactless', was '*Non.*'

[148]

I recall these trifling incidents to the notice of you young fellows – and could recall others of the same tenor were it not apparent that some of you have urgent engagements elsewhere – merely in order to impress upon you that we older men are not all as old as we look, or as you think we look, rather. We like our seniority to be recognised but not exaggerated. Do not, therefore, in your eagerness to have the great days of the past recreated for you by living witnesses, ask Mr Bleddyn Williams, for instance, what it was like to play alongside A.J. Gould. Pursue Dr Jack Matthews, by all means, for the views of an old maestro on ten-man Rugby but not, I sincerely suggest, on ten-forward Rugby.

Ask *me* about that – or Father William. We are both past caring by now.

Cardiff RFC Centenary Brochure, from a speech by H.F. Ellis.

In an age when the presence of TV cameras and microphones at big Rugby grounds is taken for granted – not to mention plug-in facilities – broadcaster Rex Alston's amusing tale of frustration in Dublin is a reminder how times have changed in the media. He had been watching the enthralling 9–9 draw of 1953 between Ireland and England.

An hour after the final whistle went I was due in a Radio Eireann studio, two miles away, for 'Sports Report'. I had made a plan with an Irish friend whereby I would wait in the ground to allow the bulk of the crowd to disperse, and would then make my way on foot to a rendezvous whence he would take me by car through the back streets to avoid the traffic in the centre of Dublin. But whether through excitement or the unprecedented number of cars, we lost each other, and there was I stranded at the other end of Dublin, with the thrilling story of the match almost burning my pocket, and the programme due to start in fifteen minutes. Traffic was still pouring into Dublin, so I stopped a car and begged a lift, but the driver was unhelpful and said he was not going my way. In desperation I tried again and this time was more lucky, though the three men in the car were from Belfast and knew no back streets. However, they took me to within walking distance of the studio, and I arrived, hot and breathless, at 5.45. A brief word from the engineer, 'You're on at 5.50; they want a minute and a half,' and I sat down in front of the mike, pulled programme and a few hastily-written notes from my brief case, put my stop watch ready (because no-one overruns his time in 'Sports Report') and adjusted my headphones. Thank goodness, it was Bill Hicks talking soccer, so I was in time. When he had finished, I heard Eamonn Andrews say, 'Our next visit is to Dublin' and then enlarge on the thrilling match which he had heard on his car radio, ending with, 'For his story of the match we call up Rex Alston in Dublin.' I had not spoken more than half a dozen words before Eamonn's voice came through my headphones, 'We can only hear a very faint voice from Dublin: let's try again.' So I did, with the same result. We found out later that a technical fault outside the studio had prevented my voice from being heard, and so, after all that effort, the best rugger story of the year was never heard on 'Sports Report'.

'International Rugby Union' by Rex Alston from *Sports Report* edited by Eamonn Andrews and Angus Mackay. Phoenix.

A few years earlier Alston had helped break in the great Welsh commentator of post-War years, G.V. Wynne-Jones, 'Geevers' to his many friends and admirers. These were the circumstances of the newcomer's debut in Paris.

We approached the ground in a stream of traffic, and to the accompaniment of wild and shrill whistling by hundreds of gendarmes as they tried to preserve order. I remember my feelings of pride at being in a car whose windscreen boasted the magic letters BBC, which worked wonders and enabled us to gain entrance under priority into the car park.

But this was the full extent of our privileges that day. If the thought of a red-carpeted entrance to the stand had lurked in the mind of a novice, the idea was quickly dispelled. The officials on our arrival were not a bit concerned, least of all the French engineers. Eventually the broadcasting boxes at Colombes were discovered. There were several of them behind the seats in the stand. We looked at one and found that a post obscured our view. We examined another, but again there was a post. Finally we liked our position, but here again our satisfaction began and ended. The window was covered with mud and dust of the War years; there was no table; there were no chairs; and the crowning omission – no microphone!

I thanked God for Alston's knowledge of French that day, for he had previously taught French at Bedford. A microphone was produced, together with some chairs. Then we were faced with the problem of where to rest it. Eventually Rex Alston searched around underneath the stand and found some odd pieces of wood, which were rigged into a makeshift table. In this country in latter years commentators have used the lip microphone. This is held close to the mouth and is designed to exclude all other sounds when one is talking. In France, however, commentators use an open 'mike' and a peculiar one at that. It is much like a narrow flower vase with the receptive part on the top. This we gingerly placed on our table in readiness.

We next had to concentrate on the timing of our broadcast. At home a commentator is given his exact time signal from the announcement, but in a foreign country this is not possible. Therefore time checks are made and a commentary starts at a given moment. In this instance it was four o'clock in Paris but three o'clock in London. Thus it was that as the stop-watch approached four o'clock I leant on the make-shift table preparing to start the commentary. To my horror, the table collapsed and everything on it – including the microphone – fell. I caught the microphone and, in my excitement, blurted out my first words on an International rugger match to the listening public in Britain. They were, 'Hell's bells!'

Sports Commentary. G.V. Wynne-Jones.
Hutchinson's Library of Sports and Pastimes Ltd.

The idea of a Fly Half Factory, deep in the Welsh countryside and camouflaged up to the hilt, was embroidered by comedian Max Boyce in 1973. Undoubtedly inspired by Barry John, though David Watkins was not long gone and Phil Bennett was Prince of Llanelli, Max recorded his ballad in 1973:

> *... My dad works down in arms and legs*
> *Where production's running high;*
> *It's he that checks the wooden moulds*
> *And stacks them forty high.*
> *But he's had some rejects lately*
> *'Cos there's such a big demand,*
> *So he sells them to the Northern clubs*
> *And stamps them 'Second Hand' ...*

[151]

But the rest of the world was not surprised to discover in 1979, that the Irish had a Factory too. Its cover was blown by one C.M.H. Gibson.

Somewhere near the lakes and loughs in the middle of Ireland, exactly half way between Belfast and Cork, is a top secret establishment. Access is difficult. There are few roads. The signposts all point in opposite directions. Only those few country folk who know the area well and the mysterious people who work there know of its existence.

The place, which is hidden among the trees and the bogs, is surrounded by barbed wire and Dobermann Pinschers. The wire is electrified and criss-crossed by laser beams. Inside the wire is a moat full of piranha fish. Inside the moat is a grey castle wall, thick and forbidding. The look-outs in the turrets are armed with machine guns.

This is the Irish fly-half factory. It is financed by sympathisers in America, as well as by the Vatican, and is an infinitely more sophisticated establishment than that much better known but rather pathetic little cottage industry stuck in a disused chapel up in the Black Mountains of Wales.

The Irish fly-half factory was set up after the last war, at about the time that an unknown Italian engineer called Enzo Ferrari decided to challenge the world's leading marques at motor racing. The first products from the two factories were so brilliant that all their rivals were aghast. Wales, indeed, felt so badly about IFF (Mark I) that they called days of national mourning to coincide with the anniversaries of those days when Ireland won the Triple Crown in successive years in 1948 and 1949. Coach parties were organised to take groups of outraged Welsh supporters up to the disused chapel in the Black Mountains to throw stones through the windows, though this was hardly necessary because the windows never had any glass in them anyway!

The cause of all this outrage was a fly-half called Jack Kyle. It is sometimes alleged that the Irish are not always blessed with startling intellect (though no one ever said that to Ray McLoughlin's face), and perhaps it was because of this that the draughtsmen working on the first prototype concentrated so much on the footballing brain.

Kyle had a mesmeric quality about him. This stemmed from the silicon chips (the Irish invented everything to do with potatoes) which enabled him to take himself down almost into a state of hypothermia. While in this state he could go to sleep, which he often did in the dressing room before a match and which he appeared to do on the field. He became virtually anonymous. This lulled his opponents. Then, when they least expected it, he would pop up out of a trap-door in the middle of the stage and win the match.

Sometimes he even did this in defence, though he always tried to avoid any such excesses, particularly on a wet day. He was always immaculate going onto the field and he was nearly always immaculate going off it. His shirt rarely needed washing, because he did not reckon to break sweat either. Subsequent generations of Irish players have always thought that it was Kyle's example which persuaded successive secretaries of the Irish Rugby Football Union that their International players needed only one jersey a season.

Heretics sometimes questioned Kyle's value to a backline, but with massive centres like Noel Henderson and Cecil Pedlow he could afford to lob the ball on at those inevitable moments when self-preservation became the dominant issue. Henderson and Pedlow are still visiting out-patients' clinics at their local hospitals, of course, but they do it as gladly as those men who have climbed Everest receive treatment for frostbite.

However, as a result of this the designers in the IFF working on Mark II decided to make some adjustments, and no doubt the result would have been something approaching perfection if the staff of the factory had not started working on a three-day week at a crucial stage of production. This short-time working was why Mick English was built not much bigger than a sand-bag, but he did have the same effect on his opponents when he tackled them.

The designers of Mark II had got some other things wrong too. They had not allowed for the possibility that Ireland might produce some backs who could run. They just sort of assumed that Irish centre three quarter play would consist for ever of men built like snow-ploughs. Undeniably this did create a difficulty, because at the time M.A.F. English was rolled out onto the starting grid D. Hewitt, A.J.F. O'Reilly, M.K. Flynn and N.H. Brophy were all somewhere near Olympic qualifying time as sprinters.

Not that this made any difference. Mick English kicked so beautifully that he passed only those balls that he did not catch cleanly! There are many classic passes in the text-book of Rugby football but no reference is made to the Mick English, which is not so much a pass as a ricochet. It deserves a place in the coaching manuals.

[153]

So does his incredible variety of kicks. Mick English had the ability to place kicks exactly, with any trajectory, to all parts of the field and to all points of most acute embarrassment to the opposition. He did this without any regard to the quality of the possession. Good, bad, indifferent – away it went.

He had to return from the Lions tour of New Zealand in 1959 suffering from a mysterious stomach complaint. He braced himself to face the rigours of a five-week boat passage, travelling first class, and then went to see his doctor who promptly diagnosed obesity and put him on a regimen which cured him in a matter of weeks. Still, no-one who was ever tackled by M.A.F. English was ever in any doubt that he was the original flying picket.

It was at this point that disaster struck the Irish fly-half factory. In seeking to make those delicate adjustments necessary to correct the very minor faults apparent in their first two models the designers got the mix all wrong. This sometimes happens even in the brewing industry, and the result is always very painful for Irishmen.

What happened was this. The factory was programmed to the name English and it made an English type fly-half by mistake! He was fair-haired and blue-eyed. He liked training. He liked tackling. He didn't smoke. He didn't drink. He tried to pass the ball. He sometimes played as a centre, and even did a lap or two as wing and as a full back. The machine had gone berserk. There were malfunctions everywhere.

It was a horrible moment. Sirens wailed. Red lights flashed. Alternate puffs of white and black smoke poured out of the factory chimney and added to the confusion. The work force was in uproar. They pulled levers. They pressed buttons. They threw switches. The factory controller fell out of the pub and called a full scale emergency alert. It took years to repair the damage.

When production was resumed, it was complicated by several factors. Levers which should have been pulled in the emergency had been pushed. Dials which had been set to fine degrees of moderation were turned up to full, and as if all that was not enough there was a regrettable misunderstanding when the factory turned over to metrication. No-one had a conversion chart from inches to centimetres and so the same figures were used. In some aspects of the production, therefore, Mark IV turned out to be 2.54 times as big as he should have been. Still, in the middle of all this over-correction, the designers did at least get the name right. They called him Barry

John. It is true that they also stuck McGann on the end, but that was probably just one of the designers wanting to sign the product, like Botticelli.

Irish fly-half Mark IV was an outrageously talented games player. Another Barry John, literally a much lesser Barry John, was eventually produced in a much less significant part of the Rugby world, and a lot was made of his remarkable abilities, but our Irish Barry John was something again.

If I may address myself to the Welsh nation for a moment, I would assert that our Barry John was a better golfer than your Barry John, he was a better soccer player (League of Ireland, no less), he was a better darts player, he was a better ping-pong player, and even though it may cut Cefneithin to the quick, he was a better snooker player. He may even have put in a bid as a Rugby player too but for that unfortunate fault in his metabolism which gave him a weight problem for most of his career and which, as I say, was due entirely to the trouble at the factory about metrication. Even so, from within that ample frame, an enviably effective footballer invariably struggled to emerge.

A board meeting was held at the Irish fly-half factory after the emergency alert in the sixties and the members were asked for suggestions which might be incorporated in the re-building programme. One of the members, who wore dark glasses and sat in the room with the collar of a light raincoat turned up and a felt hat pulled down over his eyes, said that he felt the time might be ripe to introduce a blueprint stolen some years earlier by one of his double agents, a man of the name of C.I. Morgan who had infiltrated the disused chapel in the Black Mountains of Wales.

This agent, who hailed from the Rhondda Valley and then from Cardiff, was working for British Wire Ropes in Dublin at the time and playing for Bective Rangers, but this was only a cover. In reality he was pulling strings of a much more sinister kind. Not only did he steal the master blueprint from the Welsh fly-half factory, but he pinched the mould as well. This was the world's supreme stroke of industrial espionage.

As everyone knows all Welsh fly-halves look exactly the same. Just like Chinamen. Small, dark, dodgy, big banjo eyes (developed originally for seeing in coal mines), they have an inherent ability to walk on water and win matches by scoring record numbers of points as kickers.

Well, as the whole of Wales must have realised, Ireland now have the original. Anthony Joseph Paul Ward, of Ireland, is the real McCoy. He is quite the most important Rugby player in Ireland. His legs are far more important to his country than even those of Marlene Dietrich were to the film industry. A little hairier, maybe, but a pair of absolute winners. Lloyd's of London have been asked for an insurance quotation on them and have had to to ask for the backing of the gnomes of Geneva and the mandarins of Hong Kong to cover such an enormous risk.

Phil Bennett holds the world record of points scored in international Rugby. He should make the most of it. Tony Ward is over-hauling him fast.

'Double Agent Passes on Secret Welsh Blueprint' by C.M.H. Gibson from *Wales v Ireland Match Programme*, 1979. Programme Publications Ltd.

After their Cup Final victory over Cardiff in 1977 Newport RFC were guests of Welsh Brewers Ltd at the annual banquet which used to be thrown jointly for the Cup-winners and the club finishing on top of the *Western Mail*'s unofficial championship table. That year the latter was Llanelli, and during his speech Newport skipper Colin Smart, later capped at prop by England, could not resist the temptation to poke a little fun at the Scarlets present.

'From Stradey Park we constantly hear reports about the immense sophistication of the club's forward play,' he said. 'We are told that the latest medical guidance on correct motivation is obtained regularly, and that their trainer went behind the Iron Curtain recently to study East German methods of preparing athletes for big occasions. We are even informed that Llanelli props go frequently for psycho-analysis!

'Well, I must admit that had we not won the Cup Newport might have developed an acute inferiority complex about all this!

'Good heavens, we have forwards who are still being taught to read and write!'

PLACES

Towns, tours, clubs and grounds

It can be argued, and frequently is, that Rugby Football on television is infinitely superior to Rugby Football viewed with the naked eye. The camera positions are prime, and the big close-ups surpass even the insight lent by powerful binoculars. A comfortable armchair is preferable to the best grandstand seat, let alone a cramped position on a terrace.

The fact is, however, that rugby supporters defy such logic and even when an International match is being televised live they prefer to be at the game. The hunt for tickets is the appetizer which sharpens palates for the hoped-for feast; and then there is the incomparable atmosphere in the great stadia – intensely partisan but still mercifully benign and good tempered.

By leaving the fireside and flocking together in huge numbers, therefore, rugby people incontrovertibly demonstrate their enjoyment of the companionship that is part and parcel of their game. But that is no accident. The 'togetherness' of International day is simply something which transplants itself from the great amateur network in which the game is rooted and from which it derives its energy: the clubs. Hence this section is about them and their character as well as about some great rugby cities and stadia.

Perhaps we may be forgiven for starting in Wales, since so many of the other nations speak of Cardiff Arms Park as offering an incomparable experience. But times are changing, have changed; the scenes described by Gwyn Jones, though within the memory of many keen spectators today, are already sepia in tone.

Shelton, who runs the Cwm Colliery, his wife Louise and a friend called Broddam are seated together in the grandstand.

An old white-headed man waving a stout stick ran out from the ringside seats and began to conduct with great sweeping strokes. First one group, then another, joined in, made contact, surrendered themselves, and forty thousand voices in one mighty choir sent 'Cwm Rhondda' pouring through the restless air. Some were singing in English, some in Welsh; chapel, church and disbelievers – 'Bread of Heaven, Bread of Heaven, Feed me till I want no more – Feed me till I want no more.' They sang like men who find heartease in singing, sustained and chant-like. More than two-thirds there were from the hills and valleys, and in their voices one felt the austerity of toil, the passion of mountains under the stars, the sadness and grinding of their crude livelihood. The tune was changed. 'Jesu, Lover of My Soul,' whitehead announced in a high, lilting voice, and the regimental band was with him. Louise prepared to scoff, grew still and tense. Much that she had found in this people – its meanness, ugliness of life, and oftentimes savage hypocrisy – for the time she forgot, at the stupendous outpouring of the cry of sorrow for the New Jerusalem. The hymn died away like a universal supplication – and then came comedy. The next song dissipated tears and religion together. 'Sospan Fach,' cried whitehead, and only half the band could play for him. The gates had been shut long before this, and the kick-off was near. When they sang the Welsh national anthem, all those sitting in the stand rose, and most took off their hats. Louise rather resented this. It was like standing for the Marseillaise or something equally foreign. Yet when the words had been twice sung, there were tears in her eyes. The ocean-swell of sound flooded the sky, poured into the thin blue, and was oddly over. Then it was time to start.

The Scots came on first, generously, even uproariously, greeted, and then came the glorious scarlet of the home team. This was rapture.

'There must by a couple of hundred from the Cwm here today,' Shelton told his wife.

Personalities were pointed out. Carbright – fastest man in the game; Fisher – standing by the gaunt forward Bob Llewellyn – best forward playing today. MacAndrew and Burns, their halves; Seaforth and Tom Rees the backs. The whistle blew, Gaels and Celts combined to sing the national anthem, and then the game started, Scotland playing from the river end. Without much success Louise tried to follow her husband's explanations. She heard that Scotland had scored after ten minutes and again after half an hour, but what she really enjoyed was the way the two packs set at each other towards the end of the first half. It needed no technical knowledge to appreciate this elemental matching of strong men. Patricians are never slow to turn down their thumbs. Skuse, that mighty blacksmith's helper, came staggering through in front of the stand, three men clinging around his neck and waist. She saw his chest heave up and out, and then he crashed like a tree, dragging his

[158]

parasites with him. They all wriggled clear, and he scrambled up, his jersey in ribbons. Off it came, and there was the bulk of the man, his back light brown, with red blotches from the scrummages, his barndoor chest clotted with black hair. As his arms went up into the sleeves of his new jersey, there was a rolling of muscles throughout his torso, a rippling of elastic and steel. Bulges came out across his round ribs, a pattern of power and drive. 'Shouldn't care to stop him,' Shelton grunted. 'By gad, no,' echoed a stranger next to him. For the present Skuse was Shelton and the stranger; they were Skuse. So the hammering went on. Minutes wore themselves to tatters, and play had finally settled in the Scottish twenty-five. A long, muttering roar played over the banks and stands. There was a scrum down under the posts, MacAndrew put the ball in, it came out slowly on the Scottish side, held in the back row, Llewellyn broke away from the scrum, threw himself at MacAndrew as he gathered the ball, it bounced back awkwardly, Shand snapped it up and drop-kicked as he was sent sprawling. The ball hit an upright, there was a groan, bounced onto the crossbar in deathly silence, and fell over for four points amidst a howl of triumph.

'Eight-four,' Shelton explained. 'Shand dropped a goal – that's four points.' He saw with delight that his wife was adding her handclap to the applause.

There was no further score before half time.

The second half was desperately hard. Laughter, groans, chatter, cheers, objurgations, some drinking from bottles brought into the ground, and several horrible swayings, showed that the crowd was on its toes. 'Come on, Wales!' Louise heard a clear tenor voice shouting from behind the Scottish line. 'You'm playing towards the pubs, ain't u?' There were stoppages. 'Man out!' Rees had crash-tackled Magraw. A little man with a cloth cap ran on with a sponge, the water dripping as he ran, but before he reached the place of combat Magraw was up, shaking his big head. 'Gertcher!' jeered the crowd, and the little man ran back again with his hand held high. The forwards played murderously – one moment bearing down with the inhuman pressure of a steam-roller, the next disintegrated, crashing and sprawling. Louise found herself looking for Ben, and cried sharply as he came through the centre, slick as a slice of fat bacon, was forced sideways, and finally hurled winded into touch. They rubbed his belly, shoved his head between his knees, he shook himself like a dog, and the game went on. Six minutes to go. The

[159]

game settled on the Scottish line. A good touchfinder carried play back to the twenty-five. Three minutes to go. Shand took a long line-out. The players seemed to have straggled half way across the field. Llewellyn jumped up as though he would tear down Olympus, grabbed the ball and flung it back. Wretchedly it was kicked ahead to Burns, who sliced his kick away to the right. For a moment no-one seemed interested in the ball, all the players seemed to be standing still, and then the ground was pandemonium. A figure in a scarlet jersey was coming from nowhere at the ball. It was Fisher. 'By Great God Almighty!' someone yelled behind Louise, 'he's going to get it!' Seaforth, too, ran for the ball, and the most knowing held their breath as they saw that he was going to fly-kick. As his boot drove forward Ben dived for the ball, insanely, got his hands to it, missing death or injury by an inch. His body was flung across Seaforth's knees, and the full back went down with a screech. But Ben was up, running with his head back, like the madman he was. He saw Burns in front of him, checked himself, stumbled almost on one knee, cleared him in a queer, doubled-over fashion, pulled himself upright, and then, as Magraw caught him by the thighs and Johnson by the head, threw the ball hard and true inside him to Shand, who took the ball on his chest and was over the line for a try under four forwards. Three men were out at once – Fisher, Shand and Seaforth with a twisted knee – but it was a try. You could hear the row all over the town. Strangers hit strangers' hats off. Men punched each other for joy. No-one was sitting down: there had been an unparalleled lurch towards the one corner, and dozens of spectators were overcome by the pressure. It was almost an anti-climax when Tom Rees and Llewellyn arranged the ball as carefully as if it were a big diamond, and Tom, deaf to the crowd, inhumanly cool, took his short run and deftly kicked the two points that brought the score to nine-eight and a victory for Wales. 'We've won,' cried Shelton, on his feet like the rest.

'I'm so glad!' said Louise, who had forgotten with her husband that they were English.

Times Like These. Gwyn Jones. Gollancz.

Since 1948 it has been a tradition for major touring sides to play a farewell match against the Barbarians at Cardiff Arms Park. The occasion is charged

[160]

with sentiment that wells up from the crowd and seizes the players. The most experienced journalists can be carried away by it.

Players stood, hands joined, in the middle of Cardiff Arms Park and there were 50,000 lumps in 50,000 Welsh throats as the miners from the valleys and the men from the cities sang their farewells to the All Blacks.

It was just like the end of a going-away party any of us might have at home . . . just as intimate . . . just as personal . . . just as sad.

This was one of the most moving moments I've ever had in sport, a moment that none of us, least of all the New Zealanders, will ever forget.

It came quite spontaneously, quite uninvited, at the end of the finest match of the tour, a match in which the All Blacks beat the Barbarians at their own game by 19 points to 5.

No sooner had the giant choir stopped and the players were being cheered and chaired off the field than a chant of 'We want Scott' started. No wonder.

Robert William Henry Scott, Great Scott, had surpassed all other full backs. Men who played against the 1905 invaders say there has never been a better, and I cannot conceive that there ever will be.

This man, cool and tantalising in defence, dangerous in attack, and capable of dropping goals from fifty yards, is the nearest thing to perfection to wear Rugby boots.

Daily Sketch. Laurie Pignon.

All Black tour sides always contain lots of Scottish surnames – McCormicks, McKechnies, MacRaes and so on. This may explain the special fascination exercised for New Zealanders by the city of Edinburgh. The excerpt that follows dates back to 1954.

For a day or two before the test match against Scotland the All Blacks stayed at North Berwick and then, on the morning of the match, went on to Edinburgh in time for lunch and to settle in at the hotel. They had previously visited the castle on its commanding and rocky height overlooking the city, and had seen Holyrood House and the famous Princes Street with its trams (cars, the Edinburgh people call them) which are some of the last to be seen on any streets in the British Isles.

And it was not only those in the party with Scottish antecedents who expressed appreciation of the peculiar quality of Edinburgh – the warmth and friendliness of it and its people, the venerable, historic associations breathed by its cobbled streets and ancient solid stone buildings – but anyone who knew Dunedin seemed to see some sort of resemblance in the very air of the place which seemed to link the two Scottish cities, spaced more than 12,000 miles apart.

This was not just sentimentality: there is a very real and distinct character, a rich, warm character, about Edinburgh which is somehow familiar to a New Zealander – quite distinct from any other city in Britain, or probably elsewhere in the world, except, as I say, to some extent in Dunedin. To go across the North Bridge, spanning the valley in which lies Waverley Station, and then to walk in the street that is the Royal Mile, particularly if you pry into the side-alleys and inspect carefully the separate buildings as you go down the long gentle slope from the Castle to Holyrood House, is to feel the nearness of the historical events with which the place is linked. And as if to remind the visitor – perhaps its own inhabitants, lest they forget – of that ancient lineage, there booms out from the castle battlements every day at 1pm the sound of one cannon which, when you do not expect it, is apt to cause mild surprise. On days when the mist and reek (smoke) are not too thick there can be seen the towering dominance of the hill called Arthur's Seat, and if you are very fortunate some Scot will take you on a tour of the city, which will include the circumnavigation of this remarkable hill.

The Fourth All Blacks. John Hayhurst. Longman, Green and Co.

The British Isles tour manager of 1974, Alun Thomas, likes to recall the visit paid by lock Gordon Brown to a Durban 'Burns Night' arranged by local exiles in honour of Scottish members of the Lions party. 'Broon of Troon' was superbly clad for the occasion in his clan regalia complete with kilt and sporran.

From a female South African admirer came the inevitable question, 'What is worn under the kilt?'

Drawing himself up to his full six feet four inches the British Lion answered sternly, 'Madam, nothing is *worn* under the kilt. Everything is in perrfect worrking order.'

The all-purpose sportsdromes which are common on the Continent comprise a running-track which encircles the central acre of turf on which soccer and rugby are played. Thus the crowd may be as much as thirty metres from the action and their exhortations are inevitably remote from the participants.

What a contrast with the older generation of purpose-built rugby grounds in England and especially Wales. At Stradey Park, for instance, spectators on the popular bank and enclosure are no more than a few paces from the players. The sense of theatre is acute. The teams are like actors on an apron stage – and the First Wallabies of 1908 have by no means been the only touring side to find the ordeal too much for them. Here is a local Pressman's scene-set and summation of the exchanges.

The ground was in a perfect state, except that the grass in some places was too long. In honour of the occasion the goalposts were decorated with saucepans and every committeeman wore a saucepan as a badge in his coat collar, ornamented with a little red ribbon.

It is unnecessary to say that the visit of the Wallabies created great commotion in the town of the tinplaters, and the supporters of Llanelly [sic: the spelling changed in the sixties] made no secret of their confidence in the ability of their men to put up the stiffest game the Wallabies have yet had to contend with on their tour, while there were some enthusiastic souls who were sanguine enough to believe that Llanelly would win – several of the Llanelly players had had the advantage of seeing the tourists play at Neath on Thursday.

Such was the pressure of spectators that some of the youngsters and more agile enthusiasts climbed up the high trees surrounding the ground and thus commanded a clear, uninterrupted view of the battle royal.

Special flags had to be ordered for the touchline and for the touch-judges, emblazoned with the red dragon in a white setting and the inevitable saucepan in each of the the four corners. The Wallabies were the first to take the field at 3.20 and treated the Llanelly men to a war-cry as they entered the enclosure a minute later.

In their opposition Llanelly brought out the great surprise of the season, and one can imagine the news of their victory ringing through and through the football world tonight. Llanelly won absolutely on their merits, and whatever disappointment may mingle with the local rejoicing there is no disputing the fact that the Wallabies today were opposed to a better team, and like good sportsmen they will find consolation at any rate in that.

One cannot help feeling an instinctive sympathy with the Colonials at having met their Waterloo at such an early stage in their tour, and there is no knowing what moral effect the result will exercise on their play in future matches. For the first time the Wallabian forwards met their masters in every department of play except in the line-out where the two packs were very even.

The scrimmaging of the home forwards was really magnificent and commanded unstinting admiration. They gave a demonstration of the fact that the Australian players, clever though they undoubtedly are in footing and heeling, can be beaten at their own game by a pack of skilled and resolute forwards. The solid and scientific passing of the Llanelly eight, and their unerring deftness in securing the ball, enabled them to heel out to their half backs in three out of every five scrums, and the ball came out quickly and cleanly. Some of the rushes of the Llanelly forwards were of that irresistible order which one usually asssociates with a pack of Irish forwards at their best. Time and time again they swept down the field in solid formation at terrific pace, only to be stopped within half a dozen yards of the line. Tom Evans, who led them in great style, played the game of his life and his try from the line-out, from which the goal was kicked, was the winning point of the match.

South Wales Echo. 'Forward'.

In 1969 the Welsh Rugby Union began the re-development of Cardiff Arms Park into a national ground worthy of the name. This meant the demolition of obsolete superstructures which were rusting and rotten and their replacement with symmetrical tribunes of pre-stressed concrete. Some complained that the atmosphere of the place had been impaired for ever; but as time goes by it appears that despite modernisation there has been no diminution in the level of noise or excitement within its ramparts. The singing of hymns no longer dominates proceedings; but then nor does it any more in the wider Wales beyond.

Here, an England full back reflects on a day at Cardiff, where more than two decades of defeat were to follow his country's victory of 1963.

I only played one International match at Cardiff – in 1969 – but it was a day packed with enough action to last a lifetime. We arrived

OPPOSITE: Bob Hiller, one of the game's most consistent place-kickers and an England full-back who also became a British Lion. His only appearance against Wales at Cardiff was in 1969. (*Colorsport.*)

at the Arms Park to find that the stands on one side of the ground had fallen down. This was no surprise to me because I had played in a game for the 'Quins versus Cardiff at the same ground a few months earlier when John Coker and P.L. Jones had opposed each other on the wing and I was amazed to witness a physical confrontation the like of which I have never seen since. Six of the tackles went into the red paint area on the seismograph at the Science Museum in London as major earthquakes. I thought at the time that the vibration would take its toll of the stand's foundations, but little did I expect such devastation as greeted us on the day of the International.

The Welsh Rugby Union put a brave face on the whole affair and pretended that they were re-developing the ground, but we know the truth. We changed in a temporary building behind one of the stands. This gave us quite an advantage because, instead of having the crowd shouting and stamping above us as they would have been in the old changing rooms, in our wooden hut, which was some way from the pitch, it was just possible, by putting your fingers in your ears and covering your head with a towel, to pretend that there weren't 50,000 Welshmen outside singing and baying for blood.

This small crumb of comfort was soon snatched from my grasp when I walked outside. As I passed through the gangway on my way to the pitch a head appeared over the top of the balustrade, stared me straight in the eye and said, 'Ten minutes, you 'Iller – that's all you'll last.' He immediately diverted his gaze away from me and continued singing 'We'll Keep a Welcome in the Hillsides' at the top of his voice – some welcome.

The game itself is but a blurred memory to me, a seemingly endless succession of Welsh tries and goal-kicks. During the game I contrived to break a bone in my hand. 'Budge' Rogers, whose main medical qualification stemmed from the fact that he was wearing more elastoplast than the other twenty-nine players put together – more, even, than Michel Palmie, who surely must have been sponsored by a bandage manufacturer – made the diagnosis and I was sent to the sidelines where a 'pain-killer' was injected. I don't think it was very effective because it wasn't until half way through the after-match dinner that my hand went numb – and Welsh beer has that effect on me anyway. I don't know how they spell it in Wales, but we always called it 'Feeling foul'.

Between the match and the dinner I was taken to Cardiff General

[166]

Hospital for an X-ray, and a plaster cast was needed. A young student nurse made a terrific job of plastering my arm from fingers to elbow. She was very nervous, as she had to do all this under the constant scrutiny of a very important-looking consultant, who checked every detail. As she finished she looked up at me, obviously very pleased with her work and said, 'That should do the trick – what do you think of it?' 'Marvellous,' I said, 'but don't you think you should have taken my wrist-watch off first?' We had to bring her round with smelling salts to explain that I was only joking. Still, that's show business for you.

It would be invidious of me not to pay tribute to JPR on this occasion. His contribution to Welsh rugby and to rugby throughout the world has been enormous and his play has set new standards. I for one will be pleased when he retires because I will at last be spared the embarrassment of seeing JPR, on numerous television replays, constantly brushing me aside as he scores on the blindside against England.

On the occasion of his fiftieth cap the BBC managed to show him scoring that same try no less than twelve times in one week. I didn't mind them showing it on 'Grandstand' and 'Sportsnight' or even on 'Nationwide', but I thought it was a bit much putting it on 'Jackanory' as well. That particular week did my ego no good at all – surely there must be one clip of me tackling him somewhere in the BBC archives? Come to think of it, someone in the BBC told me recently that the only film they had of me tackling had been moved to their 'very rare' section together with film of man's first landing on the moon.

To play against Wales in Cardiff is always the high point in any player's career and to win there is a rare achievement for a player of any nationality. A win for England would not only secure a permanent place in Rugby history for each individual player but would enable taunted Englishmen in clubs, offices and common rooms throughout the world to hold their heads high again.

Everything has gone wrong for England recently. Our economy is in ruins, our unions are revolting and Wales has just voted to remain part of the United Kingdom. Woe, woe, woe! All this can be put right in eighty minutes. Good luck, boys!

'Of Course, I Only Played This Game For Kicks' by Bob Hiller. *Wales v England match programme*, 1979. Programme Publications Ltd.

Richmond, Blackheath, Bristol, Leicester and Fallowfield in Manchester were all venues used by England at the end of the nineteenth century and during the first decade of the twentieth. The search for a national ground, however, co-ordinated by Billy Williams, a member of the RFU committee, resulted in the acquisition of the celebrated 'cabbage patch' at Twickenham; and since the third Saturday in January 1910 all England's home International matches have taken place there.

'Without doubt the loveliest of grounds,' wrote D.R. Gent in the Twickenham Jubilee brochure. But some see it in another light.

It is a tiresome place to get to, a most uncomfortable, poorly nourished, and gloomy place to sit at, and a penance to escape from on a crowded 'National day.

This is the ground of which a famous International, in his year of Presidency of the R.U., said in a public speech that it 'gave him the doldrums'.

Not a doubt about it, it was no easy matter for the R.U. to make their choice when the time came, about 1906–7, to find a home. The best ground, and turf, of all, that of the Athletic Ground, Richmond, they could not have then, as it is Crown property. Even if the Rectory Field at Blackheath was available its inaccessibility was not in its favour. But on that score the famous 'cabbage patch' (which was Hamish Stuart's name for Twickenham) was little better than Blackheath.

From the very first 'National at Twickenham in 1910 when England beat Wales by 2 goals (1 pen) and 1 try to 2 tries, the ground has been a very lucky one for the Rose. There is no doubt whatever about this in the minds of the impartial.

The weather, for one, and a most important, thing, has invariably been kind – I have never seen a really wet 'National there. Which fact, apart from the possibilities, in the event of a downpour, in the 'squishy' character of a turf that is never hard and fast, meant shekels all the time. The first was a 2 tries all game, yet England won 11–6!

The second, against Ireland in 1910, was a 0–0 draw; and the first Calcutta Cup there was won well by 2 goals and a try to a goal and a try. Only 3 tries to 2, but England, captained by A.L. Henniker-Gotley at scrum half in his first match for England against a Home Union (he had played *v* France a fortnight earlier at the Parc des Princes, Paris), were certainly the better side. It was curious to find

[168]

Henniker-Gotley captain in his second 'National, with A.D. Stoop in his thirteenth and John Birkett in his seventeenth match for England behind him, with C.H. Pillman in his eighth and R. Dibble in his fifteenth in the pack. But these things just happen, and players whose hearts are in the right place take them as all in the day's march. Henniker-Gotley was not captain of Oxford that season nor, so far as I am aware, had he ever played before with Stoop as his stand off. His partner in Paris had been H. Coverdale.

England's luck clearly was in evidence in that first game with Scotland at Twickenham. The score had reached what was to prove its final figure, 13–8 in favour of England with only a few minutes to go, when G. Cunningham (now at centre though usually at stand off both for Oxford and Scotland) broke clean through the English defence; but in evading England's full back, S.H. Williams of Newport, he had his breeks almost wholly peeled off him. He was then half-bare and a bare 10 yards from the line, 15 from goal, no opponent near! Rather than anticipate the nudist movement he incontinently sat down – and Scotland lost a try close to or behind goal, and with it the chance of drawing the game.

Rugger: The Man's Game. E.H.D. Sewell. Hollis & Carter. Reproduced by permission of Bodley Head.

Given that the commissioning of articles for match programmes must take place before teams are selected, the invitation to Tony O'Reilly to write about Twickenham from an Irish viewpoint in 1970 was inspired. The wing had last played for his country seven years earlier, since when the bulk of his considerable flair and energy had been deployed to found a successful business career. Suddenly he found himself plucked from the board room and thrust back (as a stand-in for his originally-chosen compatriot Bill Brown) into the hurly-burly of an International match at 'HQ'. He is thus almost certainly unique in having contributed a programme essay for an International match in which he actually took part.

NB: His cheerful presence could not motivate Ireland to victory. England won the game 9–3.

There they are – the entire staff, male and female, of the National Health Service, the British Army from Private Rafferty to Montgomery, bean barons, hole diggers, McAlpine Fusiliers, doormen, doctors

Tony O'Reilly: his terse instructions on line-out signals were, 'OK, Riley, let's have it the usual way, low and crooked.' (*S & G Press Agency Ltd.*)

and lawyers – Irish to the core, *united* by the only thing that can unite all Irishmen – which is Englishmen.

Twickers on the day is a sight to lift the heart of any patriot. To the English it is a game of Rugger – to the Irish an historical pageant, the continuation of centuries of loose rucks, crooked into the scrum and bad refereeing, including a particularly nasty period when England were strong up front and had Oliver C. at fly half, 'a very mean fella with the boot and elbow and distinctly anti-clerical when he got you on the ground', as a decaying Irish wing forward was heard to remark.

My first appearance for Ireland at the Holy Ground was in 1956. An icy day, anti-frostbite underwear with the compliments of Jantzen and a 20–nil defeat for Ireland summed up a day to forget. Tom Reid ruefully hazarded the old chestnut 'and lucky to get nil'.

Prior to the game he was observed in the dressing room performing prodigies of endeavour in the warm-up session. ''Tis the first run I've had since Pretoria,' he replied to an enquirer – a reference to the Fourth Test in South Africa for the British Lions six months previously. An angular granitic second row forward from Garryowen, he deserved immortality for the remark that summarised the unspoken fear of every second row forward: 'the deep and mortal dread of being found with the ball in me hands in the middle of Twickenham'.

It is often said that England start five points up at Twickenham. Stephen Potter would delight at the many ploys devised to reduce this handicap – like the mis-shapen Irish front row forward breaking into the English dressing room when Eric Evans, wearing a red rose and matching face, was giving a final harangue to the English team: 'Remember our history! Waterloo! [with an Irish captain] Alamein! [with another one]. Order and discipline will defeat Irish individualism,' he said.

'Excuse me, lads,' interrupted a friendly Irish face, 'but has anyone got any hairy twine for me boots?'

That particular English side required little harangue. Jeeps, Butterfield, Davies, Jackson, Thompson – surely one of the great English three quarter lines of the post-war years. Jeeps, Butterfield and Evans have now matured to the Olympian isolation of being England selectors. All indignantly deny the rumour that if you are picked for England you stand a damn good chance of getting into the Northampton first fifteen.

Nowadays, with five-year forecasts, discounted pass-flows, squad training, group think and pre-production planning, the game has become very much more scientific. Gone is the time when my sole communication with the Irish forwards was a terse instruction on the line-out signals from 'Billy Wigs' Mulcahy: 'OK, Riley, let's have it the usual way, low and crooked.'

Indeed the game has progressed in efficiency, organisation and work-rate to the point where very soon the Four Home Unions will be able to consider playing and possibly even beating Romania – which all goes to show that if we are not careful the spectre of professionalism and sponsorship will attack this last stronghold of amateurism.

The mind reels at the thought of the Irish team taking the field all wearing a number (would you believe 57?) and England emerging

'The uncertain Celtic flame' burns brightly: Brendan Mullin scores for Ireland against England at Twickenham. (*Colorsport.*)

from the tunnel sponsored by Cadburys – proving that Roses even grow on forwards. No. It won't do, and the sooner we get back to our rightful place behind the New Zealanders and Springboks, not forgetting the Romanians, the better it will be for all of us who train once a month.

The pity is that today you will not be seeing the former Irish fly half, Michael Anthony Francis English, in action. Straight from 'the Experiences of an Irish RM' it has been rightly said that he would gladly sell you a spavined horse for £25 and make you feel under a compliment to him.

Michael was marking that 'eligint Englishman' J.P. Horrocks-Taylor in a closely fought game at Twickenham. England won a narrow victory 8–6 through a last minute Horrocks-Taylor try. English, the most resolute of tacklers, had missed him.

A court-martial was held in the dressing room afterwards. 'There

I was,' he said, 'with 50,000 pairs of hostile eyes fastened on me. I went for the tackle, the Horrocks went one way – the Taylor went the other and I was left holding his hyphen.'

And so England go into the fray, gifted, resolute, swift and just a little apprehensive that the uncertain Celtic flame may burn brightly today – a flash of Gibson's genius, the ubiquitous Goodal!, the substantial competence of McGann, the elegant Bresnihan, and the Grey Fox at full back could combine to lift Irish hearts to victory. Additionally Ireland this year have the virtues of Dawson's coaching and thorough tactical approach to the game.

A win is a first step towards the Triple Crown and a chance to join the Golden Year boys – Mullen, McCarthy, Kyle, Henderson, McKay and O'Brien – in the history books. (Is it really twenty years since we last won the Triple Crown?) Indeed the mind of a former international is a psychologist's dream. One confided to me the other day, 'Ye know, I must be getting old – I almost want Ireland to win today.'

Sam Johnson was right. The Irish: a very fair people – they never speak well of one another.

'A Funny Thing Happened On The Way To Twickenham' by A.J.F. O'Reilly
from *England v Ireland match programme*, 1970.

Tony O'Reilly's great friend and compatriot Andrew Mulligan also contributed to a Twickenham match programme. He was writing for the 1962 Varsity match, however, having been the Cambridge scrum half a few years previously. Here he plots the course to a coveted Blue.

Grange Road is a long road. Whichever way you leave the ground the dreary pedal home is tiring, in itself a laborious extra after the afternoon's training – I imagine Iffley Road is the same.

After one such session I had a companion. He was a herculean Welshman with curly black hair and open boyish face. For the umpteenth time that term we weighed our chances of getting that elusive Blue. Inevitably the conversation turned to the captain – the autocratic leader of the totalitarian state which is Varsity rugby. 'Nice fellow, X,' I panted inanely. My companion grunted, 'Best way to get a Blue, bach, say b—— all and use your loaf.' I wondered about the captain's attitude to exiles.

When I recall the behaviour of Varsity players suffering from the

[173]

pressures and psychology of winning a Blue, I wonder that Theodore H. White hasn't written a companion to his epic on Kennedy. He should call it 'The Making of the Blues Any Year You Like'. There is stuff in this.

It all starts as a freshman. The sales talk of your sportsmaster varies from 'Odes to a Budding Scrum Half' to slick jargon like 'his hands impeccable; kicks special; running unsurpassed'.

Trials – freshmen's and senior alike – come and go. And from the first one is aware of the great powers vested in the captain of Varsity football. His word is law, his ideas sacrosanct. It is necessary to be his friend, rugby suicide to be his enemy. At the same time it is sound to recognise his heir, for the captain's reign is a short one – about four months of term-time – and if this isn't your year then the next may be. One must be aware of all the political forces at work in order to gain that Blue. Does the captain dislike you wearing suede jacket and bow tie? What does he think of your College? How adaptable is he? How aloof should you be from him, how friendly? What is his attitude to booze and birds? All these tiny (and at the same time subconscious) factors condition the behaviour of a potential Blue.

As the term progresses the captain is less and less willing to change his team. The boys realise this and by November he settles his side for Twickenham and begins to prepare them for their ordeal in the match itself. Then the boot changes foot and the skipper's problems set in. These are mainly psychological with players liable to hypochondria or developing nervous ticks!

After training (every day) we congregated in some college room where tea tables were sagging with food – crumpets, fruit and eggs. These were wolfed and then we waddled away into the night.

There is a curious habit at this stage of going to buy one's Blues equipment which in all costs about £30. Quite a lot for a blazer, scarf, rugby jersey and socks, much of which will only be worn once – that is, for the photograph and for the match itself. Cambridge blazers are so bright that they can only be worn on a tropical tour (they rival the feathers of a parakeet) or at the after-the-match ball. The boys look pretty pleased with themselves and their outfits in the photo.

My large Welsh companion was now joined in the team by another pygmy addition. He was as small as the other was large. They operated as a pair. Of course, they used to turn up for training, but after that they disappeared. They were never seen in college or at lectures; and we discovered that they spent the rest of the term in the cinema – in case of injury in the street. Any remaining matches were a hideous ordeal. The night before the match they didn't sleep a wink. They strutted in front of the wardrobe mirror in their blue blazers.

One photograph I have would not have disgraced a Pan American calendar of Waikiki beach, we were so pleased with ourselves. This augured badly and it wasn't our fault – it was that naughty Press again. They had told us and the world that we were the greatest thing since, er, fried bread. Not even Cassius Clay could have been as cocksure as we were. Cambridge would beat Oxford by twenty points minimum. The result? We were beaten 3–0.

As I write both Varsities have returned to their campuses to eat, sleep and dream of winning this match at all costs. They become principal actors on a stage lit by the glare of publicity, produced by the system of Oxbridge rivalry and directed by their captains. The public see only two superbly fit teams composed of youthful and supposedly intelligent rugby talent from all over the country. They cannot comprehend the pressures which require victory. That college porter who needs a win so that he can boast to his pub companions that you, his friend, were a hero. The 'bedder' who deigns to pick the sods from between your studs with a skewer. Your tutor, who has temporarily pardoned a scandalous term report on compassionate grounds of sport, must be able to present you at High Table as a good influence in college. Then your family, fleetingly hauled into the hurly-burly of Varsity rugger; and that most ardent of fans, one's mother, with needle poised over ever-shortening, ever-whitening shorts.

If you can survive all this and remain intact until the whistle blows, you have won a Blue ... not quite enough to make you a Prime Minister in these bad days: but it will definitely open a few doors later on. Could close a few too!

Grange Road is certainly a long road but Twickenham is longer – and the match itself is the longest eighty minutes of all.

'The Birth Of The Blues' by Andrew Mulligan from *Oxford v Cambridge match programme*, 1962.

Twickenham is by no means reserved for International and Varsity matches.
There are the Middlesex Sevens, the Inter-Services games, Trials, Schools and
Colts Internationals, and the club knock-out Final. What is more the Harlequin
FC were allowed – indeed encouraged – to play fixtures at 'HQ' from the start
as part of the RFU's campaign to familiarise supporters with the new stadium
in south-west London.

In addition, the Harlequins were the first team to play a match on the famous
turf. Richmond were their opponents, on 2 October, 1909, nearly three months
before England met Wales in the first International game at the ground.

So: what is so special about the Harlequins? Let H.B.T. – 'Teddy' –
Wakelam, pioneer of rugby commentators and a stalwart of the club, explain.

The history of any particular body is a systematic account of its
origin and progress. The facts of such things can probably be dragged
out of old documents and books by laborious and not very interesting
research, but usually relief can be found from this routine by con-
sulting history's junior partner, lighter-hearted legend.

Official records state that a club called 'Hampstead Rugby Club'
was formed in 1867, and that this club changed its name to 'The
Harlequin FC' in 1870.

As far back as 1911, when the compiler of this book first became
a Harlequin, he was told that we came into being under a lamp-post
at Hampstead at two o'clock one morning, his informant going on
to add that this probably accounted both for our colours and name,
and also for our motto *Numquam Dormio*.

A most unusual birthday story indeed, but quite untrue, for our
real 'Mother' was a dictionary, as the opening section of our story
will show, and our motto and monogram those of the old Hampstead
Club itself.

With this dictionary origin in mind, then, it is only just to look
into the various definitions and descriptions of 'Harlequin' as they
appear in books of reference.

The word seems originally to have been derived from the old
French *hellequin* – 'a devil in medieval legend' – to appear in the later
French form of *arlequin* and the Italian *arlecchino*, much used for the
name of a comic character, full of surprises, in the lighter types of
old Italian plays. Shakespeare has it as 'harlekin' – a 'mountebank
zany', whatever that may mean; but we are perhaps getting a little
closer to the mark when we find in the *Encyclopaedia Britannica*: 'a
person who makes funny moves'.

[176]

The *New Standard Dictionary* is still more explicit, for it says, 'fantastic and surprising like a Harlequin and his tricks', a definition well rounded off by *Webster's* with: 'a fantastic player of tricks' and 'a waggish trickster'. (A further definition, 'a peculiar type of small black dog' somehow does not seem quite to enter our particular realm!)

Here, surely, is food for thought. Have we been influenced, consciously or unconsciously, by our name and its meanings? Did it affect the mind and style of our forbears, to bring forth the great 'Stoop era', and did it influence Stoop himself in those inspired days?

In short, do not these dictionary definitions give some kind of clue to our methods, our unorthodoxy, our snapping-up of a half-chance, our attacks launched from nowhere, our 'Harlequin' game?

Harlequin Story. H.B.T. Wakelam. Phoenix House.

On major tours abroad players are usually allowed a fixed number of free telephone calls home each week which are monitored from their hotel bedrooms. Above and beyond this number they are required to pay the often steep charges themselves.

The story goes that one very homesick, very broke prop who had used up his ration of free calls decided on an attempt to beat the system. Bursting with the desire to hear a homely accent he sneaked along to the team-room, picked up the telephone, and asked for a number in the United Kingdom.

'It'll take a few minutes – I'll have to ring you back,' said the switchboard girl. 'May I have your name?'

'Oh, er, this the team-manager – Mr, er, Smith,' answered the prop hastily.

'Please replace the receiver,' came the instruction.

The tourist sat twiddling his thumbs and was soon far away in thought dwelling on the delights of his homeland. When the telephone rang it brought him abruptly back to earth.

Said the operator, 'I have the United Kingdon on the line – a call for Mr Smith of the rugby party.'

The prop looked blankly around the room. 'Very sorry,' he replied. 'Mr Smith's not here at the moment.'

Leicester could claim to be England's leading club in the early eighties, on the basis of both playing record and the number of players supplied to the National XV. In the twenties, too, they were a formidable combination, with men like A.M. Smallwood, H.L.V. Day and F.D. Prentice on strength. In contrast, as in all clubs, some playing members doubtless affected an off-hand attitude to training and club discipline; and such a one, if you would believe him, was Henry Grierson. In truth, he was by no means as disorganised as the title of his memoirs would have you believe. His was the Leicester of the inter-War years.

On or about the fifteenth day of August, if you are a player, you will receive a p.c. informing you that practice begins on the following Tuesday at six pm. Awful thought!

You will go to the changing room at the appointed time and find all the others doing the same thing, and as your kit is all ready laid out for you, as if you had played only last week and it had been sent to the wash in the interval, you take off your clothes, wish you were ten years younger as most of the side do, put the old jersey, shorts and stockings on, look carefully inside your boots for those crisp fivers you always find there daily and twice on Sundays, curse yourself for a silly old ass not to have given up the game after the War, and lace up your boots!

Before going further with our intensely interesting narrative we'll have a look at the ground. It is situate in the angle formed by two wide thoroughfares – Welford Road and Aylestone Road – both of which contain double tracks of tram lines.

The ground is therefore easily accessible and, what is far more important, can be emptied in five minutes. You walk straight in and you walk straight out. There is an enormous cement motor park at the back of the reserved stand, and as all cars are made to enter from the Aylestone entrance they can, after the match, drive off at once into Welford Road.

To see the crowd leave the ground at the conclusion of a game – the gates are invariably ten thousand – is a revelation to those whose only experience of this kind of thing is Twickenham.

Adjoining the ground is a large building – the Junior Training Hall – where dances and exhibitions are held and, being equipped with up-to-date kitchens, hot luncheons and six-course dinners can be, and are, provided for visiting teams.

The ground itself is a fine one – perhaps a trifle short from goal line to dead ball line – but that's only a detail. The stands can accommodate about eight thousand and the ground thirty thousand. The players' dressing-rooms are first-rate and the referee has a properly-furnished room with a private bath.

Having now laced up our boots I'll talk about training. We believe in sharp bursts of running and passing, a hot bath, followed by a hard rub down. Tom Goodrich, our bagman and himself an old Trial Cap, does this last for us. We wind up with a hot cup of tea.

After a considerable number of years of stern but fruitless endeavour to become a decent club forward, I have formed the opinion that nothing ruins the wind more than cigarettes. That, I suppose, is why I invariably smoke them. A pipe's the thing every time. As to food, it doesn't matter much, so long as you only eat a moderate quantity of starchy stuff. If you take strong drink, stick to good bitter beer. You get rid of the effects quickly. Spirits are poison, and I don't think more than the odd glass of port does one any good. Neither do gin and Italians, Martinis and the rest.

The massage, to which I have alluded, is a capital thing, and if you cannot get it I advocate a Turkish bath. If you play in Town it may be difficult to get practice, but if you can run about anywhere in the evening, indulge in short bursts, not long distance stuff, that is to say, after you have got your wind more or less right. This will make you quick off the mark, whereas the other tends to slow you down. But, whatever you do, go steady with the smoking.

After about the middle of October don't train at all. It only makes you stale.

The Ramblings Of A Rabbit. Henry Grierson. Chapman & Hall.

Local rivalries still wax and wane in Rugby Football, as they have from the start and always will. Evidently in turn-of-the-century Yorkshire the settling of grievances was not confined to the field of play.

Headingley were playing Pudsey 'A' in the 1897–8 season at Pudsey. It was my second visit to the ground; on my first I had received two black eyes, and they were a rough and tough crowd in those days – though Headingley could give as well as take.

Pudsey, for some reason I never found out, was always a joke in the West Riding. It used to be said that if a stranger arrived in the town one Pudsey lad would say, 'Who's yon across t'street, Bill?' Bill would say, 'A stranger,' and the reply would be, ''Eave a brick at 'im.'

To revert to the game, from the beginning it was a rough one and I received my usual black eye. Afterwards we went to the pub near the station to hoist a few 'Woolsorters' before our train came in. I and my pals Toddy Mellish, a very likeable and mischievous chap, and Harold Mawson, heavy and powerful, were sitting at a table when four of the Pudsey lads came in looking for 'the beggar wit' t' light coat', which was yours truly. Well, they would not have a drink with us, but wanted a rough house, so Toddy Mellish told them I could lick them at 'rat trap and ball', whatever that may be. They were up at once wanting to have a go at me, but this brought in the landlord who asked me to go with him as he did not want the police in.

He took me out and guided me to a side door telling me to get into the station waiting room and wait there until the train came in, as they were a very tough lot. When the train arrived we all three made a mad rush and just got on in time, or I suspect I should have had at least another black eye.

Memoir by Billy McLaren, club captain 1892–93, quoted in the
Headingley Centenary Brochure.

At the other end of England the dust rises when Cornishmen and Devonians take a tilt at each other, some of the most rousing battles being fought out at Redruth which claims (in the face of dissent from nearby Bodmin) to be the Duchy's oldest club.

Nor would many outsiders dispute the 'Reds' status as the most formidable. Certainly not the author of the piece that follows, writing from a safe base in Plymouth about an excursion to the west bank of the Tamar.

When the Plymouth team had boarded the train the guard locked the doors. 'Sensible chap,' says I. 'He intends to keep the Redruth fans out.' 'It isn't a bit like it,' replied the baggage man. 'He isn't keeping them out, he's keeping you in. You're playing scrum half today.' Unfortunately there were no tranquillisers in those days. Apprehension soon turned to fear, fear then became consternation. I had never played at a ground where there were hundreds of spectators with hungry looks at one end, but not one at the other.

I couldn't find a red jersey around so I donned Plymouth colours and the game began. Albion's Bill Webber was soon over for a try and received VIP treatment from then on. He didn't like the odds, so he implored me to have a go on my own nearer the scrum and attract the Cornish hounds. That's what I thought he called them. I had a go. Talk about grievous bodily harm! I know how a porcupine must feel when its spikes are hammered inwards. After that anybody could have the ball.

The reason for the freak crowd distribution became clear once the second half began. Redruth belted the ball upwards towards their fans. Up and up it went. When it seemed that it would come down with snow on it I shouted, 'Yours,' and fled. 'Ginger' Collins of Camborne refereed. A mass of flesh rolled over the line, but he didn't award a try. Brave man. Next time there was a roll-over I was under it. Somebody must have dragged me in.

Collins awarded a try that time. Two successful kicks and Redruth were in front; and it stayed that way, even when Arthur Brigstocke kicked a penalty goal from sixty yards. A fox terrier behind the Redruth posts barked. There was no other sign of approval. I then got a directive from Bert Sparks, Albion's England hooker – 'You've rocked 'em to sleep; you must have a go now.'

A young lad straight from school played fly half. This was before the likes of Brian Clough and zone defence. Rugby players were educated to mark their own men, and young Goldsworthy was no exception. Sparks heeled, a beauty! I shot off in the direction of the youthful fly half and showed him the ball. He took one stride towards his own man. It was enough. Roy Jennings screamed a warning, but he was too late. You can forget all about even-timers – loiterers! With the hot breath of the Redruth forwards on the back of my neck I broke all track records. I swear that Bill Webber was laughing as he took the scoring pass. Albion were back in the lead, the margin just enough to be tantalising.

What followed beggars description. Hell-fire at all corners! Strong men turned pale. I was Daz white. Francis St Clair Gregory went through his wrestling routine. Plymouth forwards flew in all directions. You might have said that things couldn't get worse, but they did. The cunning swine in the Plymouth pack figured that Roy would have a go on his own. The last throw. They opened a gap for him and he fell for it, smack into the Plymouth pack. Talk about ambush! He survived. I never knew how. Plymouth won.

At the end we tried to give the referee a measure of protection, but one little lad broke the cordon. He can't have been more than seven years of age, and the look of hate on his face can rarely have been equalled. 'Collins,' he hissed, 'you red-headed .....!' Mark you, we had only tried to take a few points off them. Supposing we had tried to take away their ground completely! Hitler was wise to call off his Cornish invasion. I put on a pair of sun-glasses and strolled towards the station. When I heard a train steaming along I deemed it dignified and prudent to run. I made it.

'A Taste of Honey – Cornish Style' by Ted Mercer from *The Centenary Of Redruth Rugby Football Club 1875–1975.*

What, then, of the other side of the coin, when local rivalry is by definition wholly absent and local derbies unknown? Does some kind of happy mental release take place?

It seems to be a characteristic of the so-called 'Exiles' clubs – the London Scottish, Welsh and Irish – that they play an uninhibited, exuberant brand of rugby which may owe something to their detached status in the rugby world. Certainly this was true of London Welsh under John Dawes in the late sixties and early seventies. London Scottish, too, have had their golden eras.

The Scottish took risks and threw the ball around. There were some very talented and original players, and on our day we took the pants off the greatest and the best. It was sweet to take over 20 points off the Harlequins at their peak with an all-International back row (remember 'Jyker' Travers and Bob Weighill?), or to run rings round Cambridge University in a successful season.

Of the memories at home I shall always treasure the chairing of old Ken Marshall off the field at Bath. It was the filthiest wet day I can remember. Rumour had it that a salmon had been picked up from the deep end of the flooded pitch on the eve of the match. Certainly every collapsed scrum brought danger of drowning. The opposition got a lot of ball and, as running was hopeless, peppered the full back with every kind of kick. Ken was 40; he had played for Scotland before the War and not a great deal since. He fielded every kick that skidded at him down the squalls of hail, whether the ball bounced off frozen mud or ducked and draked across the freezing puddles. Each time he gained forty yards with impeccable screw kicks into the wind. Finally the two fiercest Bath forwards chased a

[182]

monstrous Garryowen aimed a yard in front of our posts and arrived almost with the ball. Ken caught it at speed a foot from the ground. He skidded straight between and below the clutching arms of the two charging rhinoceroses as if he were on skis, emerged on the other side and got the longest touch of the match. It was an unforgettable display.

It was a joy to play with my elder brother Rab. He and I were both of the generation whose rugby careers suffered from the War. He was twenty-four at the outbreak of hostilities, and had just been capped three times for Scotland; I was nineteen. So the War took away most of our best years and, perhaps, the chance to play for Scotland together. For that reason we got particular pleasure from playing together for the Scottish, and I learned a lot from him when he was a veteran of thirty-five or so. He was or certainly had been lighter and quicker than I, more modest and self-effacing; perhaps less strong on his pins, certainly less selfish, and he liked to set things up for his younger brother. He was usually at centre and I was at stand off.

On the wings were, initially, two thunderous players whose presence was a great comfort to us frail mortals: the great Doug Smith and T.G.H. Jackson. Jacko, also, did not play long for London Scottish, having cartilage trouble and being moved around in his military career. He was even larger and faster than Doug if one can imagine such a thing, though he was marginally less ferocious of countenance and style. At sixteen stone and six feet two inches, and with a hundred yards speed of 10.1, he was hard to hold. He had two famous tricks: one was his side-step – no wonder his cartilage collapsed! The other was a reverse back hand under arm spin pass of fifty yards or so (he was a great discus thrower) which would flash with unerring aim straight from the blind side wing to the opposition's fastest man.

I remember Doug Smith best for his incursions into the centre. If we had starved him of a pass for ten minutes or so, he would growl with impatience and roar up between Rab and me snorting like a steam engine. To say that he took it on the burst would be an understatement. I always wondered whether it would be his blood vessels, the ball or his opponents that would burst first. Having shot through clear into the wide open spaces it often seemed to spectators that he was overcome with frustration and loneliness, and that he positively sought out an opponent into whose softer parts he could lower a shoulder, so that he might leave at least one prostrate figure on his triumphant gallop to the line.

'London Scottish post-War Years' by Logie Bruce-Lockhart from *The First 100: A History Of The London Scottish Football Club 1878–1978.*

For forty-eight hours incessant heavy rain had been drenching the top end of the Rhondda Valley. Treorchy's Schweppes Cup tie against senior side Pontypridd seemed doomed to postponement but when the skies cleared early on the Saturday morning, leaving the pitch and its surrounds like a swamp, the two teams decided to play the match in order to free themselves for an arduous programme of Christmas fixtures.

Spectators wearing gum-boots sloshed their way to seats and terraces through huge puddles and mini-streams of water with which the field was awash. When the players came on their boots immediately sank into the top layer of what had once been turf, and soon practically every man was plastered with chocolate-coloured Welsh mud. To add to everyone's misery heavy rain began falling again soon after the interval. It would have required a superhuman effort to produce anything resembling rugby football in such conditions and not surprisingly the score was limited to just a Pontypridd penalty goal to nil.

So people had had nothing much to ease their misery until a few minutes from time when an official switched on the loud-speaker system, addressing himself to the wretched gathering huddled on the terraces with water trickling down their necks and into their shoes, socks and even underwear.

'At the final whistle,' he intoned earnestly into the microphone, 'would spectators kindly refrain from running onto the playing surface.'

Even the Barbarians FC have to move with the times, and a proliferation of close-season tours by the Home Countries making extra representative demands on their top players means that the Easter tour has been truncated since Nigel Starmer-Smith wrote his official history in 1977 – Penarth RFC no longer feature on the fixture list at all, while the annual game with Newport has moved to the autumn.

Nonetheless the Baa-Baas are still the most revered touring club in the world. The passage that follows includes some of the reasons.

The Barbarian FC is delightfully disorganised in many respects but the end certainly justifies the means. It is a free and easy club, imbued with tradition, though the 'alickadoos' expect a certain standard of courtesy and good behaviour from the playing members. The word 'alickadoo' is the endearing but respectful term used to denote a senior Barbarian member and committee man; by definition, and tradition, he may pontificate, patronise, praise, organise, criticise and participate, but not play – 'all-he-can-do' is talk! The rules are minimal, and during the Easter tour the only ones that the 'alickadoos' ever seem to bother about are that 'players are expected to be in bed by eleven o'clock the night before a match', and that 'players are requested not to play more than nine holes of golf on the morning of a game'!

The overall organisation, or lack of it, is enchanting: for intance, the famous back and white jerseys are kept in a cupboard in 'Fergie' Ferguson's office and the club records are preserved in charming disarray in an old tin trunk and several battered suitcases that belonged to 'Jock' Wemyss. Nor have the Easter traditions changed, though travel arrangements are now more sophisticated and players more independent in that respect – no longer is there the same ritual foregathering for the party at Paddington, and the reserved railway coach to Wales. There is still Herbert Waddell's 'compulsory' Sunday Knockout Golf Tournament, one bag of clubs to each team of four players, taking turn and turn about; the Saturday night revelries; the friendships struck, the pervading atmosphere of relaxation, good-will and fun. Emile de Lissa once remarked, when he heard Cliff Davies singing 'Jerusalem' at one o'clock in the morning, that he had been forty years on tour and never before heard a hymn being sung to a captivated company of Barbarians at that time of day! Such things still happen.

But most significantly of all, the style of rugby that characterises

[185]

their play has not changed either – the factor which has ensured that the Barbarians have retained their popularity and unique standing. Barbarian policy is to attack from every possible, or even impossible, position – taking the risk even if the odds are against it succeeding. There are never any recriminations. However, with the great strength of the teams opposing the Barbarians, especially in South Wales in the early years, and the overall improvement in standards of club rugby that has been apparent in recent years, it has not always been easy to play 'Barbarian rugby', neither is it easy for a scratch side nowadays. Winning is important, but far from being everything, as Herbert Waddell explains: 'We are, of course, tremendously keen to win, but we have not got all the inhibitions, national or otherwise, which are inevitably involved in an international match. When we are beaten nobody goes into sackcloth.'

The colours and insignia of the club are known the world over. The jersey has wide horizontal black and white bands with the black monogram on the left breast, a monogram which in the first season, 1890, consisted of a skull and crossbones, with 'BFC' underneath. That was changed a year later to the monogram only that exists today. The tie was introduced in 1895, dark blue and light blue broad stripes with a narrow white line between. Curiously, this was presented to the club by the Blackheathen F.Mitchell, being the colours of the cricket side which he took to the USA earlier that year. The pocket badge of the blazer was originally embroidered with two lambs gambolling with a rugby ball, until in 1930 I.M.B. Stuart drew up the present design – surely the finest of any sporting body. It is made up of two shields, one with the Rose, the Thistle, the Shamrock and the Prince of Wales' Feathers, emblems of the Four Home Countries, the other with the Silver Fern of New Zealand, the Springbok of South Africa, and the Waratah of Australia. Surmounting the shields are the two lambs, the Baa-Baas, in pursuit of a rugby ball. It is a magnificent emblem, symbolising the worldwide fellowship of the Barbarian Club – a club with a very special character, a remarkable history, and a proud tradition. It is small wonder that the honour of wearing the famous black and white jersey is generally recognised as being second only to that of representing one's country.

The Barbarians. Nigel Starmer-Smith. Macdonald and Jane's.

Let us end our brief whirl around clubs and countries, in Dublin – just about the only capital, in many people's view, where it is actually possible to believe in the lip-serviced ideal that the Game genuinely matters more than the result.

In recent years the social emphasis on International day appears to have shifted to the newer hotels out near Lansdowne Road itself where finding shoulder room, let alone elbow room, to lift a pint of post-match Guinness, is a major problem.

The essay by Patrick Campbell which follows harks back to more gracious days in, some would say, more gracious surroundings. Alias Lord Glenavy, Campbell was Quidnunc in the Irish Times *for some years before he emigrated to London and the* Sunday Times *where his weekly column was a feature of the leader page. Campbell's Dublin centres on – perhaps it would be truer to say revolves around – St Stephen's Green and the sturdy, elegant buildings nearby. Some of the landmarks survive; some, alas, are gone for good.*

After a really punishing loose maul in the mud-stained remnants of my mind I still find it curiously difficult to get the ball – as it were – out and as far back as Lansdowne Road in the middle thirties.

I can see in my mind's eye, blurred as it is by many a belt from life, shivering figures in green jerseys and almost white shorts down to the knee standing roughly to attention as the Garda Si'ocha'na Band blasts out 'God Save the King', their blowing and banging affected in no way by lashing rain, whilst fifteen Englishmen, all in immaculate white, stand ramrod straight in front of them, their eyes closed in homage – not too easy to spot from the Grandstand – to their very own George V.

Or could the musical excerpts have been provided by Mary Comerford and her Girl Pipers, even if they came on for 'The Soldier's Song'?

One thing is certain, in my memory. Every man-jack of us wanted to get the music out of the way so that our lads could get at the other fellas, and especially on the occasion of the England–Ireland match.

In those days, of course, we weren't searched for bombs as we came in through the turnstiles, nor were there Gardai' with machine guns patrolling the pitch. The only weapons required for the coming war in the middle were hands, feet and a judicious elbow, and a guaranteed peace after the final whistle.

I must have attended quite a lot of Internationals at Lansdowne Road with my father, as expert and as silent an observer of Rugby as he was of racing. His first plan to stand treat to his whole family was kicked miles into touch by my mother and sister, on the grounds that even watching Ireland winning was no compensation for spending a whole perishing afternoon sitting on hard wooden benches, so that the Lord and I would go alone.

He was always well equipped for the event. A muffler, a good thick woollen rug, a silver flask of modest size and an encyclopaedic knowledge of the names, plus past and present form, of every single player on the field, including data on personnel as remote from my adolescent world as Welsh scrum halves. As I have said, he was a remarkably quiet watcher of sporting events. As, infrequently, he saw his selection first past the post at Leopardstown, Baldoyle or Phoenix Park, his demeanour would be as gloomy as though it had come in – as it very often did – an exhausted fourth.

He was the same at Lansdowne Road. With everyone around him bawling abuse or exhortation the Lord, fanatically devoted to the game and a sage on its finer points, would greet a faulty pass with the severe comment, 'Somewhat erroneous tactics,' and follow it up with a discreet sip from his flask.

It might have been this, or just plain curiosity, that led me into the social activities in Dublin that surrounded an International match, both for several days before and often a week after the event. The result of this was that I actually got to Lansdowne Road for round about one event in every three.

Our mornings would begin outside the door of the Buttery in the basement of the Royal Hibernian Hotel, almost always as early as 10.25 a.m., to be there in good time for the throwing open of the portals at 10.30. Once inside service would be held up by George and Jack behind the bar in discussion with the older members about 'What would be good for it?' 'It', of course, was the accumulated result of the two days and nights of conjecture about the possible result of the coming match – not a matter to be lightly dismissed.

It would have been round about 11 a.m. that a number of us would decide it was high time to see what was going on in Davy Byrne's just around the corner, followed about 11.45 by an investigation into Bailey's Hotel, almost opposite, a smooth flow that led us into Jammet's back bar as early as 12.30. Seeing that at this chilly hour it was much too soon for lunch the more socially-minded of us nipped around the corner of Nassau Street and back into the Buttery, where to many of us it seemed we had been only a minute or two before.

[188]

From there, some time later, we were propelled by the surge of events back around the corner of Duke Street and into a re-visiting of Davy Byrne's, followed by Bailey's Hotel, for the purpose of finding out whether Oliver St John Gogarty was still telling the story he'd been embarked upon during our first lap or, more probably, had begun again at the beginning.

All this wasn't simply a vulgar, drunken route. It was much more the vulgar excitement of feeling that the whole city was *en fête* – that hundreds of thousands of people had abandoned care, work, wives and other encumbrances and were making devotedly, if circuitously, for the ultimate Mecca of Lansdowne Road.

Rather too often lunch got in the way, in establishments as remote from the beaten track as the Red Bank or the Dolphin, where we would realise, as we took our first Irish coffee, that the whistle must have gone, miles away, for half time, so there would be no point in breaking our necks to get there for the final touch-down. That looked after the rest of the night.

But I did get there, at least twice, to witness two of the greatest athletic feats that the Rugby world has ever seen. I must admit it's quite possible I was never there at all and heard about them from my father, a bit warmed up, thereby making them my own stories for ever. Like the one about Jammy Clinch, that heroic Irish forward, the only man made of solid concrete from head to toe who could still run quite fast despite such unusual anatomy.

Was it not Jammy, looking, as usual, for trouble in midfield, who suddenly found the ball in his hands, emerging from some unknown source, and started to gallop, instantly, for the Welsh line? Did not two Welshmen climb aboard him in their own twenty-five, slowing Jammy a little but not significantly? And did not their full back add himself to Jammy's load so that all four of them fell like a double-decker bus over the Welsh line, between the goal-posts, leaving a crater the outlines of which can be seen to this very day? It's a well-known fact that all this happened, no word of a lie.

Nor is it a word of a lie about Ernie Crawford, our own little hunchy full back. Remember the day when Ernie was there with the sun in his eyes and the wind in his teeth and a big lolloping punt coming his way with three bullocks of English forwards thundering down on him and Ernie palmed the ball as if it was a marble, side-stepped and kicked for touch, while all three Englishmen ran into one another and fell down. And what happened to Ernie's kick?

[189]

Bounced off the head of a bewildered three quarter, got snapped up by the English scrum half and shovelled out to Serge Obolensky right out on the other wing, who set out like a Maserati for the Irish line. What did Ernie do? With his crab-like lightning run he covered the whole width of the field in a single second, caught hold of good old Obo, tied him up into a neat little parcel and threw him right into the orchestra stalls, two feet short of our line.

If anyone wants to question the veracity of these epic tales, with niggling demands for dates, times, teams, weather conditions and so on, let him not come to me.

I've been in exile so long that were I to find myself in Dublin again I'd be hard put to it to find Lansdowne Road itself.

'The Middle Thirties' by Patrick Campbell from *Ireland v Wales match programme*, 1978. John Rattigan Ltd.

MATCHES AND MOMENTS

Great Games, Great Scores

'The Rugby game is full of possibilities and it is hard to pin-point the one absolute essential,' wrote O.L. Owen, for many years the Rugby Football correspondent of The Times. *'But one thing at least is certain. No-one wants to see more than an occasional match lost and won by penalty points.'*

Thirty years later, as the whacking over of penalty goals from fifty and sixty metres became commonplace, people were expressing this sentiment more fervently than ever; and still the authorities found the great equation as difficult as ever to solve: how are offences on the field to be suitably punished without allowing matches to be decided *by those punishments?*

The answer of rugby's lateral thinkers is that the real solution lies with contestants on the field: they must 'want to play'. It is in order to make a small contribution towards that motivation, therefore, that we end with a sampling of games and scores where audacity and daring have won the day and the thud of boot against ball had perforce to take a back seat.

Partly because of the controversial disallowed 'try' by Deans, New Zealand's only defeat of their 1905 tour in Cardiff has had plenty of light shed on it down the decades. For that reason the tremendous battle fought out at Inverleith a month earlier is less well remembered outside Scotland. But what an epic struggle it evidently was.

Scotland 7 pts, New Zealand 12 pts.

The New Zealanders set the seal on their fame as Rugby Footballers in Edinburgh on Saturday when, after being one point to the bad five minutes before the call of time, they by a great effort found out a weak spot in Scotland's armour and scoring twice in rapid succession actually finished up five points to the good, after the most exciting finish ever witnessed on the Inverleith ground.

With only a quarter of an hour to go Scotland led by one point. The crowd became too excited to cheer. All those who possessed watches were anxiously marking the flight of time, and those who did not were informing the referee that the game was drawing near its lawful close. The Scottish backs were playing for safety and giving nothing away, kicking into touch whenever possible.

Ten minutes to go, and Scotland still in front! Would the referee never give his final whistle call? The minutes seemed like hours to the anxious Scotsmen, and like seconds to the supporters of the Fern Leaf.

A succession of scrums looked as if Scotland would succeed in keeping the ball close to the end, but at last when it seemed all over bar shouting the ball came out to the New Zealand backs. In a flash it went along the line to Smith on the left and that player, setting his teeth with grim determination and calling upon every ounce of his strength, ran straight for the goal-line.

Owing to the cleverness with which the movement had been started the only man who had a fair chance of tackling Smith was Scoular, the full back. It was a trying position for a young and comparatively inexperienced player like the Scottish full back to find himself in, for success or failure meant either victory or defeat for his side, and Scoular is more to be pitied than blamed for allowing Smith to get past him.

A wild yell from the students in front of the Press stand announced the fact that Smith had got over, and all doubts were set at rest when his colleagues were seen to be crowding round him, almost falling on his neck in their delight. No-one troubled much about the place-kick. Whether it was converted or not did not much matter. The All Blacks had pulled the game out of the fire and secured a two points' lead.

As a matter of fact the place kick was not successful, but to clinch matters in the very last minute of the game the New Zealanders scored again, Cunningham touching down after a brilliant piece of play by McDonald.

It was not one of the New Zealanders' best displays. Their backs never got properly together, and both Wallace and Hunter seemed bothered by the state of the ground. In fact the last-named has never been so ineffective. The hero of the day was Smith, who in the absence of MacGregor played on the left wing, Deans filling the centre position. In addition to scoring two fine tries, one of which decided the match, he played with rare judgement throughout.

On the Scottish side the two outstanding figures were K.G. McLeod and E.D. Simson, but all the forwards worked with unflagging energy.

The ground, frost-bound and slippery, was all against the New Zealand style of play, which depends for success upon the smartness and combination of the backs. On such a ground swerving and dodging were well-nigh impossible, for the man who attempted such a feat generally lost his balance; while the ball, blown out almost to bursting point and of an unduly elongated shape, was extremely difficult to pick up and still more difficult to hold.

The consequence was that the brilliant series of exchanges to which the New Zealand three quarters have accustomed us were frequently rendered abortive, the men either slipping up when endeavouring to take their passes or else knocking on.

In this connection it may be remarked that Mr Kennedy of the Irish Rugby Union, who refereed with the utmost impartiality and fairness, was at times unnecessarily strict in his interpretation of the knock-on rule.

With the ball rime-covered and slippery as a piece of ice, it was inevitable that fumbles should at times occur, but these were not necessarily knocks-on in the strict sense of the term and considering the state of the ground a little more latitude might reasonably have been allowed. He treated both sides exactly alike in the matter, but as the New Zealanders had the ball more frequently among their backs than did their opponents they were inevitably the greater sufferers.

Not once or twice, but many times, were Hunter and Stead tackled before they could get rid of the ball, which was either torn from their grasp or else carried on in a mad rush in which Scottish forwards and New Zealand backs struggled for possession.

Finding these tactics so successful the Scots became more aggressive still and, controlling the ball with remarkable skill, made a series of incursions which the New Zealand backs appeared for a time to be quite unable to check. It was from the fiercest of these inroads that McCallum scored Scotland's try after a combined movement in which the whole of the Scottish pack took part.

But to begin the story of the match at the beginning. From the start of the game it was soon evident that whatever the result might be it was by no means going to be a walk-over for one side or the other. Scotland at the last moment decided to play Greig, of the Glasgow Academicals, as a third half back instead of having a fifth three-quarter and this plan worked admirably. The visitors, to borrow a cricket phrase, appeared unable to time the ball on the hard ground, and so faulty was their picking up and so frequently were their passes intercepted that Scotland might easily have scored in the first five minutes.

The score was not long delayed, however, for after the Scottish forwards had crossed the line but had been whistled back for some irregularity the ball was got away smartly from the scrum by Munro and whipped out to E.D. Simson who in a twinkling had sent it flying over the bar with a clever snap-kick.

This early reverse appeared to act as the necessary goad required to stimulate the New Zealanders to give of their very best, and for the next quarter of an hour they had all the best of the game. It was only the magnificent defence of the brothers McLeod and the good touch-kicking of Scoular which saved the Scottish citadel.

After a series of protracted assaults, however, the inevitable try came at last, Glasgow managing to scramble over. The place kick was unsuccessful, however, and the supporters of Scotland breathed again, for their men still led by one point.

But their joy was short-lived for shortly afterwards, the Scottish defence having been skilfully drawn to one side of the ground in typical New Zealand fashion, Smith was left with a clear run-in. Wallace again failed with the kick, but the All Blacks were now two points up, a fact which their comrades in the stand below the Press-box noted by the waving of flags and the making of hideous noises on an antiquated and out-of-date trombone.

Back again to work went the combatants hammer and tongs and they kept at it with varying success until the Scottish forwards put in their magnificent rush and McCallum scored the try referred to above. The place kick, like every other taken during the day, proved unsuccessful, but sufficient had been done to enable Scotland to regain the lead and half time arrived with the score 7–6 in their favour.

But while they were unfortunate in just getting beaten on the post after holding the lead for the greater part of the game, it must be admitted that the New Zealanders would have been still more unlucky to have lost, for on the general run of the play they were undoubtedly the better side.

'Anon', 1905. *Scrapbook newspaper cutting.*

To claim the scalp of a major touring side is not an ambition confined to national XVs. Clubs and combinations at all levels are fired up for their meetings with overseas visitors, which provide for the majority of participants perhaps the sole opportunity in their lifetime of competing against International opposition. That touring sides sometimes make heavy weather of such fixtures is to be expected, since for them it is just one in a progression of high-pressure engagements.

So all such victories are special, but some are more special than others. The Barbarians' 6–0 victory over the otherwise invincible Springboks of 1960 is an example; but perhaps an even better one is the remarkable win in 1931 of the Midland Counties over the Third Springboks. The match took place at Leicester.

It has been called the greatest game to have been played at Welford Road, and seven Leicester players took part, one of them George Beamish, captaining the combined side. It was possibly Beamish's finest hour even though the big lock had already collected eighteen of his twenty-five Irish caps and was well-known as not only a rumbustious forward but a talented captain.

The Springboks arrived in Leicester on the morning of the match, 14 November 1931, and in the afternoon cars stretched all the way up Welford Road and spilled into the side-streets as 25,000 people made their way to the ground. 'It was,' said the *Leicester Mercury*'s Cyrus, 'one of those games we dream about but seldom see'. The combined side was:

R.J. Barr (Leicester), J.T. Hardwicke (Leicester), R.A. Buckingham (Leicester), R.G. Brumwell (Bedford), L.G. Ashwell (Bedford), C. Slow (Northampton), B.C. Gadney (Leicester), A.H. Greenwood (Leicester), D.J. Norman (Leicester), R.J. Longland (Northampton), T. Harris (Northampton), A.S. Roncoroni (West Herts), W.H. Weston (Northampton), G.R. Beamish (Leicester), E. Coley (Northampton).

Osler rested himself for the game, which must have helped the counties' cause since so much of the Springboks' play revolved around his kicking, and the tourists fielded J. Tindall, F. Venter, J.C. van der Westhuizen, B.G. Gray, M. Zimmerman, M. Francis, D. Craven, L. Strachan, J. Bierman, P.J. Nel, J. Deld, F. Louw, G. Daneel, S. du Toit, P. Mostert.

Barr, brave and solid as a rock, had now established himself as Leicester's last line of defence while Hardwicke had impressed as a clever wing since joining from Stoneygate two years before. Buckingham's quality was well-known and Gadney was on the threshold of a brilliant international career. Beamish and Norman were established players while Henry Greenwood had earned his position with hard, no-nonsense play.

The counties went into an early lead thanks to a dropped goal by Charles Slow, and they never lost it. To many people this has always remained Slow's match and after the Springbok wing Zimmerman had crossed for the first of his four tries, the Northampton fly half went through for a try which was converted. Louw left the field for treatment to a knee injury, returning just before half time, but by then the counties led 19–6.

A dribble and pick-up by Buckingham had laid on a second try for Slow, Weston converting, and though Zimmerman scored again a punt ahead by Slow enabled Hardwicke to cross for the counties' third try to which Weston again added the goal points. Zimmerman opened the second half scoring but then Weston broke away and sent Beamish off on a run to the line for a try greeted with tremendous enthusiasm and converted by the faithful Weston.

Down by 24–9 the Springboks responded but Barr survived all the pressure placed on him. Nevertheless the tourists scored through Gray, following a dribble, and then Francis dropped a goal to narrow the gap to eight points. Gray made the break for Zimmerman's fourth try and a conversion by Francis made it 24–21. It is not difficult to imagine how great a moment it must have been, for the players and the crowd, willing their team on. The counties shook off their lethargy, with Buckingham in exceptional form, and Weston kicked the only penalty of the game. Then Snow dribbled through and Buckingham crossed in the corner to put his side out of reach, the counties winning 30–21. The thirty points scored by the counties was a record for a British team against any major touring side and still is.

Although Slow – a late addition to the original XV after Greenlees and Coote dropped out because of injury – was man of the match, the plan of the match was Beamish's. He had played for the Combined Services against the Springboks the week before (and was to captain Ireland against them). Buckingham remembers his pre-match instructions: 'Beamish said to Brumwell and me, "I don't mind if they have the ball, but I want you two centres to hit them so hard they won't know what's going on." As soon as they got the ball we did just that. I've never known anything like the atmosphere of that match. It was so close and after I had scored the last try I could hardly get off the ground I was so tired.'

Leicester Football Club. David Hands. Leicester FC.

With the exception of a period in the early seventies the twentieth century has been dominated by the southern hemisphere countries. When South Africa's contact with the Home Countries became more tenuous the progress of Australia to the standing of a world force in the game provided continuity.

The try described below came in the 1949 Test series between the Springboks and the All Blacks, with a post-War 'world title' at stake. As it turned out there was only one nation in the hunt, South Africa achieving a 4–0 whitewash. The same combination of players was to march triumphantly through the British Isles in 1950–51, with Hannes Brewis a key man at stand off half.

There was a scrum near the grandstand touchline and deep into All Blacks' territory. Jorrie Jordaan hooked and the ball flashed into Hansie Brewis' hands. For a split second it looked as if he would drop for goal and the All Blacks thought so too. A battalion of defenders charged down on Brewis, but in the wink of an eye he changed his mind and streaked around the blind side with his opponents caught off balance and going the wrong way.

He was now very near the goal-line, but again his way was blocked. The quickest brain in rugby was working with computer-like efficiency and he feinted as if to kick towards the corner flag. The All Blacks hesitated for a fatal instant and suddenly Brewis was off again like a rocket.

A few yards from the line he was threatened once more and this time Brewis dummied to the inside, fooled yet another defender, and then he straightened out and went over with Scott too late to do more than just brush his shoulder.

The more than 70,000 spectators went raving mad; most of us who were there were hoarse for days afterwards. Of all the great moments in sport that I have seen since, from Newlands to Madison Square Garden, there has never been anything that could approach those fleeting seconds just after 12 minutes past four o'clock on the afternoon of 13 August 1949, when Hansie Brewis gave back to the Springboks their self-respect.

Springbok Saga. Chris Greyvenstein. Nelson & Toyota.

When the Springbok party of 1950–51 reached the United Kingdom Scotland had the misfortune to be the first Home Country to experience the full might of what many critics consider the most formidable and well-equipped side ever to undertake a major tour in Europe. The celebrated Scottish reaction to their heavy defeat – 'and we were lucky to get the nil' – has gone round the world.

Although the score-line is a large blot on their copybook, subsequent games have seen the Scots more than holding their own, and their overall record against South Africa is superior to that of England, Wales or Ireland.

Scotland 0 pts, South Africa 44 pts.

The South Africans have many triumphs to their name on the Rugby football field, but they surely have never won a game against opponents of international class so brilliantly and so conclusively as that against Scotland at Murrayfield on Saturday.

The score, made up of seven goals, one dropped goal and two tries, has been exceeded only once since the modern scoring values were adopted in 1905. This was in a match of a missionary kind played by Paul Roos's original Springboks against the French when Rugby football in France was in its infancy.

One recalls an afternoon in Dublin just before the War when England scored seven tries, and another some years before at Swansea when in storm and tempest the French line was crossed seven times by Wales. Just after the first War, at Cardiff, Wales scored eight tries against England.

But modern history shows no parallel to the scoring of nine tries by one side in an international match since W. A. Millar's South Africans made ten against Ireland in 1912.

Almost from the moment of the first try there appeared between the two sides such a wide and ever-growing disparity that the game developed merely into an exhibition. In this spectators, as soon as the first disappointment was behind them, seemed to revel in a detached, unemotional way oddly out of keeping with an international occasion.

The strange thing was that the portents were slow to show themselves. In the first minute a footrush by the Scots and a pick-up by Kinninmonth would have led to an almost certain try by Hart, the new cap on the right wing, if he had been given a takeable pass.

What might have been the effect of such a start can only be conjectured, but the moral impetus must have meant much to a side playing before 65,000 of their own countrymen.

[198]

At all events there followed seventeen minutes which were not without occasions of peril to South Africa as well as to Scotland before the first try came. It was followed within two minutes by another, which was converted, and after five more minutes by a third, converted likewise.

That was the end of the contest. There were two further scores before half time, including a lovely left-footed dropped goal by Brewis, and Scotland changed over 19 hopeless points behind.

In the first twenty minutes of the second half South Africa touched down four times more. That gave them 39 points with still a quarter of the game to go.

But they seemed sated now, and began to take such liberties that the Scots for a while were able to scramble out of their troubles, and even to instigate an odd attack or two. It was three minutes from the end when the ninth and last try came. Thus for the forty minutes in the middle of the game when the pressure was at its hottest the South Africans ticked up virtually a point a minute.

An analysis of the scoring gives as sure a clue as any to the course of the play and the reasons for the victory. One try was the result of an interception and one other came from an orthodox movement following a scrum.

These were the only tries made and scored by the outsides. Forwards were responsible for and touched down the remaining seven, two following cross-kicks and five from short passing in the loose.

The South African pack was tremendous. It had the ball most times in the tight (Scotland heeled only twice from set scrums in the first half), and the points specially apparent here were how low these big fellows managed to get down, and with what precision they straightened their backs and timed the shove when the scrum half showed them the ball. But of course after repeated possession had gained them the attacking position it was the strength and backing up in the opposing 25 that yielded the tries.

Scotland had no answer to the weight and speed and determination near the line of such men as Du Rand, Koch, Fry and Van Wyk. Nor were the men with the less spectacular parts far behind them. Dinkelmann and Delport both were among the scorers, and nothing seemed to please the South Africans more than the try scored by their hooker.

Muller was everywhere. The South Africans are adept at thrusting quickly when an opposing move has foundered, and in this harassing-cum-opportunist role the acting captain is in a class of his own.

Yet the backs had a greater share in the success than might be supposed from the bare narrative. The understanding between Du Toit and Brewis generally ensured that no clear chance should go to waste, and it was the speed over the first few yards of Brewis that so frequently made his centres a danger.

It will be assumed from this chronicle that Scotland were over-whelmed by an assault against the intensity of which they were almost helpless. That, indeed,was the case.

Daily Telegraph. E.W. Swanton.

At Cardiff the Springboks were able to defeat a Welsh side which was in between two Grand Slam years by six points to three. Much of the good quality possession won by the well-drilled Welsh pack was squandered by the indifferent kicking of the back division, including the young Cliff Morgan who came under constant pressure from the vastly-experienced flanker C.J. 'Basie' van Wyk.

On the firm South Africa pitches four years later Morgan was at his peak as an attacking stand off half and the boot was on the other foot. In the nail-biting First Test, won 23–22 by the British Isles, Morgan played his old enemy out of International rugby with a superb display of generalship which included a try scored beneath van Wyk's nose. J.B.G. Thomas relished it.

The magical moment came early in the second half. The Lions had crossed over only three points in arrears and attacked from the first whistle that announced the resumption. Unfortunately, O'Reilly was pushed into touch in the right corner and a line-out ordered, at which Higgins fell awkwardly to suffer a severe injury that kept him out for the rest of the tour. His departure from the field of play demanded an increased effort from the remaining seven Lions' for-wards and they did not fail in their task. The ball was won at the next scrum, near the right-hand touch-line, and a good heel enabled Dicky Jeeps, playing like a veteran in his first representative match, to get a long, swift pass away to Morgan.

The Welshman liked to receive the ball from his partner well in front of him so he could run onto it with opponents in his line of sight. Again, like a good outside half, he liked to take the ball at speed in attack to give himself an initial start against back row defenders. He had mastered all this in the years between and with a

[200]

slight outward jink was through the initial line of defence, racing across the Springbok 25 line diagonally with van Wyk chasing after him. He moved round in a great arc, leaning over as he crossed the South African goal-line, to turn in behind the posts as the despairing van Wyk, Morgan's great rival, came thundering up to admit defeat with a sporting smile. Morgan had avenged Wales and had set alight a brilliant piece of attack by the Lions which eventually brought them the greatest victory by any British team abroad.

Fifty-Two Famous Tries. J.G.B. Thomas. Pelham Books.

No apology or explanation is necessary for the inclusion of a second piece by J.B.G. Thomas. Taking into account his thirty-one books, regular columns and match reports in the Western Mail *for half a century, and innumerable contributions to other publications, there can be no doubt that Bryn's output is the most prolific in the history of media rugby coverage. Nor would many people dispute his standing as one who has seen more big matches in more major venues than any other spectator.*

His great respect and affection for New Zealand rugby was founded in the thirties when he watched the Third All Blacks as a youngster. As an objective rugby critic and yet a passionate Welshman he found little to cheer in his country's later exchanges with New Zealand opponents; but there was an unforgettable day in 1953 when his beloved Cardiff beat an All Black side for the first time in their history.

The All Blacks accounted for Cambridge University, London Counties, Oxford University and the Western Counties before crossing the 'Border', as they called the River Severn, into Wales. On arrival they admitted having been given much advice about Welshmen, and had heard the time-honoured forecast 'Wait till you get to Wales'! They won at Stradey Park, defeating Llanelli by 17 points to 3, and in the stand were Cardiff officials and leading players, watching and noting all the weak points in the Tourists' make-up. On return to Cardiff skipper Bleddyn Williams held a council of war and asked his pack leader Sid Judd for two fifths of the ball from the scrum and line out and to try and contain the All Blacks' pack in the loose. On Thursday morning the two teams were announced. Unfortunately Bob Stuart was not fit enough for the back row but the two fastest breakaways Bill Clark and Dave Oliver were played in an attempt to cope with the speedy Cardiff backs. Stuart's absence in this and several succeeding matches was to prove a big handicap to the side.

Haig, a rather slow and cumbersome first five-eighth, took over the captaincy and little did he realise that he was to decide the fate of the match. Cardiff played an all-International threequarter line behind Morgan and Willis, and included the veteran prop-forward Stan Bowes as the corner-stone of the scrum, which was to prove another vital factor. Bleddyn Williams planned his attacks and felt confident that if his forwards could hold the massive and mobile Tourists in front the match could be won – but only just! The morning of the match was fine and the Arms Park was full long before the kick-off to provide the largest crowd ever to watch a Rugby Union match in which a club side was engaged – 55,000. The rich notes of the two National Anthems were lofted high into the November air, and all sang lustily in anticipation of a great match. Then came the thrill of the All Blacks' 'Haka' – war-like and fierce yet very much a part of the special occasion. They won the toss and kicked off towards the Westgate Street end, but in the first minute Welsh hearts were low as the fabulous Bob Scott essayed a penalty shot from the half way line. However, it fell short into the arms of Morgan, who dashed away before kicking to touch, and hinted by so doing that Cardiff were going to attack whenever they had the chance.

After six minutes a scrum was formed on the Cardiff 25 line, a place from where New Zealand did not anticipate a Cardiff attack, but Willis sent Morgan galloping away with his short, snappy strides and when half way through the gap he short-punted. The kick was rather low and ricocheted off a defender into the air. Morgan was beneath it with the speed of a satellite to gather and shoot ahead again. The defence was completely disorganised, for Morgan was supported on each side by eager colleagues. The safe and accurate Alun Thomas was there to take a good pass and then send Rowlands down the right wing, but he had a long way to go! When he got to the All Blacks' 25 line, he kicked high infield towards the posts and there was a scramble on the tourists' line when the ball fell, but the watchful Judd had gathered and fallen over for a try amidst a mass of heaving bodies. Referee Llewellyn came steaming up to award a try when he found Judd on top of the ball over the goal-line. Cardiff had scored, and Dr Rowlands, with the coolness of a surgeon performing an operation, kicked the goal.

New Zealand girded their loins for action following this audacious attack which had pierced their defence. They bulldozed their way into the Cardiff half and, when the home side were penalised for off-side at a loose maul, ace-kicker Jarden relished the opportunity of a long kick at goal. He placed the ball delicately some 50 yards from the posts and near the right-hand touch-line before moving back to line up his shot. He ran and kicked – a superb goal – and the crowd cheered his effort. The real battle was on! Could the Cardiff backs do it again? They answered the call readily, and from a scrummage on the Cardiff 10-yard line the pack got the ball and Willis sent the bobbing Morgan away again. Once more he cut through, before handing on to Bleddyn Williams, who put in a short but well-placed punt with his left foot. The ball bounced perfectly for Alun Thomas as he raced through, and he gathered it with magnetic hands. Thomas was almost up to Scott before the startled All Blacks were fully aware of the danger to their line. As Scott moved in to the tackle Thomas sent a perfect pass, long and swift, to right wing Rowlands. Back went his head as he lengthened his stride, and the sight of defenders diving at his heels over the remaining 30 yards to the goal-line had the vast crowd on its feet yelling like mad!

Rowlands got there for a great try, but he could not convert it. Still, his try meant that the All Blacks would have to score twice to gain the lead. There remained 60 minutes of play and the All Blacks had not really unleashed themselves. Their forward effort was growing in power but their backs, with more of the ball, could not penetrate because Haig was too slow. Once again Morgan went through, only for Rowlands to be grassed ten yards short of the line. Then Rowlands was just wide with a penalty attempt, and the interval came with Cardiff holding on sternly to their five-point lead. The second half opened with a fierce New Zealand onslaught, but Judd and his men were equal to it. They fell and stopped, tackled and rushed, and all the time the crowd roared words of encouragement. It was tensely exciting. Cardiff rallied to attack at intervals and once Bleddyn Williams almost managed to dodge his way over before the All Blacks were back again, Haig going just wide with a drop at goal.

Twenty mintes to go and the effervescing Scott was trapped dealing with a rolling ball from a well-placed kick ahead. Then John Nelson was hurt in saving before the whole weight of the tourists' pack before Alun Thomas relieved with a long and accurate touchfinder. John Llewellyn dropped for goal, Thomas almost crossed in the corner, and the All Blacks must have wondered how they could break out of the vice-like Cardiff grip which halted their fierce forwards and contained their mediocre backs. The end of the match was drawing near and the constant roar of the crowd beat tantalisingly in the ear-drums of the tormented tourists. Bowes was playing above himself, and Collins held Tiny White in the line-out. Willis stood up to all, while Morgan popped the ball back into touch from beneath the very noses and feet of his opponents! Williams, as skipper, was there, ever steady, until there came the last All Black onslaught. Scott, sensing that orthodox methods would fail, proceeded to bombard the Cardiff posts with prodigious drop- and place-kicks. All sailed wide, but one was knocked on by poor Llewellyn at full back.

A desperate scrum followed outside the Cardiff line. 'Risk the penalty,' shouts Judd to Beckingham, 'but get the ball!' Beckingham struck, and won it against the head – never did he win a more vital scrum, and Morgan had cleared to touch! The final whistle went and the roar of approval from the crowd made normal speech impossible. Cardiff had won 8–3. Bleddyn Williams was hoisted up to the broad shoulders of Stan Bowes to head a triumphant procession off the field. The All Blacks were stunned, and at first unable to accept defeat, but they mellowed with the warmth of the occasion as the tension left them, for it had been no ordinary match!

Great Rugger Matches. J.B.G. Thomas. Stanley Paul.

The great Hennie Muller was a major figure in mid-century loose forward play – the 'windhond' South Africa fondly dubbed him for his great speed and the way he hunted down opponents. Very seldom could he be out-paced, even by the sprightliest of backs, and any try scored against a defence which included him had to be a bit special. Such a one was scored by the Wallabies against the Springboks at Cape Town in the Second Test of 1949.

It came from a loose ball, some ten yards from their own goal-line. Brown immediately started a movement and when Solomon came into the lineup to pass to Stapleton the Springboks were in trouble. The big wing ran up to the 10-yard line before giving his partner Garth Jones a pass so perfect that the lanky Queenslander could take

[204]

Hennie Muller (left), the 'windhond', leads out the 1951 Springboks against London Counties led by J.R.C. Matthews. On this occasion the tourists went down to a rare defeat. (*S & G Press Agency Ltd.*)

it without any slackening of his pace. Johny Buchler, the Springbok full back, made the mistake of not trying to force Jones infield where Muller, in full chase, might have had a chance of getting him in his sights.

Instead Jones found himself with a long but clear run to the Springbok line feeling, as he put it afterwards, 'Muller's breath on my neck every inch of the way'.

All along the railway stand side of Newlands the two ran, Muller just too far behind to risk a desperate dive-tackle. Muller was then well past his best, nearly 10 years older than the wing, but he kept pounding after the flying Australian, the gap neither closing nor widening. Finally Jones crossed the line and collapsed behind the posts, completely exhausted. Muller pulled up a few feet behind him, shoulders hunched and knowing for the first time in his Test career what defeat tasted like.

Springbok Saga. Chris Greyvenstein. Nelson & Toyota.

[205]

In the days before International Championship fixtures rotated either Wales or Ireland would frequently be in pursuit of a Triple Crown by the time of their annual March meeting. The frustration of one or the other's hopes would represent pure delight to the opposition as the following report shows. The buoyancy of the writing owes much to unbridled partisanship!

Ireland 11 pts, Wales 3 pts.
We shattered Welsh dreams of winning the Triple Crown yesterday, when Ireland's rejuvenated forwards led our team to a deserved victory by one goal, one dropped goal and one penalty goal to one penalty goal.

The Welsh were shocked – and we were shocked too. Not since 1948–9, when we won 5–0 in Swansea, has Ireland beaten Wales.

Even their most ardent supporters would not have dared to predict beforehand that the Irish fifteen would so completely outplay their opponents in every phase of the play as they did. When Ireland won the first scrum from the supposedly all-star front row of the Merediths and Williams we thought it an accident.

But when Robin Roe got the next two in a row, and went on to win the strike six times out of the first nine scrums, we had to acknowledge that this Irish pack did not intend to allow itself to be knocked about as were its predecessors in the French, English and Scottish games.

Much of the credit for the rejuvenation of our pack must go to Robin Thompson. In line-outs, loose mauls and foot rushes he provided the encouragement, advice and leadership which enabled the Irish pack to play as a unit rather than as eight individuals.

We got a fright after only twelve minutes, when Wales forced a scrum almost on the Irish line. A long pass from Brace out to an eager Morgan – but too eager, for to our whole-hearted relief it slipped through his fingers.

Yes, Kyle's immaculate drop-goal will certainly never be forgotten but for me neither will that fumble of his in the twenty-ninth minute.

There he was, neck-and-neck with O'Reilly as they raced up the centre. Only Owen to beat and the crowd already cheering the first score of the game. Owen goes for the red-haired giant, the ball goes to Kyle, but with a heart-breaking fumble Jack dashed our hopes.

With the score 3–3 it was a tonic to see Cecil Pedlow send that kick high and clear between the posts.

A sickening feeling came upon us as the stretcher was called for

Tim McGrath ten minutes from time as he lay concussed in the arms of Kyle. Would Wales even yet take the honours? But no – Tim refused to rest on the line, and played a gallant part to the end of his first International appearance.

All praise then to our eight forwards who gave of their best for the full eighty minutes. They did Trojan work and every ounce of weight was used to telling effect. If I must select one for special mention it is not to be taken as a reflection on the performance of his team-mates.

I feel, however, that it would be most unfair to let Marney Cunningham's outstanding display at wing forward pass without comment. The Cork Constitution man, in my opinion, gave the greatest performance of his career and it was only fitting, therefore, that he should have scored the single try of the match.

His coverage of the field, his handling and tackling placed him on a par with McKay and McCarthy of our Triple Crown era.

Readers who were not privileged to see yesterday's game – and many of my own friends failed to secure tickets for the occasion – will get some picture of Cunningham's seeming omnipresence when I tell them that his score came from a movement which he himself initiated. He got the ball away smartly to Kyle from a line-out on the Welsh twenty-five yard line and was up to take the out half's return.

What a thrill it was as we waited to see whether his dive through the tackles of two defenders had carried him over the line and what a cheer went up as referee Dickie signalled a score.

Probably the next greatest thrill after Cunningham's try was Kyle's beautifully-taken dropped goal. Garfield Owen, the Welsh full back, who otherwise had an excellent game, marked an Irish cross-kick about ten yards short of his own line just after the interval. His subsequent kick failed to find touch.

Jack Kyle coolly fielded the ball, ran about two yards infield to get a better angle, and calmly dropped a goal with his left foot to balance the penalty goal kicked by Owen in the closing stages of the first half.

The Sunday Press, 1956. Jack Arigho.

Constant scrutiny by television cameras, exposing it to a far wider and less partisan audience, has revealed the Varsity match to be, fairly often, as pedestrian as a midweek club match in April. The will to entertain is frequently obliterated by the will to win; and moreover the experience of appearing at Twickenham can play havoc with youthful nerves and composure.

However, Oxbridge does come up with the goods from time to time, when the spectacle provided is as exhilarating as can be imagined. Sometimes, as in rugby generally, this is because of one team's overwhelming superiority – as in the 1934–35 season.

Cambridge University 29 pts, Oxford University 4 pts.
Cambridge did it. They cut loose at Twickenham and picked Oxford up and threw them down and tore them to pieces and beat them by two goals, a dropped goal, a penalty goal and four tries to a dropped goal.

A smashing victory by a great team. The swing of the pendulum, also, for this is the first Cambridge win since 1928.

Oxford started well enough with steady pressure and sound scrummaging. For twenty-five minutes they held the upper hand, and only the critically-minded observed that the ball was being passed away from the scrum so slowly that it might have been a lump of lead.

Those lobbed, sluggish passes were fatal. The Oxford attack was smothered, and then Fyfe laid bare another weakness. He ran like a lamplighter to score a glorious try, and to the horror of Oxford spectators he left Warr standing.

Oxford were vulnerable beyond a doubt. From that moment, whenever the ball flashed out to the Cambridge left wing, Oxford supporters groaned and turned their faces away. The centres might tackle like heroes, the forwards might scrummage like giants, but the Oxford attack was paralysed and there were loopholes in the Oxford defence. With that the post-mortem is complete. Lobbed passes from the scrummage, weak tackling on the wings, and the corpse of Oxford rugby is plain for all to see.

The task of praising Cambridge is altogether more congenial. How superbly the whole team played! We watched with admiration the steadily growing ascendancy of their forwards, the tremendous dash of the burly Dinwiddy, the sinewy Rees, of Lord and Bowman and Leather in the loose.

We noted the swift neatness of Browning at scrum half and the dancing menace of little Jones behind him. Jones has a secure place

The Varsity Match: sometimes the will to entertain is obliterated by the will to win. But Oxbridge does come up with the goods from time to time, when the spectacle can be exhilarating. (*Colorsport.*)

among the great 'Varsity match players. Oxford nursemaids will cow their charges with threats of his quicksilver attack for many years to come.

Then that siege-gun dropped goal of Wooller's from near the half-way line, there is a memory for us, and the deftness of Candler, and Fyfe's stabbing attack, which brought him three great tries. A grand footballer, Fyfe, with his balanced running and his short, pugnacious strides for the line.

I never saw a larger crowd for this great game. Even the north stand was well filled and thousands stood in the enclosures under the grey and threatening sky.

The breeze rippled Lorraine's handkerchief, as he held it up in midfield, and decided that Oxford should start with the wind behind them. Even the most placid of spectators must have felt a stir of excitement as Fyfe kicked off for Cambridge, and the first roar came swelling from the crowd. Away went Oxford hammer and tongs, and Guy was breaking clear until Rees stopped him, and Bowman and Leather came back with the ball at their feet.

A neat run by Candler, a balloon kick by Wooller, a touch down by Grieve, and then Oxford drove steadily to the attack. Guy, again, slipping away from the scrummage – where was that Cambridge back row? – a strong burst by Cranmer and another by Bush, but once more Leather dribbled out of danger.

Ten minutes – fifteen – twenty – we gasped as Wooller went striding through, we yelled as Lorraine shot away up the centre, with Cranmer outside him to take a pass. Cranmer kicked ahead, the ball dropped over the line and Oxford lost the touch-down by inches beneath a smother of players.

Mostly Oxford so far, but suddenly Cambridge heeled, the ball whipped across, and Fyfe leaped into his stride and was pounding for the line. Past Warr he went, past Cranmer, into the arms of the plucky Grieve. 'He's over!' we shouted, and so he was with Grieve hanging round his knees, a magnificently determined try.

Three points to Cambridge, but a minute later, after a scrummage on the Cambridge 25 Guy passed to Bush, and Bush – why, bless my soul, he's going to drop a goal! A check, a moment of doubt, a Cambridge player leaping, Bush's left foot swinging, and the ball flew high and true between the posts.

After that Cranmer drove Cambridge back again and again with vast punts down the wind, until Oxford in desperate defence were penalised near their own line for failing to play the ball. In ominous silence Parker kicked a goal, and Cambridge held their slender two-point lead until the interval.

Not much in it, but how about that wind? Cambridge had it now, and Jones and Wooller used it with long and deadly kicks to touch. Up the field worked Cambridge. Oxford took a scrum at the line out and, most bitter irony, Cambridge heeled. Out went the ball, across to the left wing, and there was Fyfe handing off Warr and bouncing over as Lorraine tried valiantly to hold him up.

A disaster for Oxford, and another followed quickly. A swift heel from a loose scrum and Jones twisted and slid through the scattered defence and passed out to Candler. Like a flash Candler was off, with Jones inside him to take a perfect pass and score under the posts. Pretty work, and a goal by Parker drove the blow home. Oxford tried to rally but Cambridge had tasted blood, and before long Rees leaped for the ball at the line-out, and flopped over for another try.

This was disaster for Oxford, and Fyfe rubbed it in when Cranmer and Warr both obligingly concentrated on Wooller and allowed Fyfe a clear run behind the posts, whereupon the merciless Parker kicked another goal. Cambridge were all confidence now, as Wooller proved a moment later when he gaily took a drop from near half way, and with amazing power sent the ball sailing high over the cross-bar. What a kick that was, to be sure, but Cambridge by then had battered the life out of the game.

What did it matter that Oxford had moved Grieve up to stand off half and changed Bush to full back? What did it matter that Oxford were still fighting, still capable of the last frenzied plunges and rushes of a firmly-hooked fish? Cambridge had won, and Johnson underlined the fact in the last minute when he handed off Rees-Jones with almost contemptuous ease, and raced over in the corner.

It was time then for Oxford men to collect the remnants of their pride, and congratulate their Cambridge friends upon a glorious victory.

Daily Telegraph, 1934. Howard Marshall.

After two or three dour seasons the 1955 Varsity match was another which reassured onlookers that rugby could trail clouds of glory in its wake. The season brought together two gifted and exceedingly creative Oxford half backs who were given their head by the skipper Roy Allaway; and the virtuoso performances through the autumn build-up of Messrs M.J.K. Smith and D.O. Brace tended to overshadow the capabilities of the Cambridge side being welded together by Jeff Clement.

On the day, therefore, cavalier Oxford were everybody's favourites. But the Light Blue roundheads nearly laughed last.

Oxford University 9 pts, Cambridge University 5 pts.
The University Rugby match came back into its own this afternoon as a great sporting fixture. It was an admirable game from many points of view; it was full of incident and variety, and its closeness, with one side always within striking distance of the other, kept a crowd in the region of 50,000 in a perpetual roar and chatter of excitement....

... For a while it seemed that the Cambridge pack might pin down Oxford so completely that they would find little running space. Suddenly, however, after the Cambridge try Oxford found themselves, and in the second and third quarters of the game they went through all manner of dangerous and attractive evolutions while Cambridge could do little more than tackle, tackle, tackle – which they did, of course, uniformly well.

It was the Oxford style of play that made and earned their success, but if one man more than another was the match-winner, I take him to be Smith.

He caught everything flung at him, at whatever range and angle; backed up not only Brace but whoever had the ball with the surest instinct for position; and was equally much on hand in defence. His kicking sent back the Cambridge forwards forty yards and more at a time, and when he saw the ghost of an opening he leaped at it with a notable turn of speed.

Brace has brought out the best in Smith, certainly, but he is a highly-accomplished all-round footballer on his own account. The one fault in his repertoire at present, and it is a vital thing, is a tendency to slow down before passing on to the first centre.

Taking the match as a whole the one basic weakness seemed to be a general failure on the part of the backs to pass at top speed on the straightening stride. This was even more true of Cambridge than of Oxford and was responsible for their most dangerous man, A.R. Smith, being starved of chances. . . .

. . . On a mild afternoon with a brisk north-westerly wind coming over their right shoulders Cambridge began the game with a hot and prolonged assault. The uncontrolled frenzy that marks the beginning of most University matches was conspicuous by its absence.

Soon Mulligan was coolly working the blind side and almost sending A.R. Smith in. It was ten minutes before Oxford briefly got a footing in the Cambridge half and a quarter of an hour before M.J.K. Smith's long boot put the Cambridge line in danger. When Cambridge thrust back and won a scrum on the Oxford line, Richards had a hurried shot at a dropped goal which, from only ten yards' range, flew under the bar.

Oxford, though hard-pressed, had not been afraid to throw the ball about close to their own line, and it was this spirit which after twenty-three minutes gave Cambridge their chance. Brace, running towards the blind-side touch-line, tried to slip the ball to Walker closely marked by Kershaw.

It bounced indeed into Kershaw's hands and he went straight and fast to the corner, earning additional marks by clamping the ball under his arm and declining to touch down until he had dodged his way around behind the posts. Thus Hetherington had the easiest of goal-kicks.

It was Oxford, rather than Cambridge, who seemed transformed by this happening. Two lovely movements closely followed one another, the ball being passed in each case through more hands than could be noted down, however hard one tried to memorise the numbers on the backs.

Brace and Smith were involved, need it be said, both times and so were half a dozen forwards. The halves were foxing Cambridge by the most baffling changes of direction, but the opposition were up quickly on to their men and their back row now began the tireless chase that ended only with the final whistle.

Five minutes before half time Brace feinted towards the open side before sending away Smith on the other. Smith made great speed through a converging gap, and on arriving at Hetherington somewhere about the 25 punted over his head.

It looked a probable score until Smith was seen to be baulked by Hetherington. By the time two Cantabs had thrown themselves on the ball a foot or two ahead of the nearest Oxonian over the goal-line the whistle had gone for a penalty. Currie kicked the goal from half way out, and it was eminently right that he should have done so.

Morally the referee might have been inclined to award a penalty try, but the law says such may not be given unless, but for the illegality, a try would 'undoubtedly' have been obtained. As it was, another penalty to Oxford before half time came near to putting them in the lead, Prodger's kick, almost from half way, failing by a few feet only.

The Cambridge try had come from an Oxford mistake and just before half time we had the reverse procedure. Cambridge, moving somewhat ponderously in midfield, dropped the ball and Reeler fastened onto it and sent Walker away with some forty yards to go. The wing swept round Hetherington with a fine burst of speed and finally hurled himself for the line by the corner.

Prodger, from touch, could not convert, but now came the very best of Oxford, so that the crowd was frequently in laughter as Brace and Smith feinted, and twisted, and turned, almost always finding someone to pass to in the end.

It was a scissors to Smith that sent him off once again with Hetherington barring his way. This time Hetherington smothered the kick ahead, but Fallon quickly gathered, and while Cambridge were recovering position sent away Reeler who, with much determination, burst for the line and though pulled down just short summoned the momentum to bounce over.

Another misconversion, and the loss of Fallon, kept Cambridge hoping. Robbins was brought out of the scrum into the centre, whereupon until the end Hodgson came increasingly into the picture. There was still some furious scrummaging on the Oxford line to withstand before, with both sides pretty well all in, a gallant game was over.

Daily Telegraph. E.W. Swanton.

'Subdue and penetrate' is the All Black slogan, and as long as the subduing is going on their rugby tends to be effective but without frills or thrills. When they are satisfied, however, that the time is right to cut loose New Zealanders can play a rhythmic and flowing style of rugby that is entrancing to watch. That was how the 1963–64 tourists swept the Barbarians to destruction in their final tour game by an emphatic 36 points to 3.

And that was how they captured the imagination of Richard Evans when the All Blacks played London Counties at Twickenham. For a prop forward, skipper Wilson Whineray had a marvellous vision of how the handling game was meant to be played. London were behind as the second half began.

A few minutes later Whineray made the decision that brought about the finest period of sustained cut-and-thrust running Twickenham has ever seen from a touring side. He told me afterwards how he had weighed up the risks involved if he opened out in a final, carefree onslaught. Such tactics, of course, leave a side open to innumerable mistakes if passes start going astray. 'But I calculated that even if they scored two tries and converted both, we would still be in front,' explained Whineray, 'so I decided to have a go.' Rugby football will ever be in Wilson Whineray's debt for that decision. It is true that the risk was not all that great, but I know several captains who would have opted for a safer path to victory – especially if they still carried the battle scars of a tough campaign in Wales. But not Whineray. Making good his pledge to play attacking rugby wherever possible, he stode over to Herewini after the little fly half had slammed the ball straight back into touch from a line out and issued strict instructions that such tactics must cease.

Never has a captain's call been more magnificently answered. From the very next loose heel the ball sped out down the line in a movement that showed superb contempt for the All Blacks' technically defensive position. But defence was a word that had suddenly been wiped out of their vocabulary, and by the time Dick took Little's pass, the half way line had been crossed. In fact, as well as in spirit, the All Blacks were now truly on the attack. I shall never forget the sight when Dick cross-kicked into the middle. It was a moment for the rugby connoisseur to savour like a rare wine. As the ball floated across the pitch the entire All Black pack were splayed out across the field in perfect formation bearing down on the London line and the remnants of a scattered defence.

How the tourists failed to score I shall never know, but an unlucky bounce, a despairing grasp by a ragged white shirt and a hefty boot into touch somehow stemmed the tide. Like the ocean taking a deep and fearful breath before each pounding wave of destruction, they withdrew to a suitable vantage point from which to launch the next offensive. This time there was to be no mistake; Clarke came up into the line as Young heeled just inside his own half and, waiting just long enough to draw a man, put Little through the gap his appearance had created. Little is not the most gainly runner in the world but he had already done enough in this match to make us realise why he had risen to fame in Auckland's Ranfurly Shield team. Now he did more than that. He gave the critical members of the Press box a special close-up of himself at full throttle. Someone murmured something about an express train, and indeed it was no time to quibble over clichés. The description fits as well as any and better than most. Little steamed past us in a magnificent burst of powerful running that carved a yawning wound in the Counties' defence, and then calmly handed on to Dick for the wing to run in unopposed. Mindful of the difficulties Clarke had been in with his goal-kicking, Dick ran on round behind the posts to give the full back the easiest of angles from which to convert. But Clarke, his appetite whetted, was not content with a mere two points. It was less than three minutes before Nathan dug another wicked claw into London's wound.

Once again the lithe, dark figure thrust his way through hapless defenders and slung out a pass to the left just inside the twenty-five. A try for Smith? Not this time. For it was Clarke, roaring up from full back, who exploded on to the ball and flung his seventeen-stone frame over the line with frightening velocity.

Clarke on the turn in defence may not be the fastest sight on a rugby field, but there is no denying the speed this giant produces from seemingly immobile legs when he is going forward in a gear his particular model was never meant for.

The conversion, high, straight and true, was one of Clarke's touch-line specials and an eleven point lead had suddenly swollen to twenty-one. The crowd were beginning to catch the All Blacks' mood and, throwing aside their partisan feelings, they joined the little band of gleeful New Zealanders, who had been waving a stuffed Kiwi on top of a pole throughout the match, in cheering the All Blacks at every turn. It was a non-stop, one-way path to glory for the tourists now, as they turned on a brand of rugby that had Twickenham's blasé clientele perched on the edge of their seats.

Next it was Nathan who went over from a line-out and the crowd, little knowing that there were even greater things to come from this incredible forward, applauded him all the way back to the centre line. There were only three minutes left by then, and as London made ground from the kick-off we prepared for the final whistle. But Nathan and his colleagues had other ideas. Again he tugged, heaved, and finally broke clear of the line-out – this time in his own half – and passed on to a forward in support. Almost slowly it seemed the movement gathered momentum – another pass, another spurt, another white shirt left groping at nothing. The half way line was reached and left behind. Someone slung a pass around Whineray's ankles and that, we thought, must be the end of it. But I do not think there was an All Black capable of dropping a pass at the precise moment. They had, for a fleeting moment in time, touched a zenith of shattering brilliance which no team achieves more than twice in a whole decade. Everything they touched turned to gold, and Whineray of course bent fifteen stones of muscle and bone with the ease of a ballet dancer, and scooped the ball delicately off his toes to keep the action flowing.

Two more passes and Nathan appeared on the scene again to finish off what he had started by diving over the line as the crowd roared with incredulous delight.

Had eight men handled? Ten? Twelve? Some wag announced solemnly that it was seventeen, and certainly from an impressionist point of view it was a fair estimate. It had been a try in a million, and it provided the perfect climax to an unforgettable display from the New Zealanders.

Whineray's All Blacks. Richard Evans. Pelham Books.

Only one provincial side, Transvaal, defeated the 1968 British Isles side in South Africa, but the Test series was lost three-nil with one drawn game. However, there is no doubt that the loss of key players cost the Lions a better record, fifteen of the party suffering more or less serious injuries. Hence the Test series was an uphill struggle from the outset, with the first-choice stand off half Barry John breaking a collar bone.

This match report is lovingly thorough, and is moreover wholly in the present tense, which gives it a memorable immediacy and even breathlessness.

It is a lovely afternoon with no hint of a breeze as the dapper Max Baise, who, predictably, had been selected by the Lions management as referee, signals to the British team that Visagie is about to kick off. The ball is scrambled into touch and a roar erupts as Du Preez, rising high to take left wing Dirksen's throw-in cleanly, holds the ball and traps O'Shea offside. A penalty from 38 yards in the opening minute! Surprisingly, because he has an aversion to taking kicks any closer in than 45 yards, Tiny Naude is called upon. With his stabbing action he kicks more ground than ball and groans greet this lost opportunity.

The ball goes into touch again, with Savage to throw in, and there it is – the short line-out. Only Young, McBride and Stagg lining up against Pitzer, Naude and Du Preez as the other Springbok forwards trot back ten yards.

A thrill in the form of a narrow shave for the Lions follows in the eighth minute. Ellis wins a line-out inside the Lions' 25 and little Olivier comes into the fly-half position to take the pass from de Villiers. He weaves his way through on the inside of Edwards and John and the surprise nature of the move all but succeeds. Kiernan, however, is alert and stops Olivier just in front of the line; and though Ellis picks up and crosses the ball has been propelled forward.

Visagie is off target with a drop and the Lions show their teeth for the first time with the Irishmen, Bresnihan and Doyle, linking from broken play and it is de Villiers (he gets through an enormous amount of covering for a scrum half) who relieves the pressure.

The three-man line-out is not proving the success hoped for and

Du Preez tears away after a clean catch to flatten Turner. The ball comes back to Visagie who, with Engelbrecht outside him, runs into the Lions' 25 before kicking over the line – a well-placed kick indeed. The ball tantalisingly eludes both the fly-half and Engelbrecht and Bresnihan touches down.

The Springboks are looking the more purposeful side but that early score has eluded them and it is John who, with the flair which distinguishes the true footballer from the journeyman, suddenly threatens danger. The Springboks are slow to react when the trim little fly half taps a penalty to himself in his own half and, going through the motions of passing, dummies his way past five or six opponents. Had John let out at the right time he might well have initiated a Lions score besides avoiding the cruel fate which was to keep him on the sidelines for the rest of the tour.

John holds on too long and, close to the South African 25, is upended by Ellis, covering back, who makes something of a desperation high tackle. John comes down sickeningly on his left shoulder and has to leave the field to a sympathetic hush – his left collar-bone fractured. This misfortune strikes the Lions in the fifteenth minute. Turner moves to fly half and Taylor comes out of the pack to play centre.

Then, in the eighteenth minute, first blood to South Africa. Kiernan, turning defence into attack as he catches a forlorn attempt at a drop by Engelbrecht, makes ground and kicks ahead. Gould is in a position to check but a loose scrum forms and a Lions forward goes offside. Only Naude has the range to attempt a kick at goal from this distance, close on sixty yards with the angle to the left, and referee Baise signals the touch-judges to the posts. The big lock forward lashes into the ball and pandemonium breaks out as the flags go up.

Meanwhile Mike Gibson is warming up in the dressing room to replace John. Four minutes later South Africa go into a 6–0 lead. Arneil is penalised for not releasing the ball in a ruck just outside his own 25 and Visagie's kick is straight and true.

Bravely the fourteen Lions fight back and close the gap to a single point with an unexpected goal in the twenty-sixth minute – unexpected because the score stems from a Springbok blunder. The Springboks are under pressure in front of their posts, but the ball is passed back to Dirksen who has ample time to clear to touch. Instead the stocky left-wing tries to run past Savage, is well and truly scragged and flings the ball carelessly behind him. Next thing the Lions forwards are onto it and the tigerish McBride has dived over midway out. Kiernan takes a lot of care with the kick; it is good; and the 'Reds' are back in business.

At last, in the thirty-first minute, Gibson runs onto the field to make history as international rugby's first replacement – he had been the first player to be replaced in the opening game at Potchefstroom.

De Villiers, playing splendidly and putting his critics to shame, breaks sharply from a line-out but his inside pass near the line is knocked down. The Springboks are having several tantalising near misses.

However, before Gibson can make any impact, South Africa stretch their lead to 11–5 after 33 minutes with an unusually simple try at Test level. At a line-out fifteen yards from the Lions' line Arneil sins by tapping back, away from Edwards, and Naude bounds through to collect on the bounce and crashes over in a fair position for Visagie to convert. As if to balance this blow fortune smiles on the Lions four minutes later. Kiernan is well short with a penalty from beyond his range but the ball dips and shoots forward off Ellis's boot. Dirksen, in front of Ellis, plays the ball from a palpably offside position and Kiernan places the goal to make it 11–8.

Mistakes abound in this unusual Test in which the Lions' persistence with a three-man line-out tends to loosen up the play. Another minute and it is the Lions' turn to err expensively.

The culprit this time is Bresnihan who, receiving the ball at outside centre on his 10-yards line, hesitates fatally in making up his mind. He is crash-tackled by Nomis and Engelbrecht picks up the loose ball to feed Olivier. The centre intelligently cuts inside to link with Bedford who commits Kiernan and sends de Villiers away with an outside pass for the scrum half to touch down at the posts – his first try in Test rugby. The conversion by Visagie is a formality and the score-board changes to 16–8.

The game moves into the second minute of injury time. A centre field scrum goes down on the South African 25, the Lions hook and hold and an impetuous Olivier strays offside. Kiernan kicks the goal from right in front and the Lions, trailing 11–16, are still in with a fighting chance at half time.

The Lions forwards, up to now, have not been outclassed, though no-one has matched Greyling in getting at speed to the breakdown point. Stagg has often got the ball back from the truncated line-out, but usually by means of a deflection which ends the line-out and enables the Springbok forwards to come through and put Edwards under pressure. The Lions take the initiative on the re-start, Gould being uncertain when tested with high kicks. It is against the run of play that South Africa, in the twelfth minute, regain an eight-points lead. Mr Baise demonstrates vigorously with his elbows at a line-out just inside the British 25 and Visagie, from 35 yards, splits the uprights with a beautiful kick.

The Springbok backs, enjoying a better service from their forwards, are the more enterprising. Olivier is a constant threat from broken play. Visagie, too, is playing with far more assurance than customary, but when Kiernan stumbles and the Bok forwards ruck the ball back the fly-half errs in kicking for Engelbrecht, who is just beaten by Richards in a desperate race to the touchdown. Visagie is also at fault in trying a drop from another quick heel with his line poised to strike.

However, the nineteenth minute brings a remarkable try by Frik Du Preez, the likes of which one has not seen in twenty years of Test rugby coverage. Myburgh wins a line-out ten yards outside the Lions' 25 on the left-hand side and slips the ball to Du Preez instead of feeding back. Executing a planned move the big, black-haired lock puts his head down and, shoulders hunched to offer less of a tackling target, he bursts round the front with the ball tucked under his left arm.

Savage reaches out with his right hand in a strictly token gesture and Edwards, with a desperate lunge, also cannot get to the flying Frik. Now only Kiernan bars the way to the try-line and he might as well have tried to stop a locomotive going at full speed. Frik swerves past the full back before curving in to dive over the line. It is a try which has the indelible stamp of greatness and, though Visagie is unable to convert, the Springboks, up 22–11, seem home and dry. The Springbok forwards show their appreciation of Frik's effort by 'walking' with their opponents from a scrum inside the South African 25. But it is not all over yet. Ellis comes up too quickly at a short line-out to be ruled offside and Kiernan kicks a fine goal from a difficult angle – 22–14.

The Springbok forwards are a far superior force in breaking into the open field and a controversial ruling deprives the side of a try in the twenty-eighth minute which would have sewn up the result. Visagie, with one of his long, relieving kicks, finds touch inside the

Lions' half. Kiernan, throwing in to himself, flings out a long ball to his centres. Bresnihan, having an unhappy day, fumbles and Olivier picks up to feed the ever-present Bedford on his inside. With Kiernan out of position the number eight runs 30 yards to dive over exultantly. But the flag of Mr Mide Odendaal, the South African touch-judge, is up and Mr Baise brings play back for a line-out.

Mr Odendaal later contended that it was South Africa's throw-in and not Kiernan's. But Mr Wouter du Toit (chairman of the South African Rugby Referees' Society) maintained that it was in the referee's power to play advantage and that Mr Baise should have over-ruled the touch-judge and awarded a try.

Be that as it may, the amazing Kiernan lands his fourth penalty – a 45-yarder from a nasty angle – in the thirty-first minute to pull South Africa back to 22–17.

Not to be outdone Naude replies with a magnificent penalty-kick from just inside the half-way line and ten yards in from touch. It carries comfortably and from kicking-point to pitch must have travelled sixty-five yards, With seven minutes plus injury time left South Africa, leading 25–17, are surely safe.

With a couple of minutes left Kiernan once more raises the flags by placing his fifth goal from a line-out penalty.

This last effort came too late to save the Test for the Lions, but it gave their captain a personal best of seventeen points out of twenty and put him within one point of Don Clarke's eighteen points (six penalties) for New Zealand in the first Test at Carisbrooke, Dunedin, in the 1955 series against the Lions.

The Lion Tamers. A.C. Parker. Bailey Bros. & Swinfen.

The 1971 Lions left for New Zealand in the usual unheralded way, virtually cold-shouldered by all but the media's specialists and doomed, they were assured, to a fate like that suffered by their 1966 predecessors who were whitewashed 4–0 by the All Blacks in the Test series. The fact that John Dawes's side confounded its critics had much to do with ability and skills, but great courage and an indomitable will to win were also demonstrated from the outset. The tourists' number eight forward recalls the vital First Test.

They say that ten thousand spectators were locked out at Dunedin on the day when, for only the third time in history, the British Isles won a Test match on New Zealand soil and, like their predecessors in Ivor Jones's year, went one-up in the series. Forty eight thousand people, though, did see McLauchlan score a try and Barry John kick two penalties, to which the All Blacks could reply only with a McCormick penalty goal. Those, however, are just the statistics. What the score-line does not reveal is that for Merv the Swerve and probably fourteen other Lions this was the hardest, most demanding game of a lifetime.

Let me admit frankly that we spent much of it with our backs to the wall. Some of New Zealand's giants of recent years like Tremain, Gray, and my number eight rival Brian Lochore had retired. But their successors on 26 June 1971 were cast in true All Black mould and just as furiously did they hurl themselves in dark, rolling waves at our try-line. But somehow, for eighty long minutes, the thin red barrier held. Somehow? It was sheer bravery and guts that pulled us through, for in most aspects of the play we were well-nigh annihilated. But the word had gone round: 'They shall not pass.' So, time and time again, big men like Sutherland, Meads or Muller would thunder their way towards the target, only to be stopped in their tracks by superb tackling. John P.R. Williams stood out, but nobody dodged his duty and even Barry John never shrank from pitting his eleven stones against the bulk of forwards almost twice his weight. Chico Hopkins, too, who came onto the field when Gareth Edwards's hamstring muscle became too painful for him to continue, also covered himself in glory.

Although I found the savagery of the New Zealand assault awesome, I must say that in one way this was my kind of game. One good tackle gives me more pleasure than ten tries, so I reckon I enjoyed myself to the extent of a thousand tries at Dunedin! Always on hand were Dixon and Taylor, and never has a defensive trio in which I played got through quite so much hard work.

People say that the Lions abandoned their free-running approach that day and took refuge in ten-man rugby. That may be true: but we simply had to. Our possession ratio was, I suspect, the lowest of the series, and most of the time Barry and Gareth were having to use the ball to kick us out of trouble. Before the Test we had demonstrated one rugby virtue which we possessed – the capacity to attack, attack and attack once more. Now, under huge pressure, we had shown that we could also defend, defend and defend again.

New Zealand's captain Colin Meads was quick to call at our

changing-room afterwards to congratulate us on our win, but deep inside he must have been baffled beyond measure at his team's inability to capitalise on their superiority around the field and score more points than the Lions. One obvious reason was the way Barry John's tactical kicking had made McCormick look a monkey all afternoon, unsettling him so much that his place-kicking was below par and he missed chances which could have tied the scores. But if Colin had taken the trouble to ask the delighted Doug Smith or Carwyn James or John Dawes, they could have told him the real difference between the sides: the will to win of the 1971 British Lions. We had taken everything New Zealand could throw at us and emerged with heads held high.

Number Eight. Mervyn Davies. Pelham Books.

A disallowed try in the final moments of the last Test cost the 1974 British Lions a hundred per cent record in South Africa. There follows the testimony of the 'scorer', Irish flanker Fergus Slattery, disappointed but typically philosophical about the referee's decision – the kind of attitude that keeps Rugby Football a balanced game with its feet on the ground.

Chris Ralston took a clean catch in the line-out and the ball seemed to move slowly across to the left wing until J.P.R. Williams joined in. I had noticed the angle of his approach and went outside to the left of him. Williams was checked near the posts and I called for the ball, but had to stop to take it. From almost a standing position I checked inside to the right towards the posts off my left foot. Piet Cronje was almost standing on the line but I did not have the time or flexibility to change as one would have wanted. There was only a space of a few yards and I had to go into Cronje and hit him with my shoulder. Unfortunately my momentum was not strong enough. He fell back onto his backside and I fell into him with the ball in my hands.

I then pulled the ball down my chest between his and my legs to ground the ball, lying half on top of him. As I was about to ground the ball I remember Paul Bayvel, South Africa's scrum half, screaming, 'He hasn't touched it. No try, no try! He hasn't touched it!'

Not for a second did I ever consider I had not scored a fair try. I never heard the referee – Max Baise – blow the whistle, and it was

only from the reaction of those around me that I knew the try had not been given. Cronje got up on his feet and said: 'I am sorry about that.' Baise was unfortunately behind Cronje's back and not in a good position to judge whether I had scored a fair try or not.

The vast majority of referees' decisions are right, and you must abide by them even if they are wrong. You must also realise that, in the modern game, television can detect what a referee cannot see. It is very easy to criticise later but if one wants to put the microscope to anything one can always find fault.

'Triple Crown Baby' by Fergus Slattery from *How The Lions Won*
edited by Terry O'Connor. Collins.

For the most part denied possession by bigger, better-drilled packs, British Isles sides overseas have been hard put to offer gifted back divisions the chance to run at their opponents. From time to time, however, moments of sheer magic have been produced by Lions sides – and not only the winning ones of 1971 and 1974. This score witnessed in the last Test of the 1959 tour in New Zealand delighted Vivian Jenkins, not least because it was one of three in a game where New Zealand's only scores were penalties kicked by Don Clarke.

So to the third try, in the twenty-fourth minute of the half, and once again it was stamped with a quality and panache that tempts one to raptures.

Mulligan, again, was the prime mover, Risman the final executant, and both played their parts to perfection. From a scrum near the left-hand touch-line, thirty-five yards out, the British Isles heeled. Mulligan, as he so often did with Horrocks-Taylor at Cambridge, ran right to the open side of the field, then slipped a reverse pass behind his back to Risman. The fly-half, with the All Blacks' back-row defence hoodwinked, switched to the blind side and found it wide open. Ten, fifteen yards he ran unopposed, then came the coverers, panting and blowing to wipe out their error. Risman, in an inspired moment, beat the first man across with a dream of a sidestep, just the shade of a fraction of a veer, and was off hot foot

OPPOSITE: Fergus Slattery, in the green jersey of Ireland, covering for dear life against France: 'The vast majority of referees' decisions are right and you must abide by them even if they are wrong.' (*Colorsport.*)

for the line with half the All Blacks' side on his heels and breathing, it seemed, right down his neck. Where he found the speed from I know not, but he did, and a final triumphant dive took him clear of the last pursuer and over the line for a try.

Lions Down Under. Vivian Jenkins. Cassell.

After ten minutes of a match between Ireland and England at Lansdowne Road, a visiting forward threw a punch which dropped an Irish forward cold – whereupon a colleague of the victim retaliated and within seconds the two packs were beating the living daylights out of each other. Only with difficulty did the referee, a Welshman, quell the tumult.

He first delivered the father-and-mother of rockets to the Irishman who had swung the second punch and warned him that the next offence would earn him marching orders. At length he turned to the Englishman, who had by now cooled down and stood resigned to his fate.

'As for you,' he said, 'no doubt you're expecting a sending-off. No such luck. I've got a better punishment for you. This game at Dublin, with the Irish pack now very fired up, still has seventy minutes to run. And you are staying on the pitch.'

If Risman was a cat-burglar on that occasion – like Cliff Jones, Barry John, Ollie Campbell and their ilk – other scorers reached the try-line like smash-and-grab thieves: Gareth Edwards and Waka Nathan spring to mind. Another category of individual scorers is the confidence tricksters, who advertise their intention of making for the line and then defy the arm of the law to halt them: think of Obolensky, Sharp, Hancock, and Jackson.

Other great and memorable tries have been team efforts, owing more to endurance and collective skills than the dynamism of one individual. Such was the movement finished off by J.P.R. Williams for the Barbarians against the All Blacks in 1973. From line-out to touch-down it took some ninety seconds.

The movement that Mike Slemen climaxed with a try for the British Isles at Potchefstroom in 1980 lasted longer: one minute and thirty-six seconds to be precise, the ball being handled thirty-two times.

[226]

John O'Driscoll palmed it back from the end of the line-out, and scrum half Colin Patterson, who had a brilliant game, spun it away to David Richards, who darted upfield. Flankers O'Driscoll, breaking from the line-out, and Gareth Williams were in support and when they were stopped Quinnell eventually got the ball away and Patterson took it to the left to Richards, who missed out Woodward to get the ball more quickly to Mike Slemen on the left wing, and full back Bruce Hay.

Hay was caught by scrum half Serfontein, another ruck formed, and again Patterson got the ball back. This time Richards moved play to the right, on to Woodward, to Quinnell, to Renwick, and finally to Rees out near the touchline. Rees's path was blocked thirty yards out, so he cut infield and was stopped on the twenty-five. For the third time in this single movement Quinnell was at hand to dig the ball out, this time seemingly from half the opposition's forwards.

Patterson moved to the left, towards the main grandstand, passed on to Richards, on to Woodward, who ran to his right and then raced back left before being tackled by left wing Timothy Nkonki, one of two non-whites in the Invitation XV.

Slemen pounced on the loose ball as a man pounces on his hat after it has been blown off on a windy day, and passed infield to Gareth Williams who, once tackled, had to release the ball.

The ball ran loose and Nkonki hacked it upfield. In fact, it looked as though the Invitation XV would take play to the other end. But Richards swooped from somewhere to flick the ball up to Jim Renwick. The inspiration was with the Lions now, for whereas normally Renwick would probably have kicked for touch – there wasn't a team-mate behind him – this time he decided to have a tilt at the opposition, as he would in Sevens. He jinked twice, heading first to his left before switching to his right where he passed to hooker Alan Phillips. Little Patterson appeared at Phillips's elbow to take the pass, moved it to Rees, and the wing, in a repeat of his move a few moment before, cut infield from the right. This time he was tackled by Moaner van Heerden just outside the twenty-five.

A ruck formed, and again the Lions won it for Patterson to dart off once more. In the crowd one could sense that something extraordinary was unfolding in front of us and we began to slide towards the edge of our seats. The scrum half passed to Richards, and the ball went on to Renwick and to Woodward, and then Hay barged into the line again, full of running. Hay had been overweight at the start of the tour, but he used his extra poundage to good effect now by crashing through two tackles and then somehow turning to slip the ball inside to Slemen. The left wing, seeing his team mate was near the touchline, showed his innate footballer's brain by cutting infield on a diagonal slash towards the posts. He took Hay's pass beautifully, ran around the despairing tackle of Wynand Claassen and touched down. Twenty yards behind him Hay, still on his knees, raised both arms exultantly.

It was one of the greatest of all tries. Syd Millar said he had never seen anything like it. Johan Claassen, the former Springbok coach, said it was the best he had ever seen. To my mind this one, which lasted one minute, 36 seconds and involved 32 pairs of hands, rated above the magnificent try by the Barbarians against the All Blacks at Cardiff in 1973 because it came after 72 minutes of play in a highly-competitive match at stamina-sapping altitude.

British Lions 1980. John Hopkins. World's Work.

William Webb Ellis's status as founder of the handling code is conceded, or at least acknowledged, by all but the most pedantic of rugby folk. It may be that he had to sit at his desk and write out one hundred times, 'I must not handle the ball'; but just imagine his inner glow of satisfaction at the approach of a deputation comprising games masters and assorted sixth formers – 'I say, young Webb Ellis . . . about this new Rule you've invented. We've been having second thoughts about it . . .'

WWE's last resting-place, as the McWhirter twins Ross and Norris found when researching the RFU Centenary in 1971, is on a warm, pleasant hillside overlooking the Mediterranean at the resort of Menton. Once they realised that the local cemetery contained his tomb the French rugby authorities were swift to honour him with a marble slab which stands up above the flat stone whose inscription was for decades concealed from general view by lichens and spreading plants.

Not that WWE's name is ever likely to be without honour. At Rugby School in 1923 they remembered him with a classical invitation match in which most participants, it seems, took the ball in their arms and ran with it (some goals were also dropped). And so nail-biting was the climax that we can forgive the eye-witness his aberration suggesting that an 'England' team containing eight Welshmen had won!

Honouring WWE seems likely to be an on-going activity. Let us hope that 2023 produces as fine a match as that witnessed by O.L. Owen a century earlier.

One of the outstanding events in the history of the Rugby Football Union was the Centenary of the Rugby game itself which was reached in 1923. An ideal setting for its celebration clearly existed in the famous Close of Rugby School and there, on 1 November, was played a unique match, which also turned out to be a great one, between England and Wales, on one side, and Scotland and Ireland, on the other.

Only 2000 people were there to watch it, but about a third of those were schoolboys suitably attired and well-nigh bursting with enthusiasm and hero-worship – and what better nucleus of a crowd could one have wished in the circumstances? The remainder were guests of the headmaster and the Rugby Union in happy conjunction and they, needless to add, had been as carefully selected as the teams themselves. These fortunate guests included survivors of the first international match, representatives of any club which had been a member of the Rugby Union for over fifty years and others representing any country that played the Rugby Union game.

Then, of course, there must have been some ghostly representatives of Tom Brown's School Days, fags and swells alike, who had squeezed in somehow among the chairs and benches which served as grandstands and those who stood around the touchlines. Their presence would hardly have been resented had the squeezing been felt.

The background was composed of the famous school buildings and the famous elms. Among those buildings and trees could be found the plaque which recorded the exploit of the immortal youngster without whom, so one has always had to believe, there would have been no Rugby football as we understand it and no centenary to celebrate. Altogether, it was a scene to fill both the eye and imagination – a scene wholly sporting in character, robustly romantic and beautiful in a way peculiar to any parts of England which are still unspoiled. Everything, indeed, seemed worthy of the past. Even the weather was in a sporting mood. A soaking wet afternoon and a sea of mud would have been unpardonable on such an occasion.

Naturally, the composition of the teams was much under discussion

OVERLEAF: When the centenary of the Rugby game was reached in 1923 an ideal setting for its celebration clearly existed in the famous Close of Rugby School, shown here during the 1890s. (*BBC Hulton Picture Library.*)

before the event. It so happened that about this time English Rugby had to provide most of the really great figures on their side. W.J.A. Davies and his partner C.A. Kershaw had played in their last Championship match but no other pair of half backs could have been imagined for such a game as this. Not far away, at centre, was the solid H.J. Locke, of Birkenhead Park, a man as hard to pass as he was to stop. In front of these were W.W. Wakefield, the greatest forward of his day, outstanding even in a pack which included Tom Voyce, G.S. Conway and W.E.G. Luddington. It was a pity that Wales had no Bancrofts, Gwyn Nichollses, Arthur Goulds or Trews available but each of her eight representatives was a player to be respected. Rowe Harding, the Cambridge wing, was a brilliant runner on occasion and men like R.A. Cornish and T. Johnson fairly represented the skill of Cardiff behind the scrummage. Newport had sent an excellent full back in F. Baker who, oddly enough, was never to gain a Welsh cap, and the powerful forward Tom Roberts. Neath contributed another player of the name of Baker, a forward, Swansea sent G. Michael and the well-known Steve Morris was typical of the Valleys.

There was little to choose between the contributions of Scotland and Ireland. The latter country had sent along with six others that rich personality and fine full back 'Ernie' Crawford, as many who only knew him from repute and afar very properly insisted on calling him. It was of course 'W.E. Crawford (Lansdowne)' on the programme. In the three quarter line were the brothers Stephenson and D.J. Cussen, of Dublin University. G.V. Stephenson, a distinguished doctor in the making, seven years later was to achieve the still unrivalled record of 42 international caps. H.W. Stephenson belonged to the Royal Navy. All three could be relied upon to make for the Anglo-Welsh goal-line good and hard offered half a chance. There were, in addition, the three lusty forwards W.P. Collopy, T.A. McClelland and R.Y. Crichton.

Scotland produced a notable and heroic figure in A.L. Gracie, at centre, still bearing the bruises and glory which had come to him in the closing stages of a battle royal with Wales. Then, as every schoolboy at any rate knew, he had not only scored the winning try but made a stupendous run when half-dazed – one of the tries, in fact, which live long after all the other details of a match are forgotten. Members of a disappointed but generous Cardiff crowd had recorded their opinion on the spot by carrying him off the field in triumph. Both half backs were Scottish, J.C. Dykes, an accomplished player anywhere in midfield and W.E. Bryce, always a gallant and lively little figure around the scrummage.

More than half the pack were Scottish, too, one of them, J.M Bannerman, having become perhaps the best leader of men his country had produced since Mark Morrison. Another was the clever and attractive J.C.M. Buchanan. The other three were L.M. Stuart, a worthy product of Glasgow, and the two Borderers D.S. Davies and J.R. Lawrie. The last was a lanky and deceptively swift winger of a type better appreciated in Leicester, to whom he also belonged, than by the purists north of the Tweed. One grim and unconscious humorist had been heard to remark that Lawrie scored too many tries to please him. Lawrie helped to score one of them in this memorable encounter.

Decidedly, England and Wales did well to amass 21 points to 16 against such opponents in a match in which the fortunes of war fluctuated in the most bewildering manner. Seldom, indeed, have the sporting hazards of a Rugby match kept both teams, along with the spectators, more relentlessly – and delightfully – on tenterhooks from start to finish. Somebody described the game as the best ever prepared for the story books but, after all, it had to be played first.

Naturally, arguments raged afterwards because the winning score contained only three tries to the losers' four. Here it is quite enough to record the hard fact that England and Wales won a thrilling encounter by two goals, two dropped goals and a try to two goals and two tries. Few story-tellers could have thought of a much better plot than that – or a more dramatic ending.

The play had a kind of unspoken prologue. The Headmaster already had been greeted by a respectful cheer and the school clock had duly sounded the half-hour at 2.30 – the time for action. Thereupon there suddenly appeared a near-Dickensian figure carrying the ball with prodigious dignity. This turned out to be Mr Jiggle who, with the aid of a stick, stumped to the centre of the field and there solemnly planted the ball as, one gathered, he had done in every important school match at Rugby for many a long year. Like Mr Jiggle himself and his name, the whole procedure seemed almost too good to be true.

The teams, sure enough, appeared in turn without any undue delay. They wore jerseys especially designed for the match. England and Wales were in white, with a 'badge in red, plume of feathers and rose', as the programme announced in the best heraldic style. Scotland and Ireland were in quartered green and navy blue and nobody needed to know why the colours had been chosen. The kick-off itself was a thrilling incident and both sides set to work at such a pace that it was clear enough they fully understood what was expected of them. England and Wales had rather the better of the earlier play, and the efforts of Davies and Kershaw especially, as might have been expected, fairly raised the echoes. Yet, when all of a sudden the scoring began, it was the men in green and blue who accomplished it. H.W. Stephenson, who scored the try, never ran with greater determination for the goal-line. The try, however, remained a try and the Anglo-Welsh XV not only struck back swiftly and with effect but seized a lead of six points through a try and two successful kicks at goal. Cornish had created the opening which led to one of Wakefield's most impressive charges for the line. Baker made this try count five points. A few moments later, following one of W.J.A. Davies's best attempts to break right through, Voyce nearly added a second try but stumbled at the critical moment. Even so the effort was not wasted for, from the ensuing scrummage, Kershaw threw a long pass out to Johnson and that player, preferring a kick to a run, dropped as fine a goal as one could imagine. The Scots and Irish, for their part, replied by scoring their second try, touched down by Davies, the Hawick forward, in support of another strong run by H.W. Stephenson. Again the place-kick failed but there was little in it at half time, when England and Wales led by nine points to six.

At the interval Mr Jiggle re-appeared bearing a new ball, and again it all seemed too good to be true. There was little time for thinking, however. The game had hardly been re-started before the Anglo-Welsh pack broke away in a powerful rush which ended in Baker, the Neath forward, touching down a try. This time the kick at goal failed but, just as the opposing pack seemed to be getting fairly into a stride, an opportunist masterpiece by W.J.A. Davies brought his side a second dropped goal and so raised the Anglo-Welsh advantage to the formidable figure of ten points.

It was here, perhaps, that the match really became a classic. By a supreme effort Scotland and Ireland drew level. A breakaway by Lawrie, supported by Gracie, sent George Stephenson over at the posts and D.S. Davies made no mistake with the place-kick. On top of this the side, now fairly roused, seized upon a loose pass by one of their opponents and forced their fourth and last try. Bannerman was the scorer and it was Crawford who stepped up to take a kick at goal upon which apparently everything depended. His cool head and steady toe did not fail him and the score, to the general amazement, stood at 16 all.

The 800 schoolboys now were really having the time of their lives and wondering, perhaps, which side most deserved their cheers. The Scots and Irish forwards were going all out for the kill. England and Wales were fighting back bravely and, what was more, with a shrewd resource. Cornish made the breakaway which, with the support of Voyce and Luddington in the loose, was to settle everything. Before the defence could solidify, the two forwards were through and over the goal-line. Voyce was credited with the actual touchdown but Luddington was awarded the honour and responsibility of adding the goal points.

Even then it was not all over. In the final moments Bannerman headed a rush which seemed to fail only by inches and no-side arrived amid a hubbub which by this time had a hoarse croak in it. England had won by five points which, a quarter of a century later when the dropped goal had been reduced in value, would have been only three.

The History Of The Rugby Football Union. O.L. Owen.
Playfair Books, for the RFU.

Index

Page numbers in *italic* refer to illustrations